VOICES OF KERRY

CONVERSATIONS WITH MEN AND WOMEN OF KERRY

JIMMY WOULFE

BLACKWATER PRESS

Editor

Deirdre Greenan

Design & Layout

M & J Graphics

ISBN

0 86121 5141

©   Jimmy Woulfe, 1994

Produced in Ireland by
Blackwater Press
c/o Folens Publishers
8 Broomhill Business Park,
Tallaght, Dublin 24.

Dedication

For a Corkwoman, my wife Breeda.

Acknowledgements

For permission to reproduce photographs the author and publishers wish to thank the following:

Press 22 for photographs of Brendan Kennelly, Dick Spring and John B Keane; Brendan Landy, Listowel, for photograph of Bryan MacMahon; *Sportsfile* for photographs of Ogie Moran and Moss Keane.

INTRODUCTION

The idea for this book was conceived by Eamon Stack from Ballybunion. During a chance meeting on the Limerick/Dublin morning train he ran it past me. By the time we arrived at Heuston Station, I had embraced the idea and was off on a solo run which was to last from November 1993 to June 1994.

The rich vein of expression contained in this book is meant to give an insight into the Kerry mind. It is signposted by the experiences and feelings of well-known daughters and sons of the county.

But while its origin and emphasis is Kerry, the openness unfolded in these interviews transcend any geographical boundary.

Kerry and its people bristle with the treasure of the spoken word.

Those with whom I spoke, represent a broad spectrum of Kerry people who play a significant role at Kerry, national and international level.

There are many more I would love to have included. My sins of omission in this regard, while certainly not venial, are I hope somewhat less than mortal. But a book can only accommodate so much.

Each of the conversations took on a life of its own with the contributors in the driving seat. The questions are not included in the text so as not to interrupt the flow of the conversation. Those I spoke with opened their doors and in many instances their hearts. For their time and courtesy, I am deeply grateful.

I would also like to thank journalist, Michael Walsh, who worked with me on the sub-editing. My thanks also to John O'Connor and Deirdre Greenan of Blackwater Press for their enthusiasm and support.

Jimmy Woulfe

CONTENTS

BRENDAN KENNELLY

(POET)

WHEN I go back to Kerry I love to listen to fellows talking about football and join in the conversation. They are great talkers. Their talk is extraordinary, whether they are talking about salt water, or warts, or cattle or football, or emigration or an ould ballad. Anything at all. I have learned one thing and that is to become a listener. Listening is something we Irish are not good at. We prefer to express rather than to absorb and I have learned to listen and I have learned that in the strangest ways.

People talk in silent languages all the time. A person comes up to you and says something. And he is really saying something else. Using, as it were, the language of silence, implying something. And if you listen deeply enough to a person you can hear the language behind the language. Teaching is partly that talent for listening to the language that is in hiding.

If I was back in Kerry I would listen more carefully and try to appreciate lovely, ordinary things rather than the romantic side of Kerry. I would continue to write and to write what I saw around me and to try and do it justice, the same as I would do if I were living in Singapore. I think I always have a special place in my heart for the people I knew in Kerry in the forties and the fifties. It has changed and if I walked down the Main Street of my native village of Ballylongford possibly everyone would not recognise me. The older people would. It is easy to sentimentalise Kerry, especially if you live outside it.

Kerry people are tough, decent and increasingly middle-class. They are very conscious of tourism in places such as Tralee and Killarney. Kerry is now a strongly materialistic society. It is also resolutely bourgeois in its approach to experience and has changed greatly in that respect. It is being filtered through a new class system where the people who can't make it either loll around at home, or are exported and emigrate. Those who can make it stay at home and live there with a resolution to continue to make it. That is understandable. There is no point saying that Kerry is a great, gamey, working-class area anymore. It is not a peasant society. It is a hardworking area. It is a place where people have to work to stay there. There is a dimension of competition in the towns especially, and this is a real change from what it was in the fifties.

There are good sides to it in that when a society becomes middle-class it discovers the Arts in a conscious way. You have Siamsa in Tralee and St John's in Listowel. All the new enlightened attitudes to the Arts are good things. Great things are happening. That is why it would be wrong of me to say Kerry was better then, than it is now. It is different. There is a complex scene there now and I see that when I go there. I feel I belong there and yet in ways I have changed. I love it and especially North Kerry and Ballybunion. I love the people and I get on well with them, they are very kind to me and I enjoy the talk. It is always good to hear about a possible recovery of Kerry football.

I was born in 1936 in what is called the Main Street of Ballylongford. It was a smallish kind of a house and we lived there until 1950. We moved down to a pub on the corner of the street and I grew up in the pub. I left the village in 1954 to come to Dublin. Like everyone I went to the national school and left it in 1948 and went to Tarbert where I was educated by Miss McKenna and Mr and Mrs Carey. Miss McKenna was a tremendous woman and she based her school on Pearse's school with certain modifications that made it more practical and extremely effective. The village itself was quiet and then, as now, was hit by emigration. There were three or four football teams in the parish of Ballylongford. There are about forty houses in the village now closed. The passion, of course, was football and it was embodied in Johnny Walsh, who was one of my teachers and who had the quality of dedication and obsession that I have always admired and have tried to cultivate in my own work.

I don't think you can achieve anything in this world without being intensely dedicated. And even then you can't be sure, as what is called 'failure' is always waiting. But I don't have much respect for either failure, or for what is called success. But I do respect somebody who realises himself or herself and brings to fruition whatever promise God gave them. And that is what I learned from Miss McKenna, do your best and trust in the weather. It's a good piece of advice.

The football culture represented the larger culture of the parish and half-heartedness was not tolerated on the field. Of all the great Kerry footballers, Johnny Walsh was one of the most totally whole-hearted players. This influenced me as I do give of my best. It is the same to me if I am lecturing in Harvard or Oxford or any place in the world, or giving a talk to youngsters, I do the same with all of them – I do my best. I don't believe in class distinction at any level. It exists and it is an unfortunate thing. It is an insult to intelligence, as snobbery is a distortion of reality. It doesn't really work although it seems to prevail in our society.

One of the things you learn from a whole-hearted man like Johnny Walsh is that you cut through the divisions implied or created by snobbery or by money or even by intelligence. I think these people, like Johnny Walsh and Miss McKenna, have stayed with me and I think of them every day. That is a funny thing, because I don't set out deliberately to think about them.

I think you have to assume in creation that people are more or less the same; socially they may be more deprived or privileged. Or they may have more or less talent or intelligence. But having said that, there is another kind of equality which dominates the moment of encounter. And it is extraordinary the way people can smell condescension off you if you happen to think that person is not as well educated as you are, or whatever. That is the integrity of the moment, that you cannot fool around with anybody. You can have the mickey taken out of you. You can be mocked. But if it is a serious encounter where two people are looking into each other's eyes and evaluating each other in that moment, there is no time for condescension.

There is no room for snobbery or condescension, because both these things are simply, as I would see them, they are denials or disfiguration of intelligence. And as far as I am concerned, one of the most important things in life is to be intelligent and good humoured, and if possible graceful. It's one of the most beautiful words of all, grace. I am not particularly graceful in carriage, but it is a quality I love in people. I met a lot of that in Kerry, particularly among the older women and among some men. It is a quality of reticence; of standing back and looking at the world. Of not judging it too quickly. Of giving people the opportunity of presenting themselves to you on their own terms and of you not wanting them to be what you wanted them to be, but of accepting them for what they are. These are the qualities that I have tried to cultivate as a teacher and as a writer.

We tend to see things through moralities, religions, social values, money and education. While all these things are inevitable in society, it is very false to judge people through them.

A person is a unique creation made by God. I believe that. And I think when you confront a person, whether it be a student, a man in a jail or a person in a pub, you are confronting a mystery who is unknown to you, a complete stranger. You can label him and say he is an eejit, a drunk, or a bore and walk out of his presence. But that is not enough for me – I genuinely try to appreciate the strangeness of others.

That is why I keep on writing poetry. Because to me poetry is about appreciating strangeness. And I got this in many respects out of alcoholism. I got it out of being in a mental hospital. I got it out of knowing that out there in society there are a lot of people suffering from all kinds of things which they can't afford to reveal to their children or to themselves. The word I use is strange, and strangeness is stimulating to me. I would never take anybody for granted. I try not to take my own daughter or anybody I know for granted because you are dealing with human dynamite; you are dealing with people who are not to be belittled, who are not to be put into cosy categories, or labelled.

We Irish have an extraordinary capacity for labelling each other. I suffer a lot from it myself. He is a Kerryman, he is an academic, he is an ad man, and that is, in the view of many people, Brendan Kennelly.

But I don't know Brendan Kennelly. I know him up to a point. I know he was a hoor for the drink. I know he is fond of women. That he admires certain kinds of women. That he admires certain kinds of men. I know he wants to be a teacher, that he wants to be an educator and I know that he is intrigued by the poetry that is all around him. At the same time if I were to meet Brendan Kennelly in the street, I would treat him the same as anybody else. I would treat myself like that. I am a stranger to myself.

Alcoholism untreated is a sustained denial, deception of self as well as the deception of other people. It is also a condition of greed that you have to satisfy this need. That time of the day goes further and further back towards morning and the need dominates all time. Either you admit it then or you don't. There are those who are mad for money and whose lives are governed by the acquisition of money. They frequently live lives of profound and subtle self-deception which they cannot admit to themselves. They will dress it up as earning a living or doing good for others. And undoubtedly they do that. But there is also the self-deception involved that they should admit to themselves, if they recognise it.

The funny thing about alcoholism is that once you admit it you recognise the extent and the depth of your own poverty as a human being and that is what I found out. I found out I am not up to much. I found out I am lucky to have a small talent which I cultivate as best I can. I found out that I can communicate, that I am a teacher. And I found that I can talk to people at some level. That doesn't mean that I am not lonely or that I don't suffer extraordinary confusion when I am alone. But I don't hoist it on other people. I try and make it clear and lucid when I am writing poems or writing prose or whatever. That is what admission does. It is quite simple. You have to admit there is something about yourself. That you are this or you are that. You can go along wearing cosmetics or masks on your face or your mind for your whole life. And we do it. I still do it I am sure. I am sure I am dishonest in ways which would surprise me if I knew it. But I think alcoholism is an education and it educated me in many ways.

I don't think there is anybody I would knock. If I was called on to try and understand a murderer, a rapist, a child molester, a mass murderer, I think I would try and understand him and I think that is what we were meant to do. I think we were put here not to condemn and judge, but to try and understand and that's what education is about. But unfortunately our education system has become mechanised and mechanical to the point where it is all about passing exams. Education, I feel, should be disciplined, but free. Exams in the Arts should be done away with. I think we should encourage meditation and not guess-work. That we should encourage people to mark their own papers. What we need is objectivity, developed intellects, detached minds who are capable of judging themselves as clearly as they are capable of judging others.

It's the oldest story in the world. The standard would come from discussions with each other afterwards. They would examine each other as well. It is an ideal state, but we are trying to cultivate honesty. The best way to cultivate it is right from the start. I am trying to arrive at the honesty which is inherent in education, or should be. It is in the mind. It is truly a mental adventure and we must reach out for that honest objectivity. It is worth striving for.

I like science and I have studied bits of it. I like talking to scientists. I read poetry, I read mythology, and I read anything from any part of the world. And it is clear to me that this world is a dream of order, accommodating the most incredible chaos, famines, mass murders, racial horrors, discriminations, civil wars, corruptions, particularly in Catholic countries in Europe. In spite of all that, it is a dream of order and that dream is as much a part of my mind as it is a part of the mind of God. That is what I mean by spiritual, a dream of order. A poem is a dream of order. A newspaper article is a dream of order. No matter how flurried we are, we have to shape them.

We have to shape things. You are only raw material for every moment of your life. For every moment you are potentially chaotic. But equally for every moment you are a natural shaper. You shape yourself. And unless you live with both the sense of your own chaos and virtual disintegration, co-existing with a dream of coherence and a desire for order, you are not really alive.

I know life is conflict and tension. I am drawn two ways. I want to drink. I want to drink every day of my life. I want to be drunk always. I am not unhappy. Unhappiness is only that which is generated by the way you live your tensions. You might get guidelines from a seanfhocal or one of the sayings of Christ. Or a phrase from the Bible or from the saying of a man in the street or from one of the works of Shakespeare. You get guidelines. But you have to discover happiness. Happiness to me is living with these tensions within me and being delighted and at times made creative by the streets of Dublin. The faces, the boys and girls I teach, the strangers who walk up to me. When I go to foreign cities I meet it in different ways. This world is amazing. It is that sense of the amazingness of the world which I try to capture in my poetry.

That is the difficulty.

Happiness for me is shaping my dreams in language. The evil in your heart is your own refusal of God's gift. It stems from that. Evil is profound frustration and this can emerge as respectability, judgementalism, but it is a wrong thing to do to yourself. If you are a good footballer try and be as good a footballer as you can. If you are a poet, try and live that as fully as you can. I don't know how well I live it, but I want to do my best and that for me is happiness. It is the loyalty I display and give to what God gave me. It is a small gift. Life is a gift.

I was right to write. I accepted it. It is easy to give things to people, it is often harder to accept. To take affection, to take love, to take a word of praise or admiration. Sometimes people find it easier to take begrudgery because they can fight back. Having been brought up in an extremely inhibited religion, it is a great thing to discover women. I just enjoy the company of women enormously. Women say outrageous and wonderful things. Women will tell you honestly what they think of you and what they think of themselves. Women are very honest. But they are not honest with eejits.

You have to tune into women. If you don't tune into women, either through condescension, or distrust, or mere sexual acquisition, just trying to go to bed with her, a woman knows all that, her body tells her. You can't go within an inch of a woman without her smelling your intention and I like that. That's what poetry is. The sense of smell in poetry is highly developed. To me getting on with women is a logical extension of how I played football. That is devilment, doing my best, but always having a sense of humour about the outcome and enjoying the company of the fellow I was marking, even when he was dirty.

Once you get to know a woman's mind, her feelings, her perspective on experience, you are into a different county altogether. And let the sexuality pour through all that experience. Sexuality should not be confined to copulation. It should run through education, religion, saying prayers. The oldest poets used say prayers to the saints which were sexual. They expressed their whole beings. God didn't give you a being to be ashamed of it.

I always admired women. I didn't express it always. I couldn't. It was a sin when I was young to be looking at them with appreciation, especially their bodies. I have never seen an ugly woman. The same is true of men. There is ugliness and sometimes it can exist in a conventionally beautiful woman or a conventionally handsome man. And that is the kind of thing that interests me. Ugliness has to do with thinking too much of yourself, disproportionate self-evaluation about your own significance as a human being.

The secret of life to me is enjoyment, pleasure. Pleasure is knowledge and pleasure is loving a man or a woman's company and it is also the reserving the right to tell somebody to fuck off. There is a great pleasure in telling some people to fuck off. That is a right and that is what you should develop in yourself. You shouldn't be that hurtful about anything, only logical. Logic of feeling is the highest logic, it is higher than the logic of the intellect, because it is generated out of your soul, out of your heart. You know you are right and you should feel that way about certain things.

I am a stranger to myself and to you. But there is a sense also that if we talk enough to each other we will be brothers. And that is what we should be doing. Are we learning it at all? Must we still kill each other in this country. Have we learned to talk to each other after two thousand years of Christianity? It is very simple. Why can't we listen to each other? That is the hardest thing in the world. I must go back to Kerry and the people long ago who taught me how to listen to words, to poems, to stories in French, English, Irish and Latin. And I have never lost that.

A life is so rich there are endless things to express from it. You can sit down there in the morning on your own and write out lines you may never use. And that is what listening does. Not just listening to other people, but listening to the voices of yourself. A man is full of voices, he has as many voices as the sea and he should be able to listen to them all. That is what writers have always done and the really great ones have done it to a degree that is almost incomprehensible.

In the Gospel of Thomas, the Gnostic Gospel that is outside the four Gospels, you will find the sayings of Jesus which are unbelievably simple. He says to people, 'Be passers-by'. Imagine if you were a pass-er-by of everybody. Glancing, bearing witness, taking it all in, moving on. Observing. Having the courage to be. Who are you? You have to stop and listen and have the courage to be. Be a passer-by in this life. That is only one thing he said. Everything he said is worth listening to.

He must have been a Kerryman.

TOMMY STACK

(RACE HORSE TRAINER)

I had my first dreams of the Grand National when I was a boy being brought up on a farm outside Moyvane on the Knockanure road. My parents William and Mary are both dead. My brother Stephen now works the farm and my sister Helen Roche is married in Rathkeale. I was the baby of the family. At national school in Moyvane I was taught by Tom O'Callaghan whose sons Bernard and Colm played for Kerry. Another son, Tom O'Callaghan, was in class with me along with Austin Kearney. I used to play for the under fourteens in Moyvane. That was the one thing which was marvellous at the time – we had a few county players in the parish. There were good players like Bernard O'Callaghan. Liam Hanrahan was a fine player. The Brosnans were famous.

I remember up in the football field every evening it was an achievement to get a kick of the ball because there were so many players there trying to get it. There would be fifty chasing it. The interest was marvellous and they were tremendously fit and hardy from piking hay all day. If some of them lads hit you a shoulder you would go through the ground. They didn't need any press-ups or weight work. To this day I am still impressed looking back at the fitness and dedication of those lads in Moyvane playing football for hours every evening. They thought of nothing else. That's why they were great footballers because they concentrated on what they were doing. That influenced me. I played but was not a good footballer. But the application these people had rubbed-off on me. Every match in the parish league was like an All-Ireland Final. The passion from five teams in a small parish!

I had a piebald pony at home and we used to tackle him to bring the milk to the creamery. I used to look after him and jump him over poles in a field. Every year at the Tarbert Carnival they held a race and I entered my pony and we won. It had a fiver prize-money which was a lot for a young lad. My first win as a jockey. I used to train the pony at night-time. I used to study the photographs in the newspapers of the way Pat Taaffe and Bobby Beasley sat on a horse going over a fence and I modelled myself on them from these newspaper pictures. I followed the racing results from England and Tim Molony was a big figure then.

One of the highlights of the year was the Listowel Races eight miles away. The school would close for the three days of the Races and there I saw the real thing. By then the racing bug had gripped me. In 1958 I was sent to Mungret College outside Limerick as a boarder and I was five years there. It was a rugby college and I loved the sport. Exams were tough because I didn't do the work. Fr Cantillon was a very nice man. Fr Jack Brennan was there and in my class the students included Bobby Barry who used ride while still a student. Barry Brogan came two years after me. When we went to Mungret first you didn't get out until Christmas. The Jesuits were great teachers and marvellous men. I loved rugby and was on the college side playing scrum-half. I played in the junior and senior sides. We had a great junior side. Bobby Barry was wing-forward. We were beaten by Crescent in the Final at Thomond Park and I never cried as much as I did after that game. We were good enough to win.

We beat good teams on the way to the Final despite being a relatively small school with only a hundred and fifty pupils. The school hadn't won a cup for thirty years. I captained the senior side the next year and I also played for the Munster Schoolboys at scrum-half. Johnny Moroney, who played afterwards for Ireland, was out-half on the Munster Schoolboys team. We played in Ravenhill and it was my first time in the North. Frank Hogan, who is now involved with Garryowen, was wing-forward on our side. The Comiskeys from Rockwell were on the team. I used also do the pole-vault and won the North Munster. I won the 110 metres hurdle as well.

I got to know Barry Brogan and his father Jimmy Brogan who trained horses and I used to go up with him and ride at the weekends. Later in Dublin I kept up the contact. Barry Brogan and Bobby Barry had amateur licences while they were in Mungret and Bobby won on Chenille War in Limerick.

Nobody actually gave me lessons on riding style. The pony at home taught me a lot. I had a track going from one field to another and I used think I was going over Becher's on the pony in a childish way. Pat Taaffe had a great style and Bobby Beasley was great from the last home. So I copied their styles. During the summer holidays I would milk four or five cows each evening.

When I did my Leaving Cert, I wanted to try and get into the Army Equitation School. I applied for the cadets and I didn't get it and I was so disappointed. It was a kick in the teeth. I got a job with Phoenix Insurance in Dublin. I was in digs in Leeson Street at first and then I went into a flat at 48 Upper Drumcondra Road, Dublin, with three lads from Limerick and one from Cork. There were two Reddan brothers, one was Brian Reddan who was on the Crescent team which beat us in the Munster Colleges Junior Cup Final. He has since died. He was a great out-half and he reminded me of Richard Sharpe, the great England out-half. He was a grand fellow and a fine player. His brother, Pat, was also in the flat and Michael Weekes from Limerick. I was working in the office and I was fine. I used go to Brogan's some week-ends. The manager of the Phoenix, Mr Johnson, asked me to join Lansdowne Rugby Club and I did. On Sundays I would go down and play for Abbeyfeale. We were beaten in the Final of the Munster Junior Cup. Dr George O'Mahony had coaxed me to play for Abbeyfeale.

A car load of us would travel down and I drove as I was the only non-drinker. There was a great team in Abbeyfeale. Billy O'Mahony who should have been capped for Ireland was on the side. I was only seventeen or eighteen. Dr George and his wife Betty were two of the most marvellous people you could ever meet. They made Abbeyfeale rugby what it is today. They won the Junior Cup afterwards, but I had gone to Dublin.

While in Dublin I decided to have a crack at the racing and I wrote to every trainer in England. I got one reply back from Neville Crump. I wanted to go over as an amateur. A brother-in-law of mine, the late Paddy Roche in Rathkeale, knew Bobby Renton to whom he sold cattle and got in touch with him. Bobby Renton said he was coming over to Dublin and we met in the Hibernian Hotel. He was an elderly man and was over with Mrs Brotherton, his main owner, looking at horses. He said come over. I handed in my notice to the Phoenix and left for England on 13 July 1965. My mother nearly had a canary over giving up my good job to go to England. My father gave me fifty pounds as my airfare back as he felt I wouldn't last long. He wanted me to get it out of my system.

I didn't know anybody in England and I had only been there once previously for two days on an insurance course. Bobby Renton sent his butler Percy to pick me up at Leeds Airport. I got digs and knew nobody there. That first year I never went out. I said I would have to work hard.

I was given a few horses to look after and ride out every day. Bobby had about eighteen National Hunt horses. After a few days he said he would get me an amateur's licence. He asked me to school a few horses which I did and he said I had done a lot of schooling. I didn't disagree with him, but the truth was I had done little or no schooling of horses up to then. You have to bluff sometimes. He got me my amateur licence and at that time he was paying me four pounds a week pocket-money and he bought me a bicycle to get into Ripon for Mass on Sundays. He gave me a ride in September and I was fourth on New Money in a handicap hurdle. I was beaten by a horse ridden by Jack Berry, now the great trainer. I had a few more rides and I had my first winner on 16 October 1965 on New Money at Weatherby. I got a tremendous thrill. That was a big day in my life.

Looking back it was a thousand-to-one chance getting the great start I got. Bobby Renton had never made a jockey before. He always employed outside top jockeys. Here was a young lad from Kerry with a trainer who had no record of cultivating up-and-coming young jockeys.

My first ride over fences was at the October Cheltenham meeting when I won on Well Packed in an amateurs' race. Brough Scott and Lord Oaksey rode in the race. My first ride over fences and I won. I won the Grand Annual Handicap Chase on the same horse at the big Cheltenham Festival meeting in 1966. It was unreal. I had broken my wrist a few weeks before and at Cheltenham I rode with a plaster right up my hand to the elbow. I stayed with Bobby Renton after turning professional in 1968.

The first two years were tough and I wasn't going well. Bobby Renton died and I was asked to take out the trainer's licence for a few months. Red Rum was in the yard so I trained him for a period which is not widely known. I didn't win with him. I then went back riding and rode freelance. Tom Jones retained me for a year, and then I went to Arthur Stephenson where I was stable jockey for the last five years of my career until I retired in 1978.

The moment Red Rum cleared the last fence in the 1977 Grand National was the most memorable moment of my life. For a few moments I had this unbelievable feeling. But after that brief feeling of utter delight, right through to the run to the line I was overcome with concern that something could go wrong. Devon Loch flashed through my mind. And even when I passed the winning post I had a quick look at my saddlecloth to see if it had slipped. I was even worrying that I might have lost some of the lead which is put into a saddlebag to make up the weight a horse has to carry.

Obviously we had been looking forward to the race for some time. I had ridden Red Rum the previous year when he led over the last and we were beaten by Rag Trade by a length and a half. I thought that was my chance of winning a National gone. Brian Fletcher had ridden him in his two previous National wins. I had ridden the horse way back when he was first run in the National as an eight-year-old. I had always ridden Red Rum and I rode him on his first run over fences at Newcastle as a five-year-old when he was with Bobby Renton. Bobby had won a Grand National with Free Booter in 1953. He bought Red Rum off the flat as a three-year-old from Tim Molony and he won a few hurdle races.

We went to school him once over fences to go chasing with him. He half fell through the first and he refused to jump the second fence. That was the only schooling Red Rum got in his career. Bobby Renton said to forget the schooling and told me I had the ride at Newcastle. He had plenty of experience over hurdles and was cute. He jumped like a cat and had no inclination to stop or refuse. He finished third that day. Then his next race was at Doncaster in a conditions race and he won. He won four or five chases. When Ginger McCain got him I won his first three races and then when he was entered in the National I was asked to ride him, but I couldn't as I was retained by another trainer, and Brian Fletcher got the ride. He won that National and the next one and was then beaten by L'Escargot third time round. Then he hadn't been running well and the owners asked me to ride the horse in the 1976 National in which we finished second.

I was looking forward to riding him in 1977 again after being pipped the previous year. He always improved as the spring went on. That day in 1977 he looked a picture in the paddock and got the best turned-out award. He really blossomed at that time of year.

I had been racing in Liverpool the day before and went home to Yorkshire that night. We lived in a village called Healaugh. I drove down to Aintree with Liz, my wife, and a friend Sarah Gardner. We stopped for a cup of coffee at the last service station on the motorway. Before a big event you get tensed up. I was going well and had a good year and was champion jockey. But still, riding a horse like this in a big race, when you knew you have a chance, it's a huge responsibility. The horse had plenty of weight so I wasn't wasting to get my weight down. I drove on to Aintree and I took a walk down to Becher's on my own. The best part of Aintree I had always felt was going out through the gates after the races, going home. Over for another year.

There is a big hype leading into the National. I was concerned that I would do my best and that the horse would get back safely and that I wouldn't be at fault if something went wrong. Before the National I rode in two races and finished placed. One of those races was the dead-heat between Monksfield and Night Nurse and I was third. That was a great race. I was third on Peterhoff. There was about an hour between that race and the National. The weighing room has an atmosphere on Grand National day different to any other. There is a cold sense of something about to happen. Nobody is relaxed. People try to make jokes and get little response. People come in looking for jockeys' autographs. The adrenalin is rolling a bit.

I was very tight and I would have been the same before a rugby match.

I would be trying to concentrate on what I was going to do. When you have something important to do, you tighten up and get tense. I think this makes you into a better professional, it increases your awareness, and the will to do your best. Before a race I would always be superstitious.

I led the parade because Red Rum was number one on the card. I went down and showed him the first fence. And as it was a cold, dry April day, I got a rug put over his loins down at the start to keep him warm. The ground was drying up fast and that suited. It's like with athletes, the longer you can keep a horse warm the better. He was on his toes and he was wound up. Whatever feeling he got at Liverpool, you knew he sensed the place. He was like a coil underneath you about to explode. Yet he was not jumping or jigging, but on his toes. With him you kept to the middle of the field for the first circuit. So there were a lot of loose horses to be avoided. Six fell at the first and another six fell at the third which is a ditch.

Going to Becher's for the first time I was to the middle back of the field and another few went there. When I looked up at Becher's there were only seven or eight in front of me and I was very surprised as I felt there should have been a lot more at that stage. After the canal turn John Williams went off a long way in front and we were about sixth, closer than I expected, but I was happy. The race is always dangerous up to Becher's first time as it is only sorting itself out up to that point with a lot of the less serious contenders falling. The novelty runners are gone by then. Going across the Melling Road there was a horse twenty lengths in front and at the Chair the second horse fell.

Going into the country for the second time I was fourth or fifth. Boom Docker with John Williams, who rides a lot on the flat now, refused after leading. That left Andy Pandy in front. He led into Becher's where he fell, leaving me in front. I had a loose horse in front of me heading for the Canal Turn. I was frightened he could take me out and I raced ahead.

I concentrated on the job. I looked back and saw Martin Blackshaw cantering about three lengths behind me on Churchtown Boy. At the second last I jumped it well and I heard a crash and I knew Churchtown Boy had hit it hard. Going to the last I didn't look back and didn't hear him coming. I jumped it well and I looked back and saw we had it.

I can't describe the thrill after the last. I had it then. I pulled the horse off the rail and everything went through my mind. I kept him up the middle. It flashed through my mind that he might duck or somebody might run out. I kept him well off the rail. You could hear the Tannoy, but not clearly as I was concentrating hard. I never touched him with the stick through the race. I think that I have never concentrated so hard as I did in the last two hundred yards of that race.

The lead-in couldn't last long enough, the policemen on horseback, the cheering crowds. It was the result everyone wanted. Things went right on the day and our horse did nothing wrong. Great credit to Ginger, he produced the horse A1 on the day and he delivered. After weigh-in there were televison and press interviews. I rode in the last race and finished third.

That night we went back to Southport to a local hotel. I don't drink but everybody was drinking. Then they brought the horse into the hotel at about eleven o'clock. It was unbelievable. I will never forget it. Ginger trained in Southport where he had a garage business. But they brought the horse into the ballroom and everyone was patting him. We travelled home that night. A marvellous day. It was one ambition I had since I started off, to win the Grand National. I thought I wouldn't be good enough to be champion jockey as I hadn't the background or the experience. I was about to become champion that year for the second time. Winning the National was the one I wanted to do, more than becoming champion jockey. It is probably the most famous race in the world.

While I had my greatest high in 1977, winning the Grand National on Red Rum, I also had one of my great lows due to a bad injury at Hexham in September when a horse turned over me in the Paddock. He broke my pelvis in about ten or twelve places and he ruptured my bladder. I had to be put in traction for three months and I had many operations. I was pretty lucky with falls: broken wrists and crushed vertebrae. I never broke my collar bone. I have big, strong bones. I have a seven and a half inch wrist and good boxers wouldn't have wrists much bigger than that. I had an accident after coming back to

Tipperary after I went out to see mares in a paddock. I got a kick in the side of the head. Another fraction of an inch and I would have been a vegetable. I was knocked out for forty-five minutes in the field and an artery was severed, but luckily the blood clotted.

I met my wife Liz through racing; she was Liz Townson and was secretary to Ken Oliver. We were married in 1975. She is a farmer's daughter from County Durham. We have two children, James, 'Fozzie' as we call him, is going to Glenstal and our little daughter Serena is fourteen months old. At thirty-two I decided to retire. I had gone beyond my wildest expectation and beyond what I thought was possible. I could have ridden for another few years as my nerve was as good as ever. But I got into breeding horses and I was involved in it and that is one of the reasons I gave up. One of my last winners was Rare Gold for Paddy Norris at Killarney. I rode in Listowel also. I enjoyed coming to ride in Kerry and it was nice to have had a winner.

When I took out my trainer's licence in 1986 I found there was no comparison between riding and training. I had a good start winning the Cartier Million at Phoenix Park with Colwyn Bay. As a trainer you have total responsibility.

For seven years or so I had more rides than anybody else in England and I was very fit. It's amazing the fitness level I got to from riding and that makes you a better jockey. That's why people say amateurs can't ride. After coming out of an office all day what chance have you against a professional?

I liked flat breeding and had been involved before retiring as a jockey. John Magnier asked me if I would manage one of the Coolmore Studs, which I did and I managed Longfield Stud. I stayed there two or three years and we bought this place. We have eighty-five boxes and three hundred acres here at Thomastown Castle in Golden with all-weather and grass gallops. There are about twenty-eight working here.

Training is far more demanding as the buck stops with you and whether you have two or twenty horses you have to deliver and you live by it. A jockey might ride six or seven hundred horses in a year. As a jockey you get on one, you get off one. For the successes you have, you have so many disappointments. I think the average person does not realise what it takes to produce a horse, fit on the day to win, and the casualties that you have along the way with horses which don't meet that goal. Owners are basically very good, but some don't understand. It is quite an expensive sport. We have some great patrons like Robert Sangster.

I'd like to win a Classic and I get a kick out of watching the home bred horses progress. In racing I will never stop learning. No matter what level you are at, you never stop learning. I like to win races in Kerry and we have had winners at all three tracks there. I like to go back with horses which have a chance because, being a Kerryman, people in Kerry expect that my horses will have a chance. Kerry people are very proud and have done so well all over the world.

It's great being a Kerryman. Something I always will be. I think that because it has been such a successful sporting county in gaelic football, the major sporting game in the country, a Kerryman or woman has to look to that and say, 'I have to do my piece in what I am doing to maintain that tradition'.

Being from Kerry I have always had an attachment to greyhounds. I had a track dog as a young lad. I am involved in some greyhounds still. I like the coursing and any part of country life.

I was born in the country and I understand it and I know what makes country life tick. I cannot understand how some city people try to run down country life when they don't understand it. They think they understand it, but they don't. I am still a country Kerryman at heart.

When I think of Kerry I think of marvellous characters like Eric Browne, the Listowel bookie. I have known him a long time, and I think he has great credibility and a marvellous sense of humour and is great company. I have great admiration for Jeremiah Carroll, the man who sent up Master Myles to win the Derby in Clonmel. A more modest man you could not meet and was never given the credit for what he achieved with that great dog. Cormac O'Leary was another teacher in Moyvane. He's a great doggy man and I enjoy meeting these people.

If you had to pick a team to do a job of work tomorrow whatever it might be, as regards loyalty you would put these men on it. The Kerry people would stand by their man, through thick and thin. You certainly wouldn't like them against you, as many a footballer found out.

The Stacks originally came from Springmount, Duagh. They bought the farm in Moyvane. My mother was a Danaher from Athea and she went to America as a child of three. The family returned when she was fifteen. So we used always call her 'the Yank'.

I remember walking cattle into Listowel, seven miles in and seven miles out for the May or October big fair day. I remember marvellous scraps and family feuds which would erupt at the fairs. Dermot Dillon and his brother Kevin are first cousins of mine. Dermot played for Kerry and Kevin played for Cork. Duagh was a great football parish. You had Dan McAuliffe, the Kerry footballer, who was from Duagh. The first North Kerry Final I saw in Listowel was between Duagh and Clounmacon. Dermot, Kevin and Paul, the three Dillons and another player was Tom Costello and Dan McAuliffe. They beat Clounmacon.

Arthur Stephenson, the man I spent the big years of my career with, was a trainer who was a real professional. A hard worker and a great farmer. He told me unless I had the will to win I would be no use to him. He was a hard taskmaster in that he expected you to deliver when he wanted you to. I admired him and was very fond of him and the entire family. He worked hard and his horses were meant to work the same. He would have one hundred horses in and would go through about one hundred and fifty in a year. To win a championship you need a big stable behind you. I rode over six hundred winners and my biggest tally of winners in a season was ninety-seven in one of the two years I became champion jockey.

I remember riding in a hurdle for Arthur one time at Sedgefield. And he said in the paddock just to give the horse a run and not to get into trouble. When he really expected a horse to win the only riding orders he would give you were, 'Don't get beat', when legging you up. Coming to the last this horse was running away and I had to let go his head and he won by a half a length. Coming back in I looked fed-up with myself and Arthur walked over alongside the horse and said to me: 'Look pleased, you fool'. Concealing our true emotions.

Since this interview, Las Meninas, trained by Tommy Stack,
won the English One Thousand Guineas at Newmarket.

PADDY CULLIGAN

(GARDA COMMISSIONER)

I was appointed Garda Commissioner in January, 1991 and I am now into my fourth year. Prior to that I was Deputy Commissioner for two years. Approaching fifty-eight, I am the youngest Commissioner to have come up through the ranks. We did have younger Commissioners but they came in from the outside. When I joined the force in 1957, and for many years afterwards, the Commissioner was Dan Costigan who had come from the Department of Justice. He had been an Assistant Secretary in the Department.

The role is one of leadership. I am divorced from operational work in the strictest sense of the word. The biggest problem in being Commissioner is not about policing at all. In fact I often say that if it was about policing, that it wouldn't be that difficult for somebody who has come up through the ranks. But it is mainly dealing with personnel problems. There is hardly a day without some serious personnel problem of one sort or another. And that is understandable, given that any one of eleven thousand men and women can do something either by commission or omission which might land the job or the government of the day in some bother. Those are the things that take most of my time. I delegate a lot to the Deputy and Assistant Commissioners.

I avail of every opportunity to visit stations during working time and to join people on social occasions such as Divisional dances.

Police work is a constant battle of wits with people out there because crime changes. Crimes such as handbag snatching, larcenies, and burglaries, all of which happened in the past, are now accompanied by gratuitous violence on a fairly sizable scale. What gives rise to that is anybody's guess, but the popular belief is that it is associated with

drugs and drug crazed criminals. Some of that may be true. Another school of thought is that it is associated with video nasties. That may well also be true. But for whatever reason it is changing and it is a constant battle.

One of the reasons we manage so well is that we are so well accepted by the general public of this country. Without that help, no police could survive and we are lucky that we command the respect of eighty-four per cent – at the last call – of the public, which is enormous. I think this acceptance has come about because Ireland is a small country and we have a national force. This gives us a great advantage in that we control every aspect of policing for the entire country. In most other countries there is a special security service. But I wear a number of hats, one of them being Head of State Security. We also operate Immigration posts at all airports and points of entry into the country. Other countries have separate agencies.

There is a lot of mythology about the man on the beat. The man on the beat, when measuring police effectiveness, solves very little crime. He may prevent it, but only in the place where he or she happens to be at that particular time. The guard on the beat gives a lot of reassurance to the public. Most of this is about perception. But studies show that the man on the beat does not do much for crime, either its prevention or detection. I wouldn't be very strong on this aspect of police work. There is a place for this. But I think we need to have a number of people on the beat, if for no other reason than to reassure the people out there to feel more comfortable in their homes and on the street. From the point of view of getting work done, you have to go beyond the man on the beat and that is why we have a lot of specialist units. The man on the beat is really a community policeman.

I would never countenance the arming of the Garda Síochána. We have armed detectives, about eighteen hundred people. This is a lot of armed people for an unarmed police force. I would wish to reduce that rather than contemplate arming other sections. I think violence breeds violence. There have been many situations over the years where guns have been used and maybe if our people did not have guns at the particular time the end result might have been achieved anyway without them. So I don't go for it, even though the number of guns now available out there among criminals has increased enormously.

You can almost date this to the early 1970s and it coincides with the upsurge of the Troubles in the North. Up to that time this country was relatively crime free. It is not a coincidence but runs along with the violence in the North. The gun culture was ingrained in the people who came down here and there were lots of armed robberies by subversives. Criminals down here saw this was a very good way of carrying out crimes with a better chance of getting away with it. From that point on the gun came in down here and every two-bit criminal can lay a hand on a gun now. You can tie it right back to that.

We have been very successful in dealing with the bigger criminals. There are a half dozen here in Dublin we haven't got to grips with, but there are other, top class criminals doing long stretches in prison at the moment.

I know many of our people on the ground are very unhappy about the fact that criminals are not locked up for longer periods when they are convicted. They are very unhappy about temporary releases. But my philosophy is that our job is to catch them and take them before the courts, and what happens after that is somebody else's business. If it doesn't work out, we should not get worked up about it. That is somebody else's problem. Those problems are well known to the people who are in a position to do something about it.

We have never failed for want of expertise to investigate any serious fraud. I should say that fraud is increasing and a fraudster will always be a step ahead of you, given the nature of it. There are no outward signs which would say to a policeman that X is into fraud because of Y and Z. Somebody has to come and tell you that there is a deficiency in their books. And you take it from there. The focus came on this three years ago that we did not have enough resources and that we should have something resembling the Serious Fraud Office. What happened at the time was one of these blips in the system and three or four very serious frauds at the same time. It hasn't happened since and hadn't happened before that. We are on a reasonable keel at the moment. We are making some changes in that area to bring us up to greater speed involving lawyers and accountants. We hired them in on a short-term basis, but the present Minister now wants full-time people working with our people and that's fine as long as there is enough work for them.

There is a lot of mythology about investigating fraud. What you are talking about is bookkeeping. You have figures in and figures out. And what you are talking about is persistent investigators going through this. One case in point: the books were being audited by a company which didn't see anything amiss. Eventually somebody said there was something funny. Another accountancy firm was brought in and they said there was something wrong, but couldn't find it. They eventually sent it to the guards and the guards did find it. There is a lot of nonsense talked about the expertise you need to do this. I think we have one trained accountant in the Squad. The Squad know a crooked book when they see it.

Subversion is the most insidious crime we have today. I made it a priority when I took over as Commissioner that we would seek out where the weapons were stored and that we would also seek out the users. Over the past three years in my Commissionership we have made good inroads into that and we are continuing. The next is the drugs problem. Outside of Dublin you don't have a hard drugs problem. That seems to be confined to Dublin. It is increasing and more kids are experimenting. You could delude yourself into believing it could be solved with policing and through law enforcement. It really is an education problem. In 1982 and 1983 when we were at a peak in Dublin with hard drugs, the government and agencies set about tackling it and did so successfully. But I believe more was done through the educational end than through law enforcement.

The message was got to kids in a big way not to abuse drugs and drug abuse went down until 1990 when it started to climb again. There has not been the same emphasis in advertising and the media in educating kids about the danger of drugs. A lot of lip-service is paid to this and the one thing I would say, without fear of contradiction, is that if you leave it to law enforcers to solve it will never be solved.

My personal and business relationship with the Chief Constable of the RUC is excellent. We knew each other for years before he became Chief Constable and before I became Commissioner. Through policing we knew one another and we meet fairly regularly and this percolates down through the system in both organisations.

The Minister is my boss and the Minister is answerable in Dáil Éireann for policing in the country. To that extent the Minister has to be concerned with what is happening on the ground. My connection with the Minister would be with the Secretary of the Department of Justice, who is also a Kerryman, Tim Dalton, and his predecessor Joe Brosnan was another Kerryman. All ex St Brendan's; we'll get a plug in there for St Brendan's. We talk on the phone nearly every day at some stage or other.

The fact that we are both Kerrymen helps, it certainly doesn't hinder the relationship. It has to be a plus, as we understand each other's view a bit better and we can deal with each other more matter of factly than if the backgrounds were not somewhat similar. The Minister would not interfere in operational policing, that is a matter for the Commissioner. The Secretary of the Department is the accounting officer and he handles all the money; I don't handle any money. In my experience the relationship with the Department of Justice has been very good.

There is a wrong perception that there is a disproportionate number of Kerrymen in the guards. I think at one time most of the guards came from the West of Ireland. We had very few from Dublin and Wexford. The east coast wasn't traditionally a strong recruiting area. All that has changed. The greatest number on graduation day at Templemore are from Dublin.

I think the greater number of women in the force has taken away the rawkishness you used to get in some stations. The number of women is growing, particularly over the past four or five years. Phyllis Nolan, Bríd Wymes, Sarah McGuinness and Mary O'Donnell down in Limerick were some of the first and great policewomen. I will bring the wrath of every woman around the country down on me but, if one was to categorise jobs as between male and female jobs, I would say that policing is more a man's job. But having said that, within the organisation, there are jobs that women do far better than men. And also jobs that men do far better than women. Unquestionably, there is a place and indeed a need for both men and women in the force. The women have brought a lot of sensitivity into the force.

I think that a seventy-thirty male/female ratio would be a good mix. We only have five per cent women now and it is increasing. At a recent graduation in Templemore about thirty-five per cent of the class was female. In looking for a person who is cut out to be in the force you are looking for somebody who gets on with people and is a good communicator, not shy, but nonetheless not too brash. You want somebody with integrity and general all-round reasonable education. Not overly educated. As one progresses you need more education and training.

Above all, I think it is essential to have your feet fairly well on the ground, to understand people and the problems they can get themselves into. It is a job that gives people awesome powers, powers to do a whole range of things; powers to stop people and search them. I would say you can do an awful lot of good for an awful lot of people in this job. And conversely you can cause an awful lot of hurt to people as well. So whatever you do in your day-to-day work, do as much good as you can for as many people as possible. You must exercise your powers with restraint and with feeling for the sensitivities of people, irrespective of what part of the social stratum they come from. It's all about common sense.

My late father was in the Garda Síochána. When I joined, he said, 'Pat, I always had one rule of thumb about whether you should or should not arrest somebody. It is common sense. If somebody you are dealing with has done something which is inherently wrong, you can be absolutely sure there is a power of arrest'.

I am absolutely satisfied with the power we have. We have enough power to do the job we are asked to do. We are not constrained from doing anything we have been asked to do through lack of power. I think the people wouldn't wish their police force to have too much power anyway, I mean the sort of power you could arrest people willy-nilly and lock them away and leave them for days without access to solicitors or medical people. You can recall back in the 1970s when the government of the day introduced the seven day detention. The people didn't like that. People within the Garda Síochána didn't like it either. Its life was very short-lived for that reason.

We are now setting out a corporate five year plan. The Minister has got funding for most of it through government. We are grateful to her as it must not have been easy. Part of that will pay for a technology package which will cost many millions. The reason for that is that we have been into computers for twenty years and we have a lot of material on computers, but they are islands of information on their own with no integration. You could have one person filed under many different headings in different computer files. So we want to get the whole system integrated and have people in every station connected into the system. We want them to access it and feed it as well. That will be a huge plus in a few years down the road when I won't be here. But at least I can feel I was part of starting it.

In rural areas our community policing gives a far better service than has been available up to now. Over the years in rural Ireland, getting back to my boyhood days in Knocknagoshel, there was a sergeant and four guards. I don't know how many there are now. There certainly wouldn't be three. In those days the sergeant and four guards knew everything. In addition it was a twenty-four hour a day, seven day a week job.

The Conroy Commission in 1970 changed all that when it said the guard should work a forty hour week and everything beyond that was overtime. And in places which worked the three relief system with twenty-four hour coverage where they work three shifts, it meant that another shift had to be put in to take account of the reduced working hours and additional rest days. Take a town like Tralee. If, for instance, you have eighty guards in Tralee, you can divide that by four and that is the maximum number you can have for duty at any one time. That is not easily or readily understood by people. Some people would say, 'There are eighty people, where are they?' When you have to provide cover twenty-four hours a day for three hundred and sixty five days you are talking about trying to spread people and spreading them thinly.

In small villages that have been reduced to one guard, that one person has to get eight days off every twenty-eight days. He is there twenty days maximum and that is for only eight hours a day. He may not even live in the place. To augment that, we have grouped three or four stations and police the area as a unit and administer it from a central point. When Gardaí are not in the station the 'Green Man' comes into play and by throwing a switch the public are in radio contact. All our people, now, either in cars or on foot, have radio and are in immediate contact.

The perception that unless you have your own station with your own guard, you are getting a diminished service is a fallacy. We are working far better now in these areas. We are giving all of these areas a minimum sixteen hours cover each day, every day, whereas up to now they were only getting eight hours for twenty days out of twenty-eight. For the other eight days there was nobody at all.

Very rarely do I get individual guards coming to me with their problems. Each division has its own welfare committee which is chaired by the Chief Superintendent with people from the different ranks and from the staff associations on it. Their brief is to look after the welfare of people who might have particular problems such as drink related ones. Rarely would anybody ask to see the Commissioner as there are so many layers which they have recourse to.

I'm sure it is a stressful job and more so for some than others. But we never knew in this job that there was any stress related illness at all up until it became fashionable to talk about stress related illness a few years ago. Maybe it was being put down to something else. There are incidents of stress and it may not be related to policing at all. It can be put down to other factors of living. In a big organisation there are spots and different jobs for different people and you can accommodate people pretty well in facets of the job that suit them. Some like nine to five, others like night duty, others hate like hell working night duty. You have a mix. We are hearing more and more about stress as you do in other walks of life.

My father, Michael Culligan, opened a station in Co Sligo in 1923. He then moved on to Limerick and married my mother when he was stationed there. She was Rita Croke and now resides in Killarney. She is from Thomondgate in Limerick and I was born in St Mary's parish, or

'The Parish' as it is called in Limerick. So if you want to hear a verse of 'There is an Isle' I'm as good as anybody. I was born on July 21, 1936 in Athlunkard Street. Dad was transferred to Knocknagoshel when he was promoted sergeant. I was only three weeks old when we moved to Knocknagoshel, so I am really Kerry.

The first twelve years of my life were spent there. It was marvellous growing up. Two schools, boys and girls, two classrooms in the boys' school and to this day I still can't understand how they did it. Miss Dillon taught from infants to second and then Master McCarthy taught from third to sixth. I have an older brother Michael, a priest in California. I was the second of nine. Kevin has spent his working life with CIE and is still with them here in Dublin. Ann is at home in Killarney. She works with SIPTU. Susan Leech is married in Dublin and teaches. Adrian is a Superintendent in Mayfield in Cork and married to Nuala O'Hara from Cork. John is a detective in Anglesea Street in Cork. Brendan is teaching in Dublin and married and Philip, the youngest, is in Dublin; he has a company in the grain and feed business.

We lived in the barracks in Knocknagoshel. One of the memories I have of Knocknagoshel is the battery radio – the dry battery and the wet battery. We were fortunate enough to have one in the station. The wet battery had to be taken on the bike to Abbeyfeale every so often to get it charged and if you spilt any of the acid out of that you were in big trouble. I can remember being in the kitchen one day and a lot of people listening to the news of a general election coming through. It would have been in the mid 1940s. Listening to the final from the Polo Grounds in 1947 is another memory. Eddie Walsh played with Kerry in those days and it was a great event when Eddie returned home after a big win because the local band was pulled out and played up the village. His father, the 'Hooker', had a pub in the village.

I have no memory of being conscious of being the local sergeant's son. My closest school friend in those days in Knocknagoshel was Connie Keane. He ended up in the guards as well and the two of us were in the one division here in Dublin for a number of years. When I was in Crumlin he was in Rathmines and at that time up the road in Crumlin was Leo Corcoran whose father was a guard in

Knocknagoshel when we were there.

In 1948 when I was twelve, Dad was transferred to Killarney and it came at just the right time for going into St Brendan's and I started there as a day pupil. St Brendan's was St Brendan's, some of it you liked and some of it you didn't. The day-boys included Johnny Culloty who became a great Kerry goalkeeper, Brendan Carroll, James Donoghue, Jim Trant and Pa O'Brien. That group seemed to pal around. Then you had people like Tim Lyons and Jack Dowling. The great Gobbo, Fr O'Neill, was our President.

I was a reasonably good footballer and in my last year I played Munster Colleges. With me in that team were Tom Long, Tim Barrett, Johnny Culloty, Noel Kelly, Brendan Carroll, Donal Hurley (Cork) and Billy Crean. St Brendan's had some good victories over the Green in Tralee which were always sweet ones. My brother Michael played on those teams as well. I usually played half-back, half-forward or mid-field. I played junior football with Kerry in 1955 and 1956 and senior with Cork in the late 1950s.

After my Leaving Certificate I joined the ESB and worked with them for three years. I started off reading meters and then I went on rural electrification, designing rural networks and surveying. There are poles in fields in Kerry and I am responsible for having them placed there. And if they were not in ditches I used to get abused by irate farmers. I spent a few glorious years. In the summer of 1956 I worked in Caherciveen and had little work to do. The ESB took over the electricity plant, which had been privately owned, and rewired the whole town. So from a design and survey point I had a few weeks work, but it took months to actually connect everything. I had a very soft few months after my initial bit of work.

I was in houses when the light was switched on for the first time. I remember one house in particular near Caherciveen. It was in an isolated place. The man of the house had never experienced electricity and he spent a few minutes switching on and off the light wondering and marvelling. It transformed rural life. I was doing well in the ESB and playing basketball with them. I played junior football with Kerry with Mick O'Dwyer and Mick O'Connell. We were beaten by Monaghan in an All-Ireland Semi-Final. I had been playing basketball from the early 1950s. Ben Campion was one of the founders of the game in Killarney and it grew enormously and there were great town leagues.

Recruiting for the guards started in 1956 or thereabouts. Don't ask me why I put my name down. I don't know to this day; maybe there was something in there in my head from growing up. Maybe it was in the blood. My father was still a sergeant in Killarney. He was quite happy about it. I was in the fortunate position that I didn't worry if I made it or not, as I had a job anyway. I got it and was called.

I trained here in Phoenix Park. On the first day I came in with Assistant Commissioner Hugh Sreenan, Jim Noone, Derek Nally who aferwards became General Secretary of the Garda Sergeants' and Inspectors' Association and Jack Hennessy from Ardee in County Louth. He and I were very good friends. He retired as Detective Inspector and is now head of security at Beaumont Hospital. Conditions were primitive enough at the time. We were more fortunate than others as we lived in Parkgate Hall down in Parkgate Street and we had the luxury of hot and cold water. Others here didn't have that. There was no such thing as a single room. The regime was strict on time and we had to be in at eleven o'clock at night. We trained here for twenty-two weeks.

In actual fact you were a fully fledged guard the day after you arrived when you were sworn in. So here you were, with all the powers of a guard, without knowing anything about it. It was a short training, but it equipped you adequately for the time.

My first station was Watercourse Road in Cork in October 1957. After a few years I went on to Middleton, from there to Abbeyleix. I then came to the Technical Bureau as a detective. If I hadn't been transferred out of Cork I might well have been still there as a guard or a sergeant. I loved Cork and I have great friends there. I played football for the guards and then with St Finbarrs. John Driscoll was a great friend in the 'Barrs. His brother Paddy played for Cork. Paddy was as good and tough a footballer as ever put on a jersey. I played for Cork in 1958, 1959 and 1960. They had come out of a very good period and then they were in the doldrums when I played for them. I continued to play basketball for Kerry and in the space of eight days in one year I played with Kerry against Cork in the Munster Basketball Final and with Cork against Kerry in the Munster Football Final. When I was in Killarney I played football with the Legion. Jackie Lyne, Dinny Lyne, Tommy Cooper, John C Cooper, Gerald O'Sullivan and Johnny Culloty are names that spring to mind.

When I came to Dublin from Abbeyleix I was with the Murder Squad for sixteen years. We were involved in nearly all the big murder cases from 1962 to 1976 and we travelled all over the country. The Squad was headed by Paddy McLaughlin who later became Commissioner, a very close friend and still is. John Paul McMahon who later became Deputy Commissioner, one of the greatest investigators the Garda Síochána ever had, was in the Squad. The late Dan Murphy who was a Detective Chief Superintendent was top-notch. John Moore was also a Chief Superintendent and Jack Hennessy was also there. There were about seven in the Squad at the time. We had tremendous success. We were very high profile and we went through one eight year period without an undetected murder in that time.

The first murder I was involved in was the McEvoy murder on the Heath in Portlaoise. I had just left Abbeyleix and within two months I was back down with the Murder Squad. A woman's body was found on the Heath in Portlaoise. I went straight from that to the Hazel Mullen case here in Dublin.

I got into the Murder Squad quite by accident. I had applied for a mapping job in the Technical Bureau as I had experience of this with the ESB. I got the interview and was called. I thought I was going into the mapping office. I was there with another good Kerryman, Teddy O'Sullivan, who played with Kerry in the Polo Grounds. I was only with Teddy for a half day when a sergeant from the investigation unit called me into his office and said I was with him. He was Tony Moroney, a Clareman, who became a great friend. He was in charge of administration. I was the district clerk in Abbeyleix and he knew I could be useful in the administrative work. I was in his office doing clerical work when the murder happened in Portlaoise and they need-ed somebody to do the administration work, so I was called in and I must have done something right because from that day on I became Co-ordinator of Investigations, putting it together and directing new lines of inquiry. I spent years at that. I went in as a guard to the Technical Bureau and I left it as a Superintendent.

The Squad grew enormously from the time I left it to about forty after the Northern Troubles. When I became Assistant Commissioner for Crime and Security we were asked to look at the whole structure and our recommendation was to reduce that Squad again. We reduced it to two Detective Superintendents and three Detective Sergeants. That's still there as a nucleus of a Squad. If there is a complicated murder anywhere they can go and set up for the local Gardaí and give them advice and direction. But essentially it is a local operation now and that is how it should be. It is a fallacy to think that you can send twenty people from here to anywhere and conduct an investigation. They had to be paired with local people to show them the different places. So essentially, the work was being done by local people and all they needed was a guiding hand. We have reduced it to that now and we have trained more people in the mechanics of setting up a big investigation, and it is working very well.

The sentence a murderer gets should not vary too much. Most murderers only commit murder once and it can be their only crime. The difficulty in investigating a murder is you can never know who might commit a murder. If you are investigating house-breaking, a particular job has the hallmark of a particular criminal. And in murders it often turns out that a most unlikely person is the person who committed the crime. Some are crimes of passion, some are committed over land, some are just family rows. There are very few who set out to kill and who will kill more than once, for a set purpose, but there have been exceptions. Somebody like that needs to be taken out of circulation for longer than a person who kills in a fit of mad rage.

Generally speaking 'life' for murder here runs for between eight to eleven years. For the vast majority it is adequate. You need to have a harder look at people who commit calculated murder in the course of a robbery. I think our courts get the balance right in sentencing for murder.

I would like the Gardaí to have an air support of its own, helicopters and fixed wing. They would be of immense benefit and that is not casting any aspersion on the Aer Corps, they are absolutely brilliant and have never let us down. You are better when you have it yourself.

I play golf at the Curragh and I am playing off a handicap of eleven. I used to play off seven. I played Waterville before it was what it now is. It was a nine hole course going into disrepair in 1956 when I was working with the ESB. Eamonn Cunningham who was the engineer with the ESB and myself paid thirty shillings to play as long as we were in Caherciveen.

I live in Naas. My wife, Carmel, is from Dublin and we have three children. My son is twenty-four and an Actuary. I have a daughter in Trinity and another daughter studying for her Leaving. We go to Kerry a few times a year. We don't holiday in Ireland because if we don't go out of the country I don't have a holiday. I get away from it all. I am a reformed smoker and I drink bottles of Guinness. I am one of a dying breed as my trademark is a large bottle of Guinness and a small glass.

TIM DALTON

(SECRETARY DEPARTMENT OF JUSTICE)

I was appointed Secretary of the Department of Justice in February 1993, taking over, for my sins, from another Kerryman, Joe Brosnan, who went to Brussels as Chef-de-Cabinet with Commissioner Flynn. I am fifty-one.

You asked me to describe this job. While it is perfectly reasonable to expect that I should be able to do so, I have to tell you at the start that it's not too easy to do so in a few plain words.

The Secretary of the Department of Justice is in a central position as regards the operation of the law and order system in the State. He or she – so far there has been no 'she' but time changes everything – is the principal policy advisor to the Minister for Justice on law and order issues.

There are a number of areas in which the Secretary is very involved on a day-to-day basis. He is the Accounting Officer, that is, he answers to the Dáil, through the Public Accounts Committee, for the money provided by the Oireachtas each year for the Department itself, for the Garda Síochána, for the Prisons Service, for the Courts, the Land Registry and Registry of Deeds and for the Office of Charitable Donations and Bequests. That money aggregates about £550 million per year at the present time. A sizable proportion of it goes towards the payment of about 16,000 public service salaries to Gardaí (about 11,000), Prison Officers (about 2,300) and various others.

The Secretary has dealings with the Gardaí day-in-day-out on current issues of concern in relation to crime and so on, as well as constant discussion with Garda management on issues of general policy. Similarly with the Prison Service.

The courts are independent in the exercise of their functions, under the Constitution, but the Department is responsible for support services, staff, accommodation etc. I am involved from time to time, therefore, in discussions with judges, with court staff and with other interested parties such as the Law Society about these matters.

The Land Registry and Registry of Deeds and the Office of Charitable Donations and Bequests operate on a day-to-day basis very much on their own – that is, without any case-by-case operational direction from the Department. The Department has an involvement of course in Land Registry affairs when the annual expenditure estimates are being framed, when issues arise which are likely to concern the Oireachtas or the Public Accounts Committee, and in relation to the more important policy issues such as the conversion of the Land Registry to semi-State status, the issue of decentralisation of its operations, legislative changes and matters of that kind.

The Department itself has responsibility for criminal and certain administrative law reform and also for immigration and citizenship. Another area in which the Department has an involvement is of course Northern Ireland – in which there is a fairly significant level of involvement mainly through the Anglo-Irish Conference process. There is then a whole host of what might best be described as 'miscellaneous' items which include pawnbrokers, intoxicating liquor laws, coroners, peace commissioners, data protection, petitions, gaming and lotteries, money lending, firearms and, believe it or not, changing the clocks for summer and winter time.

Public concern in relation to some or all of the areas for which the Department has responsibility lands on my table in one form or another on a regular basis. They tend to land together when the Minister takes oral Parliamentary Questions in the Dáil – which happens about once a month or so. We receive quite a large number of Dáil Questions in this Department – for better or worse, it is in fact one of the most questioned Departments of all. I see what the Department thinks the Minister should say in reply to all these questions. I think a lot of Departmental Secretaries tend to operate in this way because it is one very effective way of 'keeping tabs' on what is actually going on in the

Department. Naturally some Questions take more time to deal with than others and the Secretary would tend to be more closely involved in the way in which certain Questions are dealt with than he would in the vast majority of them. Much depends on the nature of the Question and the level of public interest likely to be generated by the answer. It goes without saying of course that it is the Minister who decides, in the end, what should or should not be said.

The media – newspapers, radio, television – also take a very substantial interest in matters for which the Department of Justice has responsibility. Hardly a day goes by without some sizable media piece on a matter which concerns the Department.

We are, I believe, now much more responsive towards the media than we were in the past. Because of the sensitive nature of various matters dealt with by the Department, however, there are times when we are simply obliged to be less forthcoming than the media might wish us to be. The provision of information can at times involve serious conflicts of interest – one man's right to information may, for example, conflict with another's right to privacy or with the community's right to safety and security.

The people I deal with for the most part on a daily basis are the Assistant Secretaries in charge of the various units I've mentioned – There are five Assistant Secretaries in the Department in all. When it comes to discussing core policy issues in any of these areas, such as reform of public order legislation or the law applying to refugees, prisons' policy, police structures, or whatever it may happen to be, the relevant Assistant Secretary and his staff – sometimes senior Garda management – would normally sit down and discuss the policy implications with the Secretary before the matter goes to the Minister. Contact with his Minister is of course an on-going feature of every Department Secretary's job.

It is difficult, in the course of an interview like this, to describe my work any more plainly than I have tried to do over the past few minutes of our conversation.

In truth, I have very little idea, on any day coming to work, what is going to beset the place. It depends on what the present public concern happens to be. Contrary to the public perception of the Civil Service and its ways, one doesn't always have oodles of time to think about what the Minister's or the Government's response should be to whatever problem happens to descend. It's a matter very often of picking up a dictaphone, there and then (or perhaps the night before if the likely 'flavour' of tomorrow's problem happens to emerge on the *Nine o'clock News*), and putting together a statement for the Minister or the Department as the case may be.

When you don't necessarily know what particular problem may arise, you do need to have the basic 'ammunition' or instinct to get the right response or decision together quickly. You need to know how the system as a whole ought to work. It's not just a question of knowing how the system can be got to work in a manner that is cohesive and cost effective but, more importantly, how to ensure that things are done in a manner that is proportionate, balanced and humane.

What I have described as the 'humane' aspect is particularly important in my view. It's not only that the actual exercise of law and order function should be characterised by humanity insofar as the citizen is concerned, but also that the atmosphere in the Department itself should be as tolerant as we can make it and that there should be a degree of understanding when people fail to measure up – which happens to all of us at times. The same is, I think, true of all large organisations.

I had an early experience with a Parliamentary Question which is relevant to this whole question of tolerance and understanding in that it taught me that there are different ways of killing a goose.

When I was new to the Department, as an Executive Officer, I found myself with the task of preparing an answer to a Dáil Question which, as far as I can recall, had to do with the downgrading of the Garda station in Dingle.

The Executive Officer's main job – at least in those days – was to get the Minister's background Information Note right. More senior staff would tend to concentrate on the crafting of the actual answer. By and large they would tend to assume that the background note, on which the answer is based was right or, if not totally right, was as close to being correct as makes no difference. Anyway, I did the background note, in the usual way and, as we happened to be at that time of year when most of the senior staff were away on holidays, there was little or no vetting of the content of the note I had cobbled together for the Minister's file in the Dáil. That in itself wasn't necessarily a disaster but I will not forget, nor am I ever likely to forget, what happened when the Minister stood up to give his answer in the Dáil.

One of the Opposition Deputies held up a letter and, being a good politician, proceeded to wave it about saying that the Minister didn't know what was in the letter, that it came from the Department of Justice and flatly contradicted what the Minister was now saying in the House. The Deputy, as far as I can remember, did little more than make this grand gesture but, within minutes, I got a very clear message that the Minister had been highly embarrassed in the House. He had looked in vain through his Information Note in the hope of securing an insight into the background to the 'offending' letter.

As a young fellow in the system, I didn't know what kind of misfortune was about to descend on me on account of this appalling gaffe. The general tone of the letter was known by now and I proceeded to unearth a copy of it on the departmental file. My reaction, having read it, was that it wasn't all that important and that there was no particular reason for referring to it in the note I'd prepared for the Minister.

When I said this to a more experienced hand however, he assured me, quite helpfully, that I was deep in trouble – actually he didn't use the word 'trouble'. My only defence was that if I were to put references to every letter that issued from the Department in the background note I prepared for the Minister's information, he might as well carry over a wheelbarrow to the Dáil with all the letters that ever issued about any subject that might happen to come up. This, as you can imagine, was not seen by more worldly-wise colleagues as a particularly inspired piece of defence.

The late Peter Berry was Secretary of the Department at the time and he, too, was alleged to have been on the rampage over the fact that the Minister was embarrassed. I didn't know Peter Berry at that stage, but all available folklore left me in no doubt that if he was angry about something, it would be wise for a junior official like myself to divide the remainder of his day between Novenas and drafting an abject apology.

Peter Berry, however, was a much wiser man than I had been led to believe – the leg-pulling antics of the aforementioned colleagues, you will understand, had played a considerable part in upping my general sense of anxiety over the whole incident. I was sitting in the Department at about seven o'clock that evening waiting for the sword to descend when I got a message from the Secretary, now cognisant of whatever explanation I had given, that there was no need to worry and that of course I couldn't put in a reference to everything in the Minister's Information Note. The Minister himself said nothing, but he may not have been aware of the identity of the culprit.

The episode is totally insignificant to the history of the Department of Justice – indeed to any history apart from that of my personal health – but it taught me the lesson that when you are working with people and something goes wrong, and the manure hits the fan, you should take as much as you can on yourself and avoid dumping the blame on somebody who is more junior or more vulnerable. I'm not saying that culpable negligence or gross incompetence should be covered up but simply that when there is a lapse due to human error, inexperience, or whatever, the first thought should not be to grind the offender into the mire as happens all too often, I believe, in too many employments.

Is this a pressure job? Well, yes, I suppose, but, before I answer the question, let me say something first about pressure. People in most employments, now, seem to feel duty-bound to stress the pressures they endure day-in-day-out. Different employments have almost got into a sort of competition on the subject. Unless you are up the pressure 'league table' you are out of the race.

There is considerable exaggeration involved in all of this. For me, the man or woman with no job at all and four or five hungry mouths to feed has pressure. Or the person who has to endure long term illness and the like. There is job pressure, too, and I'm not in any way denying that, but we go a little over the top on the subject.

As I've said, and subject to my general views on job pressure, yes there is a share of pressure in this job. Some would also say that it has increased significantly over the years. We now have a drugs problem which wasn't a serious issue say, thirty years ago and a more serious problem with crime generally. Pressure in this kind of job, I think, is relative to prevailing social values and expectations. These values and expectations have changed over the years. Some of these changes have been for the good and were clearly necessary but more of them, sadly, have been far from positive. But my point is that, to a sizable extent, pressure is relative to values and expectations so that somebody in the same job thirty years ago would probably feel as stressed as any present incumbent, even if we now think that life then was much more idyllic than it is now.

Yes, I bring work home at night and weekends. I have very little choice in the matter. But there are many others, in different employment, who are in exactly the same situation. And it's better in my view to find yourself bringing work home than to find yourself with no work to bring anywhere with all of the very difficult consequences which that situation entails for those who have to face it.

Your question as to whether the job gets in on me personally – the answer, in a word, is 'no'. I think that if you let any job get in on you personally you might as well pack it in. That it not to say that I don't think and worry about a share of things from time to time – things that most sane people don't have to think or worry about, but there is no point in letting it get to the point where you spend the night or the whole weekend tearing your hair out.

There are, as I say, people with far greater worries – about the fact that they have no employment, about illness and so on.

When I want to switch off I dig the garden or go out and have a few pints. Sometimes I even do both, the first as a warmer-up or as a domestic 'excuse' for the second. Generally, I suppose, I try to approach things in as balanced a way as I can, judge things as carefully as I can and take as much advice about problems as people are willing to give me. After that, if you are not doing the job reasonably well, you should be having serious thoughts about doing something else with your life.

As to my pre-Civil Service existence embracing, as you put it, some background on Dalton, the character, I've been most reluctant as you know to do any interview about myself because like most people I don't think very much about myself on a day-to-day basis. I'm no good at self analysis therefore because I have no practice at it. Some people, who, mind you, describe themselves as friends, say that I should take a greater interest in analysis – at least that's how I've chosen to interpret their advice that I should be seeing an analyst.

My father, Jack Dalton, is still alive and well and living in Tralee. He worked with CIE. My late mother whose family name was Hickey was a farmer's daughter and I spent a share of my summer holidays farming with my cousins. It might be more accurate to say that I got in the way of their farming endeavours. They still in fact farm near Tralee. I have one sister also living in the area.

With regard to schools and so on, my first school was a small country school outside Tralee which was known as O'Brennan National School. It was a two-teacher school run by a Master and Mrs Lynch. It was located on a by-road of the same name – O'Brennan Road – about six miles from Tralee, on the Ballymacelligott side.

When I last saw this academy its doors and windows had long since departed this life and the school appeared to have graduated to the status of cattle shed. The new four-legged 'pupils' staring through the ruin were, I suspect, at least as interested in sums and history as some of us were in our time at the institution. But they looked far less happy in themselves, less boisterous, less likely to produce a scholarship boy or girl, a scientist, a teacher or even a convict. A spanking new school replaced my old school several years ago.

Teacher ratios, now very much in vogue, were difficult to discern. I can recall sitting in a classroom in which about four classes were being taught by the same teacher who had blackboards on different walls. The first class looked at one wall, the second another and so on.

Looking back, it had the accidental advantage that a smart pupil could greatly advance his or her educational prowess simply by looking in a different direction from time to time whereas the older, less talented pupil could, by casting an eye over his shoulder, take consolation in the knowledge that he was at least a few steps ahead of a more junior group of wall gazers.

The school was uni-sex but we were too young and well reared to appreciate the potential inherent in that particular feature.

One of my more frightening memories of the school had to do with the old ink-wells which sat on each desk. In fact they sat in little holes which were carved out on the desk. In any event, during my first few weeks in school I managed to topple one of these containers, pouring the ink all over my hands. An older and far from sympathetic fellow-student informed me that I'd really had it and that my hands would remain blue for the remainder of my life. I'll never forget this piece of news. In fact I spent the day bawling my head off about the tragedy. Those who know me now would say that it wasn't so much that my hands were about to remain permanently coloured, but that the colour was blue. Had the ink been green and gold, everything would have been hunky-dory.

I left that school when I was in about fourth class and proceeded to the Mercy Convent in Tralee and subsequently to the CBS Primary School. I remember two teachers in particular at that school. One was Master O'Brien who managed to tell us a new story every day, each with a strong republican flavour. Brother Browne was another teacher I particularly remember because he was a stickler for high standards. I remember a number of pupils at the school and I have met many of them since – Matthew Hassett, Colm Courreen from Tralee and many others. I remember one chap called Peter Keogh who, I think, became a chemical engineer in later life. I remember him for the unusual reason that we were in constant competition for the apples and chocolates doled out by Brother Browne as work incentives.

Another pupil I remember was Oliver Whiston from Boherbue in Tralee who is now teaching in Wicklow. Oliver and I shared the same birthday and, naturally, I didn't like this because it shaded the glory a bit when the birthday came around. It meant, for example, that a teacher who might be disposed to dole out an apple segment to 'celebrate' one's birthday, could end up, instead, doling out two smaller segments. These, as you know, are matters which weigh heavily on the mind of a ten or eleven year old.

Following primary school I became a pupil at St Brendan's College in Killarney on a County Council scholarship. There I progressed steadily from being the best student in the class to being a thoroughly lazy one, something which had to do with an inherent tendency on my part rather than any fault on the part of the College. You see, I thought it better to spend a fine summer's evening dawdling through Keats or Wordsworth than grappling with the subtleties of a Greek verb, even if the latter was required for my next exam and the former required for nothing beyond enjoyment. At the College I got to know amongst many many others, Joe Brosnan who was of course my predecessor in this Department.

There are a number of Kerrymen in roles similar to mine in other Government Departments – Michael Dowling, Secretary of the Department of Agriculture, Seán Dorgan in Tourism and Trade and Paddy Teahon who is Secretary of the Department of the Taoiseach. All of these were pupils at St Brendan's as was the Garda Commissioner, Paddy Culligan, with whom I now have regular dealings and the newly appointed Governor of the Central Bank, Maurice O'Connell.

Kerrymen holding similar positions who did not attend St Brendan's are Seán Brosnan, Secretary of the Department of Defence, John O'Mahony, Chairman of the Office of Public Works, and Cathal MacDomhnaill, Chairman of the Revenue Commissioners. Both Cathal and John are from Tralee.

The net effect of this recent Kerry invasion at the top of the Civil Service is that we displaced the Cork Mafia, but there is ample evidence that they still haven't given up. For example, they have given us absolutely nothing on the football field since we displaced them. I suppose that, in a world guided by proper values and priorities, we would give up the jobs altogether to see if it would soften the Corkmen and perhaps change our luck in the Munster Championships. But we have the reputation of being what John B Keane describes as 'cute hoors' so, for the moment, the jobs take priority over the football.

Another fellow student in St Brendan's was Paddy Kennelly who is Brendan Kennelly's brother – I hope Paddy doesn't mind being identified by reference to his very well-known brother. He wrote a book called *Sausages for Tuesday* which is set in St Brendan's. There is a character in the book called Dalton, but I am not he. There is another character, however, whose name I cannot remember, but he is definitely based on the pupil who was Dalton. He was a prominent organiser of some of the more 'subversive' escapades described in the book which, if they had been part of my CV, would not have advanced my prospects of ending up in this outfit. You will have to read the book and draw your own conclusions.

I did my Leaving Cert in St Brendan's and then went back to Tralee CBS to repeat because I wasn't happy with my first effort. At the end of that year I joined the Civil Service. One of the first people I met in Dublin was a fellow called Tadhg Tansley from Fenit who had been a fellow pupil at Tralee CBS and was, and still is, in the Department of Health. Eventually he and I together with a chap from Bandon, John Fitzgerald, now in the Department of Finance, descended as lodgers in a house in Cherryfield Avenue in Ranelagh which was owned by a Mr and Mrs Harding. I stayed there until I got married about eight years later. My reason for staying as long as I did is that we were very well looked after by a couple whose patience was often stretched but whose tolerance seemingly knew no bounds.

I didn't come to the Department of Justice by choice. At that time you were told you were assigned to a particular Department and that was it. I think that may have changed since but, to tell you the truth, I'm not sure whether it has or not.

I started work in what was known as the 'West Block' of Government Buildings. That was an exciting structure in the sense that one was always kept on one's toes as to whether something vital, like the stairs, would survive the day. That, I hasten to add, is a non-professional piece of judgment. Anyway the building survived magnificently until it was demolished and I also survived, for better or worse, to move around the Department of Justice.

One of these moves saw me assigned to a building in Hume Street where I was encouraged to walk around the edge of the room rather than on the centre of the floor. At that time I weighed about the same fifteen or sixteen stone that I seem to have weighed since birth and when I walked across the centre of the floor, the place began to shake. So much so that faithful, long-serving staff who were of a nervous disposition, but with a better eye than I for a potential tragedy, thought it best to keep me by the wall.

The man in charge of that office – where we dealt, incidentally, with Petitions and the appointment of Peace Commissioners – was one Paddy Cahill, a Dubliner, but I particularly remember another gentleman who worked in the office, Tadhg O'Donovan from Cork. He was, as far as I can recall, a cousin of Jack Lynch's. I remember him as an expert on hurling but even more so on greyhounds. He seemed to know every hair on every dog's tail in the country and regarded the study of their form – I'm talking about the dogs not the hairs on their tails – as a matter deserving the very highest priority. He counselled me on the advantages of gambling but, following a few disastrous bets, I concluded that the disadvantages probably outweighed the advantages.

There were a number of Kerrymen in the Department at that time. John Griffin from Caherciveen was head of the Account Branch. There was also Tom Woulfe, whom I still meet from time to time, and who is known to everybody with an interest in gaelic football because of his work in the removal of the infamous Ban. Probably the most interesting character in the place, however, was a man by the name of Paddy Burke, now retired – a man of very great ability who was so far ahead of his time that he was considered by many to be somewhat unusual, to say the least of it. He was always talking about some forthcoming disturbance called the 'computer revolution' when the rest of us were still grappling with the wonders of the abacus.

As happens to most decent men, which incidentally is a description I'm accused of applying liberally to Kerrymen, I became friendly, in due course, and then obsessively friendly with one Anne Doran a Dubliner who worked in the Department. Subsequently I was the cause of her losing her job because, at that time, when women Civil Servants got married they were obliged to leave the Service. She managed to secure employment outside the public service but, when the children came along, she didn't work anymore outside the home, in accordance with prevailing tradition at the time. I'd better stress of course, for the sake of my health, that she does work within the home. We have five children, four boys and a girl, the eldest of whom is working and the youngest in primary school, with the remainder somewhere in between in the educational grinder.

As regards subsequent education, I did an Arts degree by night at UCD and thoroughly enjoyed all the attendant 'shenanigans' which I need not describe. Suffice to say that the late evening 'tutorials' in O'Dwyer's and Hartigan's premises in Leeson Street were something of an educational highlight during those years. Later I qualified as a solicitor, again on the basis of studies conducted outside of office hours. I qualified in 1977 but never practised. I thought of leaving the Civil Service at the time and going into private practice but in the end I decided against. I suspect that all of our jails would be even more overcrowded had I become a defence lawyer.

I was Secretary to the Pringle Committee which recommended the introduction of Civil Legal Aid and had the privilege of drafting that Report which was published, I think, in 1979. The Pringle Committee recommended the establishment of a Board to operate the Civil Legal Aid Scheme and I left the Department to work with that Board for about years years from about 1980 to 1989. I travelled around the country during that time establishing Law Centres and the like and I must say that I enjoyed it immensely.

In 1989 the job of Assistant Secretary in the Department's Prisons Division came up which I applied for. That was a fairly tough job – some would say that any application for the job should be taken as proof positive that the applicant is somewhat unstable – but it was one of the most rewarding jobs I handled. About two years later I moved over to the Garda Division in the Department, again at Assistant Secretary level and, from there, I went to serve with the Anglo-Irish Secretariat in Belfast for about ten months. I came directly from the Secretariat to my present job.

You asked me whether rules and regulations tend to stifle civil service initiative. I think there is a lot of mythology about it. It may have been true in the past and, while it still applies I suppose to some extent, I would say that it is no longer the major problem.

I believe that in many employments, not just in the Civil Service, there is a tendency to hide behind a mysterious group of individuals called 'THEY'. 'THEY' will not permit this or that to be done, 'THEY' don't care etc, etc. As one of my colleagues in the Department says, 'Maturity arrives on the day it dawns on you that "THEY" are now "US".'

If you really want to change something or influence change whether inside the Civil Service or outside it you can do it. Day-to-day working life inside the Civil Service is now much closer to life on the outside than is generally realised.

It may seem odd, in the extreme, to hear the Secretary of a Government Department say this, but I believe that the Public Accounts Committee has made a valuable contribution to cultural change within the Civil Service. The Committee used to be, I think, something very close to being a gentleman's club in that there was a sense that Dáil Deputies were almost grateful that a Department Secretary came over and answered their questions.

That has all changed and I think it is absolutely right that Civil Servants should be asked for explanations as to how or why public money is spent in particular ways. Not only that, they should also be expected to answer to the best of their ability there and then. The more robust approach of the PAC has, I believe, been an important factor in encouraging Civil Servants to think in terms of value for money. In my case, with a total annual budget of about £550 million I think that, at the very least, the public are entitled to expect that I would be scrutinised about its use by their public representatives. My experience is that while the Deputies can be quite searching in their questioning, they are all sensible, experienced people who ask questions on behalf of the public which they judge to be right. They will accept it if a reasonable attempt is made to answer the question either at the time it's asked or by way of follow-up correspondence.

I've probably stuck my two feet in my mouth by talking in this way about the PAC. Colleagues will definitely conclude that I've gone soft or completely lost my marbles or both.

Do I have difficulty with the idea of working with a Minister who is a woman? In short, absolutely none. I think I've always been what is now called 'gender neutral' in dealing with people in the sense that I can never remember it being a problem whether I was working with a man or a woman.

The only thing that does change rather significantly is the language. You have to be a little more careful in that respect. I'm not taking about things like the frequency with which one uses swear words – which of course never happens in the Civil Service and never never amongst Ministers – I'm talking about the importance of remembering to say 'she' as well as 'he' even if the subject of the discussion is God herself. Gender is a secondary issue when you can get through the business of the day with courtesy, efficiency and a little good humour thrown in. Our present Minister fits the bill ideally in all of those respects. And, if you think I am going to expand anecdotally on that, you are mistaken.

SR CONSILIO

(FOUNDER OF CUAN MHUIRE)

ABOUT thirty years ago I started working in St Vincent's Hospital in Athy as a nurse. It was more or less the County Home. I spent most of my time in the kitchen and part of my responsibility was to look after the casual callers who needed lodgings for the night. They would then move off to another County Home and do the rounds and would be back again within a month.

There was a little house at the end of the garden which I looked after for them, and at night-time I often used go down late to talk and listen to them. I wondered how people like these, many of whom were well educated and came from good backgrounds, had drifted so far that they ended up drifting from one county home to another with a bottle of wine in their pockets.

I wondered what force inside in them drove them to this and I thought how worried my mother would be if any brother of mine was on the road like this and she not knowing where they were.

Some of these men had changed their names so that nobody would recognise them. I used always ask them if they wrote home to their mothers, because I visualised their mothers worrying about them and then I realised as time went on that they were my brothers. I then decided that somehow, some day, some place, I would have a place that they could call home and from where they could go to work. I felt it was very important that they could get back to work and get back their dignity and come home at night to a fire and a meal and somebody to love them.

I thought if they had somebody to love them, all their cares would be over. But it took me a long time and I paid a big price before I found

out that it was not about being loved, but about learning how to love. Particularly to love one's own self. And by loving I mean seeing what is best in one's own self, and then it is easy to see what is best in others. It took me a long time to realise that was the key answer to the whole thing.

I did my nursing in the North Infirmary in Cork before joining the Sisters of Mercy in Athy in 1959. Although I was a nursing sister, I spent most of my time in the kitchen as we had three hundred and twenty people and the operation of the kitchen was a major task. I felt that one of the best ways I could help was to put up nice meals. I was transferred from the hospital in Athy to the convent, but I was no time there when people began calling who had problems. I got permission to go to an open Alcoholics Anonymous meeting and a man that I met called to see me in the convent about a week later. He called once a week for about five or six weeks. I thought he was calling because he felt I was interested in alcoholism. But afterwards he told me that he found that our chats helped him, having somebody to listen to him. He told others and in no time people were calling to the convent drunk and sober, late and early.

At that time things were strict and there was night silence in the convent and the gates were locked. I had these visitors when I was supposed to be in bed. In no time lots were coming who had problems with alcohol. I listened and made tea for them and after a while I got the use of a little room near the gate and they came in. To my amazement quite a few began to get sober and we were two years in that little room. I made tea and as I was working in the kitchen I used to prepare a few apple tarts and they stayed late, because people who drink alcoholically are afraid of the night and never think of going home.

It was very difficult. You had to stay with people who had been given medication. A doctor who had problems with alcohol began coming to the meetings and he was a great help because he prescribed medication for those who wished to be dried out. I had to stay up late at night, and still be in the kitchen early in the morning. People who wanted to go for treatment had to go to St Patrick's or St John of Gods, and by the time they had their bills paid many were back drinking again.

I thought it would be great if we could have a place for people to recover without having to charge them any money. I said to one of the sisters that if she got a fridge she could give up the old dairy which the convent had at the end of the yard, rather than to be going over the yard with butter and milk.

So when I saw a big fridge advertised in the paper down in Waterford, I rang the man and told him that I badly needed it. I told him I had no money, but would pay him some time. He told me to come down and collect it. I gave the convent the fridge in exchange for the use of the old dairy.

At that stage a few tradesmen had recovered and Sr Rita had a room near the old dairy which she was not using and we started work on it. Some local people objected that we were bringing undesirables into the area. There were lots of objections as it was near the school. It was known as 'the dugout', so we felt we had to put a name on it. The late Dr Des O'Neill, who was a beautiful and great person, said we should call it 'An Cuan', the harbour. He was a great man with boats and the harbour was a safe place when boats came in and it would be appropriate. So I said that we would have to have Our Lady's name included, as without her I would have never started. We called it Cuan Mhuire.

People started coming from far and near and the amazing thing was that they began to get better. I was amazed because I knew very little about alcoholism. Mother Sacred Heart employed some of those on the recovery programme, doing work in and around the convent. They were able to send home some money to their families while on recovery. We were there for five years and we could keep about thirty people and it was getting very packed. It was too near the town and the pubs, and I felt it would be marvellous if we could move out the country, away from everyone and where we would not be coming in anyone's way.

Some land came up for sale. I asked permission to go to the auction. I had no money, but I believed Our Lady would get it for us if we were meant to get it. I bought the land for forty-nine thousand pounds, twenty years ago at the auction. I didn't have any money. It was a lot of money at the time.

The auction took place on the side of the road and I stood there with one of the men from the centre who came with me. I stood there in all my regalia, veil and all. I can't recall if it was the man who came with me or myself who actually did the bidding. The man who sold it died shortly after, so that gave us eighteen months before we had to come up with any money. I got two years' credit from builders' providers and we built the first Cuan Mhuire there, one mile outside of Athy, twenty-one years ago on forty-two acres.

Reverend Mother Sacred Heart was very supportive. Once she felt you were in the business of helping people, and not thinking about yourself, she wouldn't pull against you. As a matter of fact, she got a lot of stick over me down the years, but she never said anything. She was a great woman.

I wouldn't have a hope without Our Lady. I bought it as I believed Our Lady would look after us and we only do what we do because we believe that She will look after it, totally, completely and entirely. The old dairy was reconverted into school rooms afterwards. The new situation enabled people to do a day's work on the farm and feel well and have the space without people looking over their shoulders. After Athy we opened Cuan Mhuires in Newry, Bruree, and now in Galway. We also have a house in Dublin for aftercare.

A whole way of life has evolved without any formal plan. I believe we were shown a way. I based it on my own experience and the way I saw my mother care for a relation of ours who lived in North Cork and who suffered from alcoholism. She was a woman with a great big heart and gave without expecting anything in return. She died two months short of ninety and, shortly before she died, when she knew she was not going to live much longer, she said to me, 'I'm sorry, Eileen, I thought I would get another year to help you out. I thought I would be able to help you for another year'. Here at ninety years of age she was still giving, at an age when most people would expect to be given to. But that was her whole outlook, giving.

When I was young this cousin used to go on skites a few times a year. When he would not be well, he would send word to my mother. My father would go over in the pony and trap and collect him, and he would spend six weeks in our house. And, strangely enough, in most of the alcohol treatment programmes, six weeks is the duration. My mother would dry him out by giving him a few bottles of stout each day. And then she would wean him off and when he would be rested and back in the full of his health he would go off home.

When we started off in Athy, Dr Bertie Blake from Carlow saw from the early stages that Cuan Mhuire was the place for those with a drink problem and not the psychiatric hospital. From the early stages he sent people to us and he visited us and supported us. He felt that psychiatric hospitals were not the place for people recovering from alcoholism.

He was one of the few people who was really supportive in the early days. Instead of sending them to St Dymphna's in Carlow he sent them to me. He saw that the spiritual side was needed as well. If somebody had other problems and if they needed psychiatric care, he helped them. I believe all addictions come under the one heading, as people take substances to kill the pain of living.

Cuan Mhuire is all about discovering your own inner giftedness, goodness and gentleness. All our therapy is based on being attentive to what is best in people. We do not go in for confrontation. To be honest, I find people who come through the door in Cuan Mhuire have already beaten themselves to the last. They already feel guilty. If you were to ask me, I would never say anybody is an alcoholic. I do not like the idea of labelling anybody. I would say the common problem is that they have a poor self-image and a low self-esteem and somewhere along the line they believed they were not as good as other people. They believed a lie because, in fact, they are the finest people you could meet. They are gentle and sensitive people, easily hurt, who have been wounded somewhere along the line. They need the help to be able to look at that.

But you can't look at the pain until first you have something to stand on. Our whole idea here is to help people to come to the realisation and to experience for themselves, that the Kingdom of God is within them and that they are made in the image and likeness of God. By that I mean that there is no end to the gentleness, and the love, and the truth, and the beauty, and the kindness and the wonder and all the other gifts within the human being, and people are shown and encouraged how to give away that goodness, because it is in giving that you receive. As you give it to other people, you actually experience it for yourself. Then having experienced your own goodness, you have something to stand on. Only then, can you look at the hurt and the pain of the past and deal with it.

Life pushes up the pain. Every human being is capable of living out that pain and hurt and becoming their true and beautiful self. I see that happening in Cuan Mhuire everyday. People growing and blossoming like a plant without being pushed or being pulled or being shoved. You just give them an environment where there is just love and respect. Where everyone is considered to be unique and special. We don't look down or up at each other in this house, because everyone here is special. We run the house together. We work it out each Monday morning and get on with it out of our love and gentleness.

The time spent here varies. Each person will take his or her own time if they are wise enough. Eight weeks for some. In Cuan Mhuire it takes as long as it takes. Rather too much than too little.

We have young people getting off drugs, young girls with a lot of problems. Some little ones would need a solid year of being cared for and discovering their own gifts and taking responsibility for their own lives before they would be really ready to face out into the open out there again.

There are people who might need a few months and others who might need a year. When people come in first they may need medication but, after that, there is no medication. It is group and work therapy and one-to-one listening and the power of the love that is generated in the house and the positivity of the house.

I might be dead tired going into a morning group meeting, but I would always feel full of life coming out of it, as there is so much life generated in there. I am more interested in people than in administration. I have come down to Galway and will stay until there is a good programme going. I was six years in Newry when that Cuan Mhuire opened. I have permission from my Order to look after the Cuan Mhuires which are owned by a trust and not by the order. It is a non-profit-making trust.

I had no intention of coming to Galway, but I was at home last summer and Father Timmy Curtin, who spent some time in the new Galway Cuan Mhuire when it was a missionary house, said he felt it should be retained as a Cuan Mhuire. I was on my way to Dublin when I got a call on the car phone from a Sacred Heart priest and he said would I be interested in Cool Arne. I wasn't interested at the time, as we had a lot on our plate with two other new houses on the agenda but, off the top of my head, I said I would have a look at it.

For want of something better to do I rang Fr Screen and he said he would show me around and I said how early in the morning. I said I would be there around eight the next morning. I arrived at twenty to eight and immediately I set foot here, I knew we were meant to be here. We bought it on St Patrick's Day, 1994.

In Athy we have about one hundred and sixty on treatment at any time, about one hundred and thirty in Newry and about one hundred in Bruree. Cuan Mhuire is about a way of life and I can see it in time in many other areas taking care of people in need, journeying with people interested in discovering their own inner goodness and giftedness.

Cuan Mhuire has done an amount for me as a person and all who work in Cuan Mhuire. It is living at a deeper inner level, at a soul level rather than a head level. It's like turning on the power rather than trying to light a house with a candle.

It is so important to be happy and happiness is something we discover as we give it away to others. There is a way to be happy and it is an illusion to believe that anything outside ourselves like booze, sex, power or money or gambling can make you happy. I am not against pleasure, in its own place and in its own time. But if you are depending on pleasure to make you happy, you will never be happy. If you are a happy person, you can enjoy all these things in moderation.

We were created to know, love and serve God and we were created for God. St Augustine, who tried it all, wine, women and song, said after a terribly miserable time, and then discovering God, 'Thou hast made us for Thyself, O Lord. And our hearts are ever restless until we find our rest in You'. If anything describes the person suffering from addiction, it is restlessness. And no amount of anything will satisfy that person who is restless. Recovery is from within, and any worthwhile life is from within. Trying to live at a head level is like giving a farmer a hedge clippers to go out and mow a meadow of hay instead of turning on the rotary mower. When you are living from the neck up you are using the hedge clippers. When you are living from within, you are using the power mower, turning on the power.

I'd love to tell the whole world about the power and happiness that is experienced when you turn on the power of love, truth and goodness within each one of us.

We are non-denominational. In Newry the people of no religion were probably the quickest to pick up on this inner life. I think they were so relieved to find that God was within them and had nothing to do with denominations; that the Kingdom of Heaven was within us. The family dimension in Cuan Mhuire is also a great strength.

We got a tremendous welcome here in Cool Arne. The parish priest asked me to come and speak to the parishioners and I spoke at Mass and they gave me a great clap and welcome. I just told them what Cuan Mhuire was about and if they were happy to have us here we would like to come and that I would not like to come without letting them know what was happening. And I told them what it was all about. The local farmers offered help and they did help.

The people of Galway are extra special, like Kerry people. I know if I went to Kerry I would get a big welcome.

Before entering the convent, I was Eileen Fitzgerald. Our postal address was Brosna, Co Kerry. My children's allowance book had Rockchapel, Co Cork, on it and then our address was changed to Abbeyfeale, Co Limerick. But I have always regarded myself as a Kerrywoman. Both my parents were Kerry and the farm straddled the Cork/Kerry border.

My mother was Mary Agnes Guiney. My father married into her people's place at home. My father, Maurice Fitzgerald, came from Scartaglin. There were three boys and three girls in our family – Mossie, Johnny and Joe, Ita, myself, and Agnes who was handicapped. Ita joined the Sisters of Mercy in Ardee and is Sr Agnes. She came to help me about nine years ago and she stayed with me and now runs the house in Bruree.

I went to school in Knockaclarig and then on to the Mercy nuns in Abbeyfeale for my secondary school education. After I did my Leaving I stayed on at home for a year. My father, wisely, suggested this as he said they would never again have a chance of having a year with me. They did not want me to go rushing into anything.

I got on well with the nuns in Abbeyfeale and I just pulled through at school. I wasn't good to study. We had a very good upbringing at home. My parents were extraordinary people, they gave us a lot of freedom with responsibility. We milked cows in the evening and then I used to go to the man next door and help him with his cows where I milked four or five more. I milk the three cows we have here in Cool Arne, as we have not got a milking machine yet. Milking cows is no difficulty for me.

I really did benefit from that year I had at home. I went dancing to Abbeyfeale, Mouncollins, the Rock (Rockchapel) and Ballydesmond. I always knew that I would join the nuns. It was there within me. I'm not saying I liked the idea, but I knew I would never get away from it. Even the day I was leaving to join the nuns I was crying and heartbroken, because I thought it was the end of everything for evermore. I thought I would never again enjoy anything and here I was leaving everything. My heart was breaking.

Johnny, my brother, came to the railway station with me in Mallow. I wouldn't bring anybody with me because I was too heartbroken to say goodbye to them at the convent door. He saw the state of me and said, 'Come home out of that, you were never meant to go anyway'. I said 'no', that the nuns would be waiting for me at the station at Portlaoise and I said that when I had satisfied my conscience I would come home for Christmas. Once I went in I never thought about coming home again. I knew for certain that I was where I was meant to be and I never doubted it. The only time I doubted it was before I entered and wanted to get rid of it. I knew I would end up in the nuns, but I tried to postpone it as long as I could.

When I decided to enter I wanted to go as far as possible from home and from Ardee where my sister Ita (Sr Agnes) had entered. She told me of Athy and she said there was a Sr Dominic there and she couldn't imagine anybody being unhappy with Sr Dominic. I came to Athy and joined the nuns there. I joined on the eighth of September, 1959, a day I will never forget. My heart was broken.

After arriving at the convent you got nine free days to settle in where you could stay late in bed and go into the garden. I can remember the first morning that I didn't have to get up early. The novice mistress came up and the window beside my bed was wide open as it was very fine. She closed the window and said that I wasn't to open it. She meant that it was too near the bed and it might give me a cold. That gave me a very sinking feeling that I could never again open a window without getting permission. But it was very strict at the time and there was a purpose.

I was very lucky to have joined the Sisters of Mercy in Athy. The nuns there were very special, particularly the older nuns who really supported me and prayed for me and pulled me through in an unbelievable way. They were great people. My own group, I suppose, worried about me. We made a pact that if any of us began to trail we would tip each other off a bit. I was the only one straying and they used to try and tip me off. You need only work in a Cuan Mhuire for a short time to know that somebody looks after us throughout the day each day. And that somebody is Our Lady and the Lord himself.

Sure there is no need for me to be worrying or fretting or getting anxious, because I am only here out of their goodness, allowing me to be here to change myself. And that's my primary purpose here. There will be ups and downs in Cuan Mhuire, but there is always a great joy and a great peace and a great love. A great togetherness.

BRYAN MacMAHON

(AUTHOR)

I was born on St Michael's Day, 1909, that's the 29th day of September, in the town of Listowel. My father, Pat MacMahon, was a clerk in a law office and my mother was a schoolteacher. Her name was Joanna Caughlin. She was reared here in Listowel after her mother died in childbirth.

My mother always said she was the eldest of eighteen, because her father was twice married. There were six in the first family and twelve in the second. She had four children: my brother Jack, myself, my sister Máirín and 'Bubs' (Patrick), a doctor, the youngest.

I had a great childhood. My grandfather was weighmaster and keeper of the market and I spent much of my youth there. I was born near the station. At the age of three or four we moved to Market Street and our back door opened onto the market. I have said one time that it was like an Eastern bazaar. Everything from white trout to eels was on sale. I have written at length about that. It was a great clearing house. Listowel is in the middle of a square that is North Kerry. Everything flows in there. If you put a compass on the town of Listowel and swing it 360 degrees you would impinge on the interests of no other town. So you have the hinterland and drawing ground for the market.

That drawground is also indicated by the number of public houses in Listowel. There were seventy public houses at one time. In one street there were three consecutive pubs side by side. Where else will you get that?

I never wanted to go into teaching: I wanted to travel to the East and India. But my mother said no. She wanted me to be a doctor and I said no. I saw a man come out of a sawmill one time with his hand cut-off and I thought this might be happening every day. She told me to sit the King's Scholarship and so I prepared myself and got called for training. I did my school teacher training in St Patrick's, Drumcondra, from 1928 to 1930 and I taught in Donore Avenue CBS off the South Circular Road in Dublin.

Dublin was lovely but I applied the principles of a small town when there. I wanted to know everyone and this gave me mental indigestion. Everyone who would pass me on the street I would think it unusual that they were not saluting me at all. This I found odd indeed.

It was too exciting. I explored Dublin and I would go to a particular area on a Saturday and study it in detail. I found a McMahon Street in the Jewish area of the South Circular. Vangey O'Hanlon, my friend, was studying to be a dentist and we palled around together. We asked an awful lot of questions. So I can tell you anything about every part of the city. Vangey was called after his aunt a nun, Mother Evangelist. She called her nephew Michael Evangelist O'Hanlon. Vangey stood sponsor for my son, Bryan, who is now up in Ennis and he is Bryan Michael Evangelist MacMahon. He was a tremendous character, a sportsman who played in goal for Kerry for a while. He stopped a penalty from Con Brosnan and was famous for that. He was a boxer and also did the Liffey Swim.

We had a gaelic football school league in Dublin. The teachers were the organisers. One day in Purcell's tobacconists near Nelson's Pillar, we had a meeting. There was a whole lot of motivated people there at the time. After the meeting a few of us were asked to stay back to discuss a financial investment. About ten of us stayed on. There was a discussion about a building society because it was felt that young teachers would be building their own homes in the decade ahead. The details were explained and it was decided to form the Educational Building Society. Out of that little meeting came that great society. I was there. But after two years I took out my twenty quid and opted out of my foundation membership. I recall the first organisers: Tom Ryder, Dave Kelliher and Harry McManus. Dave afterwards became General Secretary of the INTO.

I was waiting to get into university as I had done first arts on com-

pletion of my teacher training. I was in digs in the South Circular and had a lively time. I had another great friend from Liscarroll, County Cork, Eamon Murphy. We attended lots of dances and house parties. It was a lovely life.

I was very reluctant to return to Kerry. I nearly got pneumonia while queuing for a Jimmy O'Dea pantomine and got drenched to the skin. I got very ill and came home to recover: a teaching job in Listowel came up and my mother insisted that I take it. I was about twenty-one. It was 1932. I met my wife in Lisdoonvarna. I was introduced to Kitty Ryan, a Tipperary girl, by the father of TJ Maher, old Thomas Maher.

I wasn't a man for waiting around and we were married within eight or nine months. I got married on about twelve pounds a month. I bought the house I am now living in and started a bookshop. I had five young sons and I decided I would give them the very best in education.

Education has always been held in tremendous importance in Kerry. There is a tradition of learning in North Kerry. There was once a Bardic School in Lisselton. The holdings were small and the families large. So the traditional escape was either the Church or education.

I had no problems with my sons when I was teaching them. At school they called me 'Sir' and at home I was 'Dad'. I was very involved in the locality; and at one time I held office in sixteen different organisations in Listowel. As a teacher I made it my business to know the parents. If you know the parents there is no problem. My mother used tell me if you had any success to 'walk easy when your jug is full'.

I was a founder member of Listowel Drama Group. We won the All-Ireland with *'Sive'* and we were up in the Shelbourne Hotel and there I was spouting away and I told the others to walk easy when your jug is full. Jack Lynch, the former Taoiseach, picked it up. When he got in after one election with a very big majority, one TD in the opposition asked him what he said to his TDs before entering the chamber and he replied: 'I told them what Bryan MacMahon said in the Shelbourne, to walk easy when your jug was full'. When I met him later, Jack would always remark: 'I am still walking easy'.

I was writing ever since childhood. In Dublin I started a crusade to get the big Squares like Mountjoy Square opened for public use. We had a campaign in a periodical called *'An Camán'*. It was run by a member of the famous Breathnach family. One of them, Cormac, became Lord Mayor of Dublin.

Danny Flavin's bookshop was a tremendous asset in Listowel and Seamus Wilmot was a great influence on me. At St Michael's I learned Latin and Greek, the Humanites. We had an atmosphere of literature and imagination around us always. There was a great amount of idealism around the country still from 1916 and this influenced us up to the 1930s and '40s.

The Irish language is very dear to me. It was taught from the point of view of grammar and I have condemned that method, bell, book and candle. The new Irish language TV station might be of help and has to be tried. Irish is a beautiful, sensuous instrument for expressing any emotion and now it is in danger of dying.

We are now in danger of becoming so international that we will end up as a bland mixture of everything, and maybe finish up as nothing. The language is so important. When Irish people are abroad and break into speaking bits of Irish, this shows the desire to show our own identity.

Some time in the 1920s Listowel, for a while, was designated as a place where there was as much Irish spoken as English. We had idealists like Tomás O'Donoghue and Jim Sugrue. They were marvellous people who never got their due. But these pioneers put the seeds of idealism in us and this persists to the present day. Because a cause is beaten, which it is not, it does not absolve you from serving it. The by-products of idealism cannot be calculated. It goes into the soul and provides a profound sense of motivation. The rest is up to the coming generation.

There is a Kerry identity. We Kerrymen are outgoing and a small bit daft and that is delightful to me. We call it 'creativitiy' and I like that. I go around the fairs and markets and meet old friends and I am astonished at what they say to me. I have a whale of a time every Wednesday and Thursday in the market when I meet these cronies of mine.

Ó Faoláin has said of us that when the Kerryman is laughing, watch out because behind that laughter lies a cold, calculating brain. We are crafty in a way. Being from Kerry is very important to me. I know every part of it.

I am slightly disorientated when I move outside the county boundary. Kerry should really extend to Barna Gap in West Limerick. When you have a son playing with Kerry, as my son Gary did, it is great fun. People just come up and say 'Well' meaning 'How do you think the county team will do ?'

I get letters from many parts of the world which is one of the great joys of being a teacher. Going down Broadway a voice comes ringing through the crowds: 'You're welcome to New York, Master'. The letter from a former pupil telling of the success he has met because I encouraged him to pursue his education – this is lovely. If I go to Henley Regatta or Ascot I meet old students of mine.

I have seen a former student lead in the winner of the Cheltenham Gold Cup which he owned. The other day I met an old pupil home from England for a funeral and he thanked me for convincing him at a young age that reading was important. This was at his father's funeral and I found it very moving.

I find that young people now are bored. We didn't know the meaning of the word.

When I travel abroad I like to go into schools and from what I have seen, we are as good as any and better than most in what we offer in our schools.

My compulsion to write has not diminished. I just can't stop. It's like a form of alcoholism. I won't tell you what I am working on at present because the lust to write diminishes with each telling. Most masterpieces are 'written' in the pubs of Dublin. Don't talk; write it.

My book *The Master* has made a fine impact. Looking back I had a great friendship with a printer in Listowel, Bob Cuthbertson. His father came here in 1883. They were a Scottish family who came to Limerick. Old Jack Macauley told Bob's father, Robbie, that there was an opening in Listowel. Bob used ask me to write ballads. He would give me a pen, a bottle of cut glass violet ink. 'Write a ballad,' he'd say. I wrote forty-three ballads.

There was a printer in Limerick, Garret Howard and Bob Cuthbertson was so clogged printing my ballads that he had to sub-contract the printing of them to Garret. They sold for four pence a dozen. They ran off about two hundred and fifty thousand of one ballad. I could write a book on Bob. I became a printer of sorts and from visiting the harness makers, Moss Scanlan and Paddy Finucane, I could almost make a straddle from the years watching them. I spent about twenty-five years going to Moss Scanlan every day and then twenty years going to Paddy Finucane.

I write longhand and I put in about four hours a day. I like the silence when using the pen: the noise of the typewriter would drive me crackers. Some of my original manuscripts have been presented to universities in the US where I lectured at different times. I usually awake each day at half past six. I then listen to the news. I have breakfast and then I work out what I will do. After listening to the eight o'clock news I go back to bed until half nine and get up then. I work for an hour or so and then the post and the paper arrive. Suddenly, it is twelve o'clock and then I go off down the town.

What worries me today is the amount of evasive talk that goes on in world politics. That disturbs me. I try not to let it influence me. We had great mystics: de Valera and Michael Collins. The last place I saw Michael Collins was in this very room. This house was owned by Jim Crowley, a member of the Dáil, and Collins called. I remember seeing him. One of the great tragedies of our people was the death of Michael Collins. I see good in all of them. My view of history, my view of the Civil War will prevail – there were great men on different sides.

There are too many cynics about today, knocking the creative man. I hate lies, damn lies and misquotations. Dev's quotation on comely maidens for instance. What he referred to were 'happy maidens and athletic youths'. I opened the paper one Saturday and there were three distinguished people misquoting Dev on that. What's wrong with a maiden anyway? They want to put a milkmaid connotation on it, that Dev was an antiquarian.

The biggest fallacy is to judge what happened then by the standards of today. You dare not judge what happened then by the standards of now. The prophet backwards. What we are saying and doing now in this country will be laughed at in twenty years. And the gods of this and that will be laughed at and mocked. I still hold that there are constants in every aspect of life. Even though they are at times obscured. Fashion is like fashion in women's clothes; there is also fashion in literature, there is fashion in every aspect of human life. People get tired of doing the same thing.

MICHEÁL Ó MUIRCHEARTAIGH

(BROADCASTER)

OUR family comes from Doonshean, Dún Síon in Irish. It is a small village about three miles east of Dingle, near the seaside. Like all places west of Blennerville it would be a farming area. The usual farming in West Kerry would be dairying and my father, Thady, was a dairy farmer.

My mother was a Quinn from near the Conor Pass. She was known as Katie. You notice nowadays that women tend to keep their maiden names on marrying, as part of the modern culture. But this was always the situation in the Gaeltacht. My mother was always known as Katie Quinn rather than Bean Uí Mhuircheartaigh. What is now considered modern, was part of the old Gaelic culture in Gaeltacht areas. It signified women's independence; that they were persons in their own right.

There were eight of us in the family: Pádraig, the chairman of the ESB; my sister Eileen Devane, she is a retired teacher in Dublin; the next brother, Ignatius or Nais, inherited the farm and is still at home; then I came in; and then my brother Donal who is a teacher in Dublin; Maire who is Mrs Davis, a teacher in Dublin; Siobhán died young; Kathleen Barry is here in Dublin.

We were known by our English name, Moriarty, but as I finished my secondary education at Coláiste Íosagáin in Baile Bhúirne, I went by Ó Muircheartaigh and I kept it.

As children we were always out in the open and to the present day I love to be out in the open. Anything that can be done outdoors I would opt for always. The farm gave us a reasonably good living at the time. There were about fifty acres and we had about twenty cows and two horses.

There were pleasant jobs like going to bring home the horse to take the milk to the creamery. You might milk a few cows before heading off for school. You had to be in school for nine o'clock as in those days it was a serious crime to be late. It would be no good telling the monks you had a problem catching the horse in the morning. Everybody was encouraged to go to school and learn. Even when you would be on your way to school people would say to study well and there was a genuine feeling towards education in the place. This was a great aspect to life there, this appreciation of the value of education.

In Dingle, after First Communion, we went to the Christian Brothers, known locally as 'the monks'. I did the Intermediate Certificate in Dingle and then I went off to the preparatory college, Coláiste Íosagáin, run by the De La Salle brothers. I stayed there until I did the Leaving Cert. From there I went to St Patrick's College, Drumcondra, to train as a national school teacher.

I travelled out of West Kerry for the first time when I had finished my Intermediate Cert and set out for Coláiste Íosagáin in Baile Bhúirne. This was 1945 and I was fifteen years old. I had never been on a bus before and it was the first time I had been east of Lispole. It was a very exciting journey. Seán Ó hAiniféin and I got the train from Tralee to Cork and that was also our first journey on a train. It was an exciting two days as we had to stay the night in Tralee. Tralee at that time seemed like the mind's image of New York to us: big, busy and bright.

I recall a quick trip up to the dog track in Tralee just to see it as we had a few hours to while away. The reason for the trip was a simple one. There was a famous solicitor from Listowel living in Dingle, Paddy Fitzgibbon. We used to fish with him in his boat. He had a great greyhound which had won big stakes in Tralee and I had heard so much about this greyhound I had to visit the track where he had won these races.

Cork was magic altogether when we got there. And it was the first time I heard the young lads on the street, the newsboys, shouting 'Echo'. I didn't know what they were saying. When we got to Cork we were greeted by a great man, Brother Peadar. There were two lads from Dublin, Jimmy Agnew and Jimmy Doyle. Baile Bhúirne was a very relaxed, easy going place and there was a great emphasis on football, but above all it had a wonderful Irish atmosphere and in a very natural way Irish was the language of communication. I think that all who passed through the place retained a great 'grá' for the language for evermore.

From there I went to St Patrick's, Drumcondra, to train as a national school teacher. My first school was St Finbar's in Cabra West and I went from there to the Christian Brothers in Seville Place where Luke Kelly was a pupil at the time. I taught him for a while. He was the same then as he was afterwards, funny and singing. It was a lovely school down near the docks. It had great connections with the O'Toole's football club. It was a lovely area and I spent three years there before moving to O'Connell's school. As I always liked study I read at UCD for a BA, Higher Diploma in Education, DPA and a B Comm. So I transferred to the secondary school in O'Connell's in the mid 1960s to teach accountancy mainly. I stayed there until 1980 when I decided to go into broadcasting full-time.

I got into broadcasting by chance when I was in St Patrick's College. Seán Ó Síocháin used to do all the broadcasting in Irish at that time. It was customary to broadcast the Railway Cup Final on St Patrick's Day and the Oireachtas Final in October through Irish. In early 1949 after Sean decided that he would not be doing it anymore, Radió Éireann needed somebody. Word was sent to St Patrick's and a little notice was put up and the Dean, Fr O'Neill, informed us of trials being given in Croke Park.

A crowd of us decided that it would be great fun for a Sunday. This trial had the added attraction that we would get in free. About ten of us went down. The old broadcasting box at that time was between the old Hogan Stand and the old Long Stand. The people adjudicating on us were in under the Hogan Stand.

We were all sent up for our five minute stint. It was an ordinary match for which we didn't even have a programme. Faughs were playing UCD and I knew a few lads I had seen playing the previous Sunday for Waterford and I also knew the goalkeeper for UCD. He was the bank manager's son from Dingle, Teddy Hurley, who is now the doctor to Patrickswell Hurling Club.

When I got into the commentary box for my test I hadn't the remotest idea that this would develop into anything. It was fun to us. But I can tell you, Teddy Hurley played a mighty game. Even though he was the goalie, he was everywhere. When I came back down they asked me to stay on and I was sent back up for a second run which I enjoyed.

About a week later I got a letter from Radio Éireann with a contract to do the Railway Cup Final two weeks further on. I was eighteen at the time. I met Micheál O'Hehir the following Sunday when Kerry were playing Mayo in a league game. They let me sit in with him for experience. He was more than helpful, telling me not to worry. I assumed that Micheál O'Hehir knew everything, but he asked me a few questions about the Kerry players and I think that was to give me confidence. He knew the answers to the questions he was asking me, but he knew it would help me feel at ease.

On St Patrick's Day I was in at the deep end with no training and no coaching. I knew the players anyway. I always say it is not a crime not to know something, but it is a crime if you are supposed to know it by a certain date and you haven't done so. My first broadcast took place on March 17, 1949, the Railway Cup Football Final between Munster and Leinster. Micheál O'Hehir did the hurling match. He used do the first game at Croke Park on St Patrick's Day and then get out to Baldoyle for the horse racing.

When I got to Croke Park I was still worried if I would make a fool of myself, having no experience. I went in under the old Hogan Stand and there was no-one to meet me. I didn't want to go up while Micheál was doing the first game. I went for a walk around and I was near to where the technicians were located under the stand. They didn't know me and I overheard some technician asking who was doing the second match? I think there was a bit of panic setting in at that stage. I went over and identified myself. But once the broadcast started I forgot about nerves. I remember a complimentary letter appeared in the paper a few days later about the commentary. The Oireachtas in October was my next broadcast. Tipperary had just won the All-Ireland, John Doyle getting his first of eight medals.

I continued to do the Railway Cup and the Oireachtas. I am not too sure about the date when I did my first English broadcast, but I recall broadcasting the replay of the 1956 Munster Football Final between Kerry and Cork in Killarney. Two who were later to become 'greats', Mick O'Connell and Tom Long, were playing for Kerry and I remember Niall Fitzgerald kicking the winning point for Cork.

Telefís Éireann opened in 1962 and I think I did the first ever television commentary from Croke Park. A lot of sports associations were nervous of television, fearing it could ruin attendances. The GAA was the only sports body which agreed to allow live television from its inception. They allowed coverage of the finals and semi-finals. But they put in a condition that fifty per cent of the commentary would have to be through the medium of Irish. The commentary for the All-Ireland Semi-Final of 1962 was divided between Seán Óg Ó Ceallacháin and myself.

This alternating commentary between Seán Óg and myself did not work and then somebody got the brilliant idea of doing the minor match in Irish and the senior game in English. That satisfied the requirement on Irish. I started to do the minor games in Irish in 1963 and enjoyed it immensely. Sometime in the sixties the programme known ever since as 'Sunday Sport' was introduced, with extensive coverage of many sports from different and widespread venues. It was the brainchild of Ian P Corr, current head of Radio Sport, and it has proved to be very popular. On Sundays both Micheál O'Hehir and myself would cover matches. When Micheál O'Hehir became ill in 1985 it created a big void and I had to switch from the minor games on television to do the senior games on radio.

I always held that one should never set out to imitate anybody. Do the thing your own way and let it be liked or disliked. People ask me often do I study the whole thing. I don't really, but if you have an interest you will always be working on it unknownst to yourself. You follow all the matches through the year. It's a process of ongoing learning and not like cramming for an exam. You will watch out for team selection and between that and the Sunday you know there are certain details you have to obtain.

I always have somebody to keep a tab on the score for me during a game. This is important when I have to do a radio report afterwards. This person with you can also keep an eye for off-the-ball situations.

Con Houlihan wrote one time before an All-Ireland Final that he pitied people who don't have to travel to a big game. I love going to Thurles or going to Killarney. You are at a slight disadvantage when you are in Dublin for the All-Ireland. There is no sense of going to the match. On the morning of an All-Ireland Final I have at times travelled out of town and returned with the followers. You get a greater sense of the occasion. It's not just the game, it's the preparation, the travelling, the excitement. That is important. If it's a big match in Thurles I love to walk from the Square. You might see the old Pecker Dunne on the bridge with his banjo. It's all part of it.

Another sport which I have always been attached to is greyhound racing. We had greyhounds at home and as I said earlier I can still recall the first time I stepped inside a greyhound track on that day in Tralee. At some stage RTE decided to do this programme 'A Night at the Dogs' and the secret is that it doesn't concentrate on the greyhounds alone, but on the people as well. I have watched sports commentators in America and Australia. They concentrate on giving information about the horse or the greyhound and little else. People in Ireland want to hear about the connections, and the human element. I think we are different from other countries in that respect – curious without being inquisitive.

For a long number of years now I have been looking after the Kerry players in Dublin in a very informal way. It's great to be in the company of these great players. It's easy to train a good player. Among others I had Donie O'Sullivan, John O'Keeffe, Ger Power, Pat McCarthy, Paudie Lynch, Jack O'Shea, Charlie Nelligan, Paud O'Mahony and Dermot Hanifin, and now we have Noel O'Mahony, Anthony Gleeson and the young Dara Ó Sé in Dublin. For some reason that I cannot explain the Dublin based Mayo players have always trained with us as well.

All sport is meant to be a pastime and in Kerry there is the right outlook on sport. Recently I was speaking to team managers from a few other counties and they wondered why they were going so badly. I suggested that they were spending too much time on looking back on what might have been instead of looking forward on what is possible. Anything is possible when you look forward. And nothing is possible looking back. I remember that point being made indirectly by Mick O'Dwyer one time after Kerry had lost a great game. Mick's attitude was that it was over and gone, but that the next time was still there to be won.

I have been appointed chairman of Bord na Gaeilge. I think it is now more important than ever to identify with our language. I would never criticise anything English or from other cultures. The world would be a very boring place if everything was the same. Everything has its values. I would hate to see the game of cricket die in England as, for me, it is a great British custom and tradition. We have our language, Irish music and Irish games. I'm not saying they are better or greater than aspects of culture in other countries. But they are as important to us as theirs are to them. In that way it would be a terrible pity if our language was not preserved. It should be possible for everybody to have the choice of doing their business with all state and public offices in Irish or English.

I am very optimistic about the revival of the Irish language. A quiet revolution is taking place and a growing number of people wish to become acquainted with it. Like the games and the music in the past, the language has survived a period of inertia and is now set for a dramatic recovery.

I go back to Kerry every Christmas with the whole family. My wife Helena is a McDowell from Dublin. The eldest of the family is Eamonn who is twenty-three and then there is Niamh, Aonghus, Cormac, Neasa, Nuala, Éadaoin and Doireann. The idea of moving back to Kerry to live has never entered my mind – not yet anyway.

DERMOT KINLEN

(HIGH COURT JUDGE)

I regard myself very much a Kerryman and I have always been very proud of my Kerry connections. My grandfather Tom O'Donnell was an MP for Kerry and he was a tremendously formative influence on me. He died in 1943.

The O'Donnells are still in Liscarney. Tom O'Donnell as a young man became a teacher and barrister and went for election for West Kerry. The county was divided into three constituencies in those days. As a child his father refused to pay increased tithes and the entire family were evicted. The RIC went in and removed the hearth which was the sign that the house was not to be reoccupied. That made him bitter, but the family eventually got repossession of their home situated on the Conor Pass. I have lots of cousins including O'Donnells, Begleys and Fitzgeralds. The former Kerry footballer, Séamus MacGearailt is a cousin and the poetess Nuala Ní Dhomhnaill is doubly related. My grandfather was elected in 1900 and was MP until 1918 when he didn't run.

Fr Tony Gaughan in his biography of my grandfather maintains that he was always a member of the Irish Republican Brotherhood, the IRB. The interesting thing was that after the Civil War the Redmondites sided with Cosgrave, but my grandfather was very much opposed to Cosgrave and he set up the National League which fought the election in 1927. He ran in Clare and might have been elected, but the Bishop of Killaloe more or less said it would be a mortal sin to vote for him. Their party was going to support de Valera. Not much was known about this move to support de Valera in 1927 until Fr Gaughan came up with the information in his research. My grandfather maintained, and in hindsight was proven right, that if the constitutionalists were allowed con-

tinue, Ireland would have been a damn sight better off. Not decrying the Republicans, they contributed very much to Irish history. It is seldom realised that Ireland got an Act giving it Home Rule for the whole thirty-two counties in 1914, but its implementation was postponed for one year or until the war was over whichever was longer. It did not give us a Republic but it gave us Home Rule and we might have evolved like Australia, Canada and New Zealand.

In every country you have had the constitutionalists and the revolutionaries. They are very unhappy partners, but they do produce the end results.

My grandfather had ten children and his wife, Nora Ryan, ran two pubs in Killorglin. She kept the money coming in. My mother, Aileen O'Donnell, remembered one day hearing her mother implore him to give up politics and think of his wife and family. My mother adored her father and she was so incensed at hearing this, she kicked her mother in the shin for making what she considered a treasonable remark.

My grandfather went back to the Law after losing his seat. He was made a temporary Circuit Court Judge in the 1930s in Cork and then he was chairman of the IRA pension fund. That was an extraordinary thing. There were more people in the GPO than in Tienanmen Square to judge from the number of claimants looking for pensions. Judge O'Connor, who had been seconded from Cork, became the President of this pension tribunal. My grandfather was appointed as a temporary judge to Cork. Then Judge O'Connor realised that he would have to refuse thousands of people claiming the IRA pension and he didn't want to do it. So he asked permission to go back to his job as a Circuit Judge. My grandfather was appointed to replace him. He signed all the orders for the granting or refusing of a pension. Seán MacBride brought it to the High Court on the basis that the judge who signed these orders was not the judge who heard the cases and they were all declared void. As a result my grandfather was appointed to rehear all the cases on a temporary basis, but this lasted for years.

I remember as a boy going to Griffith Barracks in Dublin to one of these pension hearings. There was one fellow who had fought on both sides. At one point he was in the British Army and then he fought on the Republican side. He had a British army pension and he was looking for an IRA pension as well. He was really playing the field. I was mesmerised by this two-faced man, a Mé Féiner looking for pensions for being on both sides of the one conflict. He felt as he had given fifty per cent of his time to the Republican side he deserved his pension. I can't recall the actual outcome.

I felt as a Kerryman that I understood an awful lot of the things that went on in the Circuit Court. Kerry can be divided very clearly and you know by the people's attitude whether they come from the North or South of the county. It goes back into history. When the Normans came in 1169 they swept across Ireland and they threw all the O'Sullivans out of Tipperary and they came down and took over all West Cork and South Kerry. There was a very important battle just outside Kilgarvan, which stopped the Normans getting into South Kerry. And today you can see the Normans in North Kerry and the Celts in South Kerry.

They have a slightly different approach to such things as the oath in court for instance. In Listowel in particular you have to watch to see if the witness is putting his or her full hand on the Bible when they are being sworn. Frequently I had people with their fingers crossed underneath the Bible, so that the oath would not apply! In Listowel I sometimes had to ask to have the witness resworn with fingers on top so that I could see the hand. This sometimes caused annoyance to the witnesses.

In South Kerry this did not apply at all because a lot of people there don't regard the Bible as having any application to this day and age and it is the same, to some extent, in West Kerry.

Kerry is great fun in court. The late State Solicitor, Donie Browne, used say it was practically impossible to get a conviction in Kerry. I used to think this was due to my brilliance as a defence counsel. But I later discovered it was as much due to the desire of Kerry juries to release people.

I'm not surprised at JB Keane producing all sorts of stories out of Listowel. We used to stay in Tralee and travelled to Listowel every day for the Circuit Court sitting. I remember one day the only barristers present were William Binchy and myself. There were three cases, one worse than the next, typical of the sort of law you would get in

Listowel. One of the solicitors asked us to the Lisowel Arms for a drink and we declined as we wanted to get back to the hotel in Tralee. As we went for the bus, William turned to me and said, 'This is an unclean town, I am looking forward to getting a shower in Tralee'.

One of the cases was between a father and son who had a dispute as to who should pay for the morphine administered to the mother who was dying. Judge Barra Ó Briain couldn't credit this. William Binchy was for the father. Barra Ó Briain asked him was it correct that the case was that his client would not pay for morphine to ease the passage of his wife into the next life. He said it was the son's responsibility as he had transferred the farm to the son.

Barra Ó Briain said he understood the legal niceties but asked if it was the case that neither the father nor the son was prepared to pay for the morphine to ease the passage of the unfortunate woman into the next life. We both said, 'Yes'.

The Judge said he understood what the case was about now. And when William Binchy realised that he was going to beat the lodgement having clocked up so much anyway, he said that his client was now prepared to pay for the morphine. Barra Ó Briain said, 'Oh no. I'm not going to let him pay for the morphine as he had asked responsible counsel to state that he would not pay a penny towards the morphine. If he wants strict law that is what he is going to get from me.' The judge said it was typical of some attitudes that unfortunately were frequently found in North Kerry. The result was that William Binchy won as he had beaten the lodgement.

So one could see where John B could be writing these plays, with people saying there was no basis in reality in them. There was a basis in reality in them.

Judge Barra Ó Briain turned to William Binchy during one particular case and asked: 'Let me be clear on this. This is a rock without a shred of grass on it, standing in the middle of a river. Is this what we are fighting about, the ownership of this rock?'

William Binchy looked up at him and said, 'To quote from *King Lear*, my Lord: "It is not much, but it is mine own." '

In South Kerry they are more easy about the Law. I personally am against the use of the Bible in court unless a person expresses a wish to be sworn and that there is silence in court. I used to be horrified at some sittings when all the guards would be sworn in together to save time. The first would have his hand on the Bible and the rest would line up with each placing a hand on the next one's shoulder. I remember an occasion when the first guard put his hand on a spectacle case because there was no Bible and the others all touched him on the shoulder. It was revolting and a blasphemy.

I remember the first case I had, it was in Tralee. And there was a businessman, a Protestant, who was a friend of mine and he was called for the jury. I felt 'Thanks be to God' at least somebody will know me and that it was my first case. I was horrified when my solicitor, Con Healy, got up and objected to this juryman. Con was a famous solicitor in Killarney. I said, 'What are you doing Con? He would be well disposed towards me personally.' He said he would explain later. On the way back to Killarney he said, 'You are very young yet Dermot, and you don't know how to do criminal cases.' (Although my client in that first case was acquitted.) But Con said, 'I will give you one bit of advice. Never let a Protestant on a jury.' I said, 'Why, what's wrong with Protestants?' Con said, 'Nothing – they are very fine people. But they see everything in black and white. Catholics see the grey areas and if you want acquittals or disagreements, Catholics are your only man.' That was in 1953 and my first case.

One of my early cases was for Kerry County Council. This was due to the kindly old Mr J D O'Connell who was the County Solicitor and had remembered my grandfather. In Killarney Tom Healy had a huge practice and he would arrive into the International Hotel with a bundle of briefs for William Binchy, William Roche, Gerry Lee and Maurice Danaher. He would dole them out like a pack of cards. We would turn over the folders to see what we got and sometimes you would have to hand over a brief as the other barrister had been involved in it at an earlier stage. But then you always got something back. You might get a guinea or two.

Among the solicitors were Joe Grace and Donie Browne, who were enormous characters in Tralee. Larger than life. Their adventures were many, numerous and they were looked after in Benner's extremely well. Donie Browne was an outstanding lawyer. The brilliant Tralee solicitor Gerald Baily said that if Browne worked a full day the rest of the solicitors in Tralee could go out of business. He died last year and was an outstandingly brilliant man and a great lawyer. A most amusing and lovable person.

To be a good lawyer, you must learn your law and know where you can find it. When we started out there were few Irish textbooks. Nowadays we have many books on Irish law. Then when you have found your law, the next thing is to know your judge.

For nineteen years I used to appear before Judge Barra Ó Briain along with William Binchy. I took silk in 1971 and William died the same year. It left a fantastic gap, as between us we had eighty per cent of the work in Kerry and Limerick. Barra Ó Briain and myself were very fond of one another. He told me one day he was going to write a book and have one chapter on the faces of counsel. He said that William Binchy's face showed that he had no faith in the point he was making but felt he should make it in case it would win favour with the judge or that the client had told him to make the point. But it would be apparent that he did not believe the point himself.

William Binchy was a wonderful fighter in a case. He was a big and powerful man, but also shy and nervous. The case might be well and truly over, but he would fight to the very end. When William Binchy lost the case he reminded me of a great Spanish galleon sinking with all guns firing. A wonderful friend too. He was a great influence on me.

Advocacy does change; I think it was appalling to do away with juries as they have done in most civil cases because it has made the law elitist. Most people don't like lawyers which is sad but understandable. They think all lawyers are making millions because a few are getting big fees which they deserve. There are lawyers in the law library practically drawing the dole. An awful lot come in and an awful lot fall by the wayside. A lot of it is a question of luck, as it was in my own case. I started off with others who were equally able. I was the eldest of the family and after three years my father said he was sick and tired of paying my hotel bills and would I consider applying for a job in Hong

Kong or somewhere? I said I would. I mentioned this to William Binchy and to John Kenny who was the leading barrister in Limerick at the time. They both went to see my father who was a builder from Wicklow and told him that I would do well if I had another year.

John Kenny asked me to do some work in Limerick as he was in the Supreme Court. He asked me what I was doing that evening as he wanted me to work and I said I was going to the pictures with a girl. When I got back after the pictures there were fourteen briefs awaiting me. I had only one brief based on a drunken New Zealand sailor for the three years up to then. From then on I had a Limerick practice.

John Kenny told them in Rathkeale I was the leading authority in Ireland on drains. I brought my wellington boots everywhere after that. I had never done a case on drains until John Kenny gave me one, which I won in Rathkeale. He put out the word that I was the man on drains.

When you were before Judge Barra Ó Briain in Killarney you would know by looking at him whether he had caught a salmon in Glencar that morning before breakfast. And if he did, it was going to be a sunny day. Everything would come up roses and you could chance your arm on anything as it would not rebound. But if he came in with a scowl, it meant that it had not gone well on the river or lake. He didn't drink, so there was no question of a hangover. Sometimes his crier would come in and forewarn us, 'He missed two this morning', and we knew immediately that it could be a rough day. But he was a very even tempered and fine judge.

Some people felt he acted as though he was the House of Lords or the Supreme Court. When he became President of the Circuit Court, he used to indulge in long dissertations. I remember in Listowel one day, William Binchy and William Roche were in a case. The case was about breach of warranty with regard to an in-calf heifer. As President of the Circuit Court, Judge Barra Ó Briain was ex-officio a member of the High Court. I went in and sat beside William Binchy and he was debating with the judge if he, as an ex-officio High Court Judge, would have matrimonial jurisdiction. I asked him if the cow was looking for divorce. He said it started as an academic point a half hour earlier and they were still discussing it. Barra used to do that, he was a very learned man and we all were very fond of him. He let us away with murder.

Now that I find myself as a Judge of the High Court I find the change total. Firstly, there is nervousness and I suffer slightly from scruples. What worries me is that there is no appeal from the High Court, except on a point of law to the Supreme Court. But the High Court has to make up its mind on facts and therefore you have to assess character and I am very bad at doing it and I am aware I am very bad at that and I keep lecturing myself on it. If somebody comes in well dressed, with a shiny face and melting eyes and is a good actor or actress, I have to keep warning myself that rogues can be like that. I would like to see a Court of Appeal established where two High Court Judges could hear the evidence again on any case that has started in the High Court. In the District Court you can appeal to the Circuit Court and that's it. You get two bites at the cherry. Or else you start in the Circuit Court and appeal to the High Court, you get two bites. But when you start in the High Court on facts, there is no second opportunity. I think it is unfortunate that we don't have two bites at the cherry in the High Court.

I think it appalling that they did away with juries in civil matters. Judges have no greater insight into the man or woman in the street than juries have. In fact far less, because judges by their nature are cut off, and that is only right. But I think that they were becoming more elitist and more cut-off from the people. Mao Tse Tung said that lawyers were an unnecessary bourgeois extravagance and that all questions should be decided by the people. The insurance lobby seemed to press the government into the view that juries were irresponsible and gave far too much damages and cases took longer. Therefore costs would go down and that premiums would come down. That turned out to be completely untrue.

An awful lot of people feel that judges are out of touch with reality. The judge decides the Law and states the Law in a court and a jury must accept that. The jury decide the facts. Twelve men and women are more likely to cop on to somebody who is trying to con them than an aloof judge.

I am greatly honoured to be in the High Court. I regret that my mother did not live to see it as she died earlier last year. I pray that I do the right thing as there is no appeal. I pray very much. It may sound pious.

Another thing I have to remind myself on the bench is to shut up in court. I have a note written in front of me with the words 'Shut Up'. After so many years of advocacy I tend to become an advocate.

I feel sorry for people who have no religion. In the middle of a case I might say, 'Please, please, Lord, let me get this right'. My decisions will change people's lives. As a barrister you just did your case and went out. I have been involved in visiting committees for prisons for many years. I am concerned about the inadequates who are put in and not properly assessed. If you have a mentally ill or inadequate person in prison they wander around and they join a godfather's gang as a foot soldier. Very few judges visit prisons, seeing it as not being part of their function. I think we should take an overview.

I think each branch of the criminal justice system should be informed about each other's functions and there should be conferences on it. They talk about sentencing policy, but far more important is who goes into jail and need they go into jail? We should have all sorts of radical alternatives to prison. Ordinary prisoners can be rehabilitated. However, drug addiction is becoming a huge national problem. Some children get drugs at three or four years of age. There is very little that can be done for them. There is some hope for an alcoholic but very little for somebody addicted to other drugs.

I haven't had to send anybody to prison as I have not yet dealt with criminal cases. My friend Kim Reilly in Sneem says that I will make a great judge, but I won't be able to send anybody to jail. In fact, he thinks I will invite them down here to Sneem.

I first went to Sneem in 1943 with my grandfather. We stayed in the Butler Arms in Waterville. He had made the match between old Mrs Huggard of the Butler Arms and her husband, Martin. One of his few Protestant supporters was Martin Huggard who supported the Redmondite party. My grandfather, when he was a barrister, used to stay in the Central Hotel in Tralee and the manageress was from Westmeath. My grandfather thought it was time she got married and brought her down and introduced her to Martin Huggard, a publican in Waterville.

Charlie Chaplin stayed there and made it a world famous hotel. She had six children and so she decided to have six hotels. She ended up with the Royal Hotel in Valentia, the Carragh Lake, the Lake Hotel in Killarney, which is run by her daugher Hilda – my godson Tony Huggard is the manager of it – then Ashford Castle, Cong and Ballinahinch Castle. Mrs Huggard bought all of those. She was a fantastic woman, a larger than life person. She had half the English hierarchy staying.

When Billy Huggard was courting, his mother Mrs Huggard had nobody to run the entertainment at night for the guests so I used to be brought down for July and August to organise trips to the Skelligs and midnight feasts on the beach. I used have free summer holidays as a university student. So I really grew to love it. I always said if I ever won the Sweep I would move, as the quality of life was so much better than in Dublin. Later I stayed there with Rene and Olive Cusack from Limerick.

I had a car accident outside Sneem in 1969 and William Binchy who acted for me said that I should buy a house in Sneem with the money, or otherwise I would just spend it giving parties and buying drink for people. I bought a bit of land for two hundred pounds and I built a house for four thousand pounds on it.

It was the best bit of advice I ever got. That house is my little paradise and it is there I spend all the time I can. People ask me how I fill in the time when I am in Kerry and I tell them there aren't enough hours in the day when I am in Sneem. I called the house 'Kinlough'. It is situated in Bunow Harbour. It means 'the bottom of the river' in Irish. Bord Fáilte objected at the time and delayed the thing about six months. I lit into Bord Fáilte over eyesores on the Ring of Kerry. They stopped objecting to developments altogether afterwards, which was a retrograde step in itself.

My house in Sneem is a well-known place for people to gather to think and chat. Cearbhall Ó Dalaigh, the late President of Ireland, was a regular visitor with his wife Máirín, who died last January. They had spent their honeymoon on the Blaskets in Peig Sayers' house. Máirín was born in Mysore in India and was sent back at the age of three to an aunt in Tralee. She really had no home life as such. She arranged to meet her father one time in Nice in France. She waited for the train and he never turned up. She returned in tears to her hotel bedroom and there was a knock on the door. There was this total stranger at the door, her father. She had not seen him since she was three.

I became a great friend of both of them. She was a MacDermott. Cearbhall, when he was Attorney General, became a friend. He was a very scholarly, lovely man. Máirín, who was very diffident and shy, never evolved as a person until after his death. This was by her own choice. They used come and stay with me and he, when President, used to stay. I have a smaller house which he called Arusin, the small Arus.

Cearbhall and Máirín fell madly in love with the place and were trying to find a house. Máirín used come down every Wednesday because that was Donie Courtney the solicitor's half day in Killarney and he would meet her at lunchtime. Fr Pádraig Fenton was a very close friend and he would cut out the sales ads from *The Kerryman*. Mairin would arrive and Donie Courtney would have to rush around South Kerry looking for a house.

Eventually they bought a house from Eddie Moriarty in Caherciveen. It was a converted schoolhouse and had been done very skilfully. It was miles from the village and too big. Another house came up which they bought.

Máirín was a Kerrywoman even though she was born in India.

Cearbhall felt that the insult from Minister Paddy Donegan was an insult to the office, not to himself.

When he was President of Ireland, he told me that he would love to go to China. But, as President, he was unable to do so as there were no diplomatic relations at that time. At the time China was very closed. I am a British barrister and I did a bit of practice in London. I have lots of English friends. They are more sincere than Irish friends. My mother used say they hadn't the imagination to be disloyal. I found English judges liked the Kerry accent I would turn on when appearing in London courts. It was great to get them on your side.

Anyway, I made contacts then in the Chinese Embassy in London. In 1976, David Andrews led the UCD soccer team to China. It was the first breakthrough. The ITGWU organised a group and then a group of doctors went with Dr Michael Mulcahy, the leading Irish psychiatrist. The next group was myself, Máirín Ó Dalaigh and a friend of hers, Mrs Maitland, a neighbour of the Ó Dalaigh's in County Wicklow.

After he left office, Cearbhall rang me and asked if there was any room on the Kinlen Tours of China. I told him we were full but I would waitlist him with the Embassy in London.

He joined us and the Irish 'Gang of Four' headed off. We had this wonderful interpreter Mr Wong. He had a Kerryman's mind. We became great friends and all four of us got to feel that we had known him for years. Mr Wong had fluent English and he was very amused by my impersonations of Winston Churchill.

One day I said to Mr Wong, 'Are you sure you come from China?' and he said, 'Why?' I told him he was a 'cute Kerry hoor'. He said: 'Whore! But Mr Kinlen, that is a prostitute.' And I said, 'Technically it is, but in this context it means something different. It's partly a derogatory phrase but it is also a grudging admiration because when I look across a room Mr Wong, I know what you are thinking and you know what I am thinking.'

Frequently after that we might catch a glance and we would both burst out laughing without any word said. I have no doubt that in a previous existence Wong was a cute Kerry hoor. One time in total exasperation he shouted in frustration, 'Would you please shut up, you Kerry bastard.' I felt I had been struck in the solar plexus. I went white as we had never seen him angry and Cearbhall remarked that he never thought he would have seen me stuck for a word. I think Mr Wong is now an ambassador somewhere in Africa.

Of course one of the great events in South Kerry was the visit of President De Gaulle to Sneem. There was a Dr O'Sullivan who, I think, was a Kenmareman, in Foreign Affairs, and there was a wonderful French ambassador to Ireland, D'Harcourt. He was here for six years. He had one leg amputated without anaesthetic by the Gestapo when he was a French Resistance leader. He went to the Skelligs against my advice in the month of January at one time and stayed there for a few days. It was extraordinary to see this one-legged man going up the mountain. He had come down with Dr O'Sullivan and selected Hern Cove as a nice secluded location for President de Gaulle to visit. There was a long avenue which was important from the security point of view.

The real reason the President wanted to visit Sneem was the fact that there was a Miss McCarthy who had been a nanny to his wife. She was in the geriatric hospital in Kenmare at the time, so he and his wife wanted to visit her.

I have a deep relationship with the Skelligs. I think it is among the most fantastic places in the world. There is a wonderful spiritual dimension to them and you feel uplifted when you get there. It's nature at its most majestic and there is something spiritual there. I have been going there every year since 1943. I did a programme for the BBC out there with Frank Delaney. It has been rebroadcast many times and I always get a cheque for twenty pounds, minus tax, when it goes out.

The Board of Works have done a great job. It had been altered in the last century by the lighthousemen who lived there. The series on BBC Television on civilisation starts off on the Skelligs and states that after the Barbarians overthrew the Roman Empire it was on cliffs like the Skelligs that civilisation clung on by its nails, because the knowledge of Greek was continued there. The whole evolution of Celtic crosses is to be found out there. I spend a lot of time in Kerry, up to four months of the year. I find it a very happy place to be. I feel spiritually much more released and much more at peace with nature in Kerry. I know Kerry people are rogues. I'm a rogue myself. Its beauty is physical and spiritual. There is an atmosphere and serenity in Kerry which you will not find any place else.

I remember a case which had an interesting development on the question of climate in Kerry. I was acting for Kerry Couny Council when an expert witness said the particular part of South Kerry which was being discussed in the case was one of the three wettest places in Europe. It involved a lake near Killarney and the County Council wanted to extract water from it. We were saying that no matter how much water we would extract that it would not affect the level of the lake because it got so much precipitation. They say you shouldn't ask a question, unless you know the answer. I asked the question as a matter of interest as to where were the two other wettest places in Europe. Oddly enough, he replied, they were also both in Kerry. I looked at the press bench, and I said, 'Ladies and gentlemen of the press, I don't wish in any way to suppress your reports, but I represent Kerry County Council and Kerry is going through a most appallingly bad tourism season because of the wet weather and I would beg you not to record that statement as it was not relevant to the proceedings and I should not have asked that question.' They all nodded.

Next day's *Cork Examiner* had the headline: Kerry Wettest Place in Europe, says Expert.

In our family I was the eldest and as I was the only one qualified when my father died, I took over the household as my mother was very dependent. I reared my brother and sister who were both at school at the time. They then left and I was left as a carer until my mother died last year. Normally a woman is the usual carer in our society, but about twenty per cent of carers are men. I don't regret this as I have had many rewards. I don't have a wife and family which is a pity, but at this stage I am definitely a self-centred bachelor. Nobody will change me now and I don't wish to be changed.

DICK SPRING

(TÁNAISTE)

My earliest memories are of Strand Road, Tralee, I was always conscious of being in a political household. It was a relatively small house and my parents had lived there since 1944, about a year after they got married. It was the centre of activity in that street and the door was always open. In those days one could keep the key in the door without worrying too much about it. My father, Dan, had a great expression on Sundays when we went for a family drive. He would ask who was going to mind the house? What he meant was, who would be around if anybody came looking for the TD ?

I particularly remember evening times doing lessons around the table. Three or four of us fighting for space with our school books and my father would be doing his constituency work at the top of the same table. There would be six children sometimes at the table. It was never a quiet house as there were always people coming and going. People would just walk in at any time of the day.

We lived next to a nursing home and in those days we had no phone, so when my father would need to make a call, he would do it from the nursing home. There was a famous Nurse Regan who used to take telephone messages for him. In those days also there was no such thing as free postage for TDs, so another memory was being sent off at night for twenty threepenny stamps and if you couldn't get them at the local shop we often had to go out to Blennerville with my father in the car where there was a small post office which stayed open late.

You ask how I opted for the Law. Well one thing I decided at an early stage in secondary school in Roscrea was that I was not going to do anything related to the sciences Boyle's Law was enough for me. I felt more comfortable with the Humanities, English, History and Commerce subjects.

From early days the idea of Law and Politics looked like a natural pattern. In those days lawyers seemed to dominate the Dáil. I think my father was keen that, if any of us was going into politics, we would have a legal training.

I did not decide for a long while which side of the profession I would go for, solicitors or barristers, but I chose the latter.

I believe my brother Donal could have been equally as effective a politician as I. But it was timing and where I was at a particular time that led me into politics. I found myself free to help in elections in my teens when I was on platforms at a very early age. I can recall speaking in Eileen Desmond's campaign when I was a student in Trinity. I'm not sure that my Trinity speeches won her many votes in mid-Cork, I must confess.

My first memory of canvassing was in Dingle in the 1957 campaign when I was seven years of age. I distinctly remember walking around Dingle which was in North Kerry in that election. It became part of the South Kerry constituency for subsequent elections. Politics was in the blood even then, but that didn't stop me from attempting to go away from it. In my twenties I wanted to be as far away from Ireland as I could be.

I went off to the States for a few years and that was to get away from living life in what I thought was a fish bowl. You were always conscious of being a TD's son. He was going before the public and he would not want us to do anything, as anything which we might do would be a reflection on him and he would ask us to mind ourselves. There was that sort of pressure. You would be conscious. It wouldn't be a fear of the law, but it was your father as he would take anything personally. He expected not to get any reports on us that might reflect on him as a public representative. This meant we were more restricted.

There wasn't a Minister in Kerry since the thirties until my appointment to cabinet in the eighties. There is an expectation in Kerry and people are very conscious of that. People, irrespective of their political affiliations in Kerry, are very proud to have somebody from the county

at the Cabinet table and that has come back to me very strongly, particularly in the past twelve months. People are entitled to believe that Kerry should get its share of the action and a reasonable share of the national cake. I am conscious of that. There is a question of balance. What you want to ensure is that you get your share and not to be forgotten and that you don't get it at the expense of others.

I have set goals in relation to certain services, hospital services, education services, access to government departments, the whole question of roads. I am not talking just about potholes but about the whole road network, as all these services have a very important bearing on people's lives. Jobs is probably the key question. If you provide jobs, a lot will follow from that. As Minister for Foreign Affairs I am obliged to travel a good deal, but on any of my trips I am always looking out for potential investors to help in our fight against unemployment.

Irrespective of politics, if you were to offer me a choice in the morning about where I would like to live, I would still opt for Kerry, probably a site overlooking Tralee Bay.

The quality of life in Kerry is as good as you will find anywhere, particularly in relation to facilities and in terms of resources. I wouldn't say to my children, you must live in Kerry. They have a great affinity with the United States where their grandparents live. They are very much half Irish and half American. Kristi and the children enjoy living in Kerry. Tralee has great amenities, close to the beaches and is a great town to live in. My eldest, Aaron, is thirteen, Laura is eleven, and Adam is seven. Aaron shows a flair for art and writing; maybe he should have a law degree as well just in case.

I went away to boarding school in Roscrea when I was twelve and I then went on to Trinity. I then went off to America; then I came back to Dublin; then back to Tralee. So here in Tralee they have always been used to me coming and going. People know I have to move at a very fast pace. Maybe on a Thursday night, the odd time, I might go down for a drink, people would see me on the television news giving an interview in Brussels or somewhere earlier that day. People know that I work hard and I enjoy working hard.

When I have a night off, I prefer to have a night at home. If I was allowed to relax I think I might enjoy two pints in one of my local pubs. If I finish early, say eight or nine at night, I really like to put my feet up and enjoy a good book. I usually read a book about the country I have just returned from, having not had the time to get to it before travelling to that country. I was in the Gulf recently and I am still reading *Arabian Sands*. I like reading political and travel books.

But for real relaxation I find nothing better than a good walk on Banna Strand which I associate with my childhood. We probably had the only car in Strand Road for a long time and my father would often take a car load of us and the neighbours' children to Banna. He would often go by the bog in Kilflynn, where we would do a few hours work. The big treat on getting to Banna would be Nash's lemonade and Marietta biscuits. Banna Strand still has a great magic for me.

People ask me if my bad car accident had any effect on my outlook. It didn't have the same effect Augustus John experienced when he dived into the river and banged his head and he started producing better quality material after it. Initially it didn't affect me, but at times you stand back and just realise that it was a close call. Even in the tightest of political adversity, it puts things in perspective. There are times in my business when you feel the world is coming down on top of your head, and you think to yourself: what if the lights had gone out in 1981 when I had that accident as I was being driven to Dublin? I think my philosophical approach is that any morning you can get out of bed is a good morning as there are many people who have been in lesser accidents and suffered smaller injuries who cannot.

Being in that kind of situation gives you a resilience; now I am not sure if that resilience had been there prior to the accident, but I feel sure it is there now. I can use it to my advantage. It is probably one of those shattering experiences which you can turn to your own benefit.

Getting back to the Dáil, the Dáil is not responsive to the demands of Irish life. For a long time in the seventies and the eighties, the courts were the main legislative dynamo in this country. People were making constitutional advances through the courts rather than through the Dáil. For a period the legislators were behind the people, but I think that has changed in recent years. I think we need a more open and tolerant society, rather than a confessional society and to let people run their own lives with as little interference as possible. I think the Dáil has improved. You wonder if a system set up and modelled on the Westminster model is the best way to get things done in an age of confrontation and mass communications. I would put a question mark there as I don't have an answer – what is the alternative? I think politicians work within the constraints of the day. If somebody came along and said, 'Look, tailor your work to the needs of the people on a day-to-day-basis', I think politicians would go with that. You operate within a system. Overall I feel that many changes are still necessary in relation to how we get things done and how government works on a day-to-day basis.

There is a huge workload and rural politicians have a totally disjointed life, some of the week in Dublin and the weekend in your constituency, working in both places. Kerry is distant from Dublin, but thanks to Kerry Airport, I can travel more easily than when I was previously in government. Then I had to spend eight to ten hours on a road trip to Dublin. Nowdays I can get up in an hour and a half without the pressure of being on the road.

Kerry is the premier tourism county, but we have to be careful to keep industrial employment and maintain the balance between industry and services. We are holding that balance. The Regional Technical College in Tralee is making a tremendous impact. Apart from employing one hundred and seventy staff and having thousands of students, it is giving Kerry a training base for prospective employers. We can't compete totally with the universities, but it does give a skills base. I would like to see a high quality tourism industry in Kerry. We will never get the mass market. The quality of the facilities will remain high. There is scope for cultural tourism in Kerry, ranging from Skellig Rock to the literary traditions of the county. FÁS in Tralee is also a very important asset.

You ask me to compare working as Tánaiste with Garret FitzGerald and Albert Reynolds. Well, you will have to wait for me to write my own book to find the answer to that one. It is well known that they are men of totally different styles, backgrounds and political interests. It is important that the Taoiseach and the Tánaiste work well together – this involves Cabinet cohesion and effective decision making. I had a good working relationship with Garret FitzGerald and have a good one with Albert Reynolds. Never forget that you are talking about two leaders of two different parties.

In the day-to-day working relationship we have exchanges every day. Our offices are only fifty yards apart down the corridor. Our staff are in close contact. Given my portfolio in Foreign Affairs, there is obviously a huge link with the Taoiseach's office. It is working. It's two people who try to get the chemistry right. But it is strictly business.

I don't see us ever going back to the single party government. I think there is a certain irony in what is happening at the moment. If we can maintain the momentum we have attained now in May 1994 and build on the achievements to date, it will be ironically Fianna Fáil who will have proven that coalitions work, despite fifty years of campaigning that coalitions couldn't work.

I think the norm is going to be parties co-operating. One of my main aspirations in politicis is to get Ireland away from the traditional divide of the Civil War. If we can work with Fianna Fáil, that may also throw up the prospect of Fine Gael working with Fianna Fáil. That may well happen in the future. I'd like to get rid of that divide. Let the parties be able to work with one another and bury what basically was the division of the Civil War.

It is still in the background. At local level there would be some enmity between Fianna Fáil and Fine Gael. Our generation has no association with it, wants to move on from that and look to the future rather than the past.

My real frustration in politics is the fact that the violence in Northern Ireland isn't stopping and that those living in Northern Ireland cannot get out of bed some morning and say we must settle this conflict, we must compromise before another person dies.

Why is Ireland on the world map? Because of the conflict in Northern Ireland. There are a lot of other reasons why Ireland should be on the world map in terms of what we are producing, not just in terms of commercial goods, but also in the Arts. There is an artistic explosion taking place in this country in all forms of drama, art and film making. That is why we should be on the world stage. For example, somebody who has just returned from Yugoslavia was telling me that all they knew about Ireland in Yugoslavia was U2 and the IRA.

Getting back to Kerry, I think the fact that we are so far from Dublin means there is this strong pride that we can do it ourselves. That is best reflected on the football field. And if you look at the administration of the State, Kerry has always had a very strong Kerry component. Numerous secretaries of government departments are Kerry born and educated. There has always been a very strong tradition in education in Kerry, looking for quality education as the key to progress.

I often talk to pupils in local schools and I tell them they are living in a country where the quality of life is as good as you will find in any other country in the world. The opportunities are limited, but if you are prepared to put in the work and get the qualifications, you can be an achiever here. But one has to have the discipline to make the effort. Why are so many Irish people successful abroad? If we could keep that energy here and get stuck into producing the goods in Ireland, it could be a lot better place.

I have no problem about people going abroad to see the wider world. But be prepared to come back. Kristi has come from Virginia to live here and I am fortunate in that she happens to be a very strong woman. I don't wish to sound condescending, but I don't think you could bring your average American woman into a North Kerry political family and expect that it would be plain sailing. But I am fortunate in being married to a strong woman who has made a career out of ensuring that our kids have at least one parent around as much as possible. She has made many sacrifices.

Ongoing innovation has marked out Tralee's annual International Rose Festival. They're a great core of people. They will have internal difficulties, but without a split. There is enormous commitment and the Festival is now well supported by the town. It puts the town on the national and the international map. The Rose selection is a great show and very professional. It is a fair reflection of how things in Kerry are done, when people set out to do things. The Aquadome is a four point four million pound project and it will probably be the most modern facility of its kind in Europe. It will be open twelve months. There is no future in eight week tourism.

Europe is not going to be a paymaster indefinitely, and the Structural Funds we are getting this time won't be there again. We have a chance between now and 1999 to build our road structure, to develop our education base. I think this is the last big round-up and what we have to make sure is that when it is over we can stand on our own two feet.

It is serious business to make sure we can compete with the best. There is a great opportunity there. We will be spending over the six year period seven point two billion, which we wouldn't have otherwise.

JERRY KIERNAN

(ATHLETE)

I had two ambitions in life. In 1964 I remember when I was eleven, being in our next-door neighbour Lizzie Sayers' house in Colbert Street, Listowel, watching the Tokyo Olympics. We didn't have a television then and I recall being mesmerised by the athletics and saying, 'That is what I want to do'. I knew in a smaller scale that around Listowel I could outrun any other boy at that time. So I wanted to run for Ireland in the Olympic Games and to run a sub-four minute mile.

I was just reflecting in the Dublin school where I work the other day. I gave the kids an essay titled 'A Wish' to write for their weekend exercise. That first wish in Lizzie Sayers' kitchen came back to me. And I remember there was a bank official staying in digs in Lizzie's and he initiated me into the whole thing of the staggered lanes on the track as we watched the Tokyo Olympics. He was Ollie Lehane who is now a very successful businessman and racehorse owner.

I remember Ollie sitting down with me and explaining the whole thing to me vividly. I remember the great Peter Snell in those Games and a Jamaican runner called George Kerr who always finished fourth. There was Billy Mills and Ron Clarke. So all these names from the athletics' world were etched on my mind even at that early age and I can't recall any football names.

My father, Pat, is a Clareman from Kilkee and I think the fact that he was from Clare and not Kerry had a major bearing on me opting for athletics and not football. Living in Kerry it is always the desire of most fathers to see their sons play football and there is this pressure to concentrate on gaelic football. But my father left me make my own choices and that was very important. And I have always acknowledged it. He was catholic with a small 'c' in his approach to all these things. Providing I behaved myself, everything was fine as far as he was concerned. My mother is Mary Downey from Brosna and they met when he was stationed there as a Garda.

I was born in my grandmother's house in Brosna and we lived then in Ballylongford and I still remember those days. I can recollect going to the local national school before we moved to Listowel.

I have one sister and two brothers. Eileen is the oldest and she is one year older than me and she is married to Denis O'Sullivan. My brother, Michael, is a Garda in Cork and my other brother Padraig works and lives in Dublin. I was born on 31 May, 1953. I was brought up in Colbert Street, Listowel or, as it is known locally, Forge Lane, because of the forges which were located there. I was there until I was about twelve and then we moved into one of the guards' houses in Ballygologue.

I loved all sports, soccer and football and we used to even improvise our own rugby. My earliest recollection was kicking football around Courthouse Road which would be impossible now because of the traffic. My friends growing up were Tadhg Moriarty, the Murphys, Dick and Jer, Pádraig Walsh from Church Street and PJ Browne. We had the town league in the national school and I was traditionally a Boro man and I remember one time being shifted from the Boro to the Ashes side just to strengthen their team and even things out. I was very distraught about it. So that shows that even at that early age there was a very competitive aspect to football in the national school.

I meet Jimmy Deenihan occasionally and he maintains that if I had not gone on to athletics, I could have made the great Kerry team of which he was a member and captained to win one of their All-Irelands. I doubt that somehow, as I was a little on the light side at ten and a half stone. I used to play midfield and I have a County Championship minor medal for Feale Rangers. That was in 1971. We beat Shannon Rangers and I got most of the scores. I got 1-7 of the 2-11. And the goal I got was of the soccer variety along the ground. The soccer was great and we used have Macha Bunyan down in the Cows Lawn coaching us and I was as interested in the soccer then as anything.

Bryan MacMahon taught us in the national school. I remember Bean Uí Chrualaigh in high infants and then we had Miss Maureen O'Connor in first class. She was a real nice lady and never smacked you. She died very suddenly and we were all very upset. There was Tadhg Joe O'Flaherty and his fiddle which he used to play in class and then Dick O'Flaherty and then Michael Keane in sixth class whom I really liked. In those days there were many people in Listowel who encouraged those of us interested in running. There was Timmy Daly who had a great interest in the young athletes. There was Gene Moriarty, the father of my friend Tadhg Moriarty, who had a passion for cycle racing. And we used be driven to meetings in Eddie Sheehy's hackney-car every Sunday.

I then went on to St Michael's and I remember looking forward to returning there after the summer holidays when I was going into Leaving Cert year, with the prospect of all the running championships before me over the months ahead. That showed the way I was leaning even then, because up to then I would have been inclined to skip running training to play football. But I was beginning to put the football to one side and I then saw myself as a runner. But that was in my Leaving Cert year.

Two of the teachers in St Michael's, John Molyneaux and Johnny O'Flaherty, were pioneers really with regard to athletics. They started off knowing nothing about running and they made it their business to do everything they could to inform themselves. I remember them getting coaches down to the college, which was almost unheard of then in Kerry because the ethos was if you didn't play gaelic football, you were nothing. I remember Robert O'Dwyer coming down to coach in the triple and long jumps. I recall that they wrote to Pádraig Griffin, one of the top coaches in Ireland at that time, for training schedules for the likes of me. Everyday they used to give up their time after school to go down the Cows Lawn with Pat O'Connell, John O'Connell and me and put us through our paces. Looking back on it, they spent an awful lot of time with us.

I played in the college football team and would have played midfield and in the forwards. I was always in the thick of things. In my final year in St Michael's we had Jimmy Deenihan and Tim Kennelly on the O'Sullivan Cup side. Academically St Michael's was very traditional. The teachers I recall obviously were John Molyneaux and John O'Flaherty and I recall with tremendous affection Fr Dan Long. I thought he was a really nice man. He was the President of the College. We were concerned with getting good results, but he used say to us that actually the education was more important than the actual results. So he was before his time in that respect.

When I left St Michael's I got what was known as the 'call' to train as a primary school teacher at St Patrick's. I remember Tim Kennelly coming to me and they had hired a taxi to bring me down to Kerry to play a game for Listowel. I was only eighteen at the time. And I decided that I wanted to give it up. I haven't played gaelic since then and I have no regrets. I don't think gaelic football could have sustained me, because there is so little fitness involved in playing it that I would need to have something far more challenging. I remember when playing senior football at about seventeen, getting thumped by much older fellows who would not have been able to keep up with me, but would have been much heftier than me. And I said to myself that I didn't need this. I just wasn't interested.

John Molyneaux constructed a six or eight lane running track in the gaelic sportsfield and I don't know how he got away with it. At the time the gaelic field was invested with a certain sanctity that no other grounds had. He weed-killered the whole place to mark out the lanes. How he got away with it! The foundation was laid and the discipline was set in my athletics career in St Michael's by men like John Molyneaux. He was a fanatic in a way and I suppose you would call him in political terms a kind of benevolent dictator. But in certain situations you need that.

When I left Listowel I lived the high life and then there was the cut-off point. I knew I could not do both and I became very disciplined. I was aware one had to lead a certain kind of life to achieve anything. While in St Michael's I won the Kerry Colleges, the North Munster, the Munster and a silver medal in the All-Ireland Colleges where I was second to Eamon Coghlan in the 1,500 metres when I was in Leaving Cert.

I was about ten yards behind and he accelerated away from me in the last 100 meters. My first teaching post after St Patrick's College was at St Brigid's, Foxrock, and I have remained there ever since. I vary between first and fourth class. This is my twenty-first year there.

The minute I went to St Pat's I went straight up to Clonliffe Harriers in Santry. I wanted to be near Santry as it had associations with names such as Herb Elliot, and I wanted to be on a track and that was the established track at the time. It was only two and a half miles up the road from Drumcondra.

I ran my sub-four minute mile in Crystal Palace in 1975. Prior to that I won the National 1,500 metres in Belfield. I do remember in 1977 running an Irish record for the 3,000 metres. That was on 18 May because I was the first Irishman to break the eight minute barrier for 3K. And about a week later I ran an Irish record for two miles. For one brief ten day period I held two Irish records. Coghlan eventually broke them. I missed the Montreal Olympics by half a second when I ran my first sub-four minute mile. I almost fulfilled two of my boyhood ambitions at once. But I got one and the other was to come in the Los Angeles Olympics.

I got into running marathons by accident. As you get older you slow down and realise where your talent lies. In 1977 when I broke the two records I got a bad injury about a week later and did no running until April 1978. It was a foot injury which I could not shake off. Eventually it righted itself, but it took me a few years to get back. In 1980 I began to show a bit of promise at 5,000 metres and in 1981 I cracked a fast time in Cork. I was not getting the races that I needed at international level. I am in the unique situation where I have run all my fast times, except the Crystal Palace run, in Ireland. All the other great Irish athletes have done their good times in big events abroad. I never got onto those Grand Prix meetings. Two or three nights a week I trained with Coghlan and in 1980 I was the fourth fastest 5,000 metres runner. The first three went to the Moscow Olympics.

I was stymied and there was no place to go and I started to turn to ten mile road races. At that time if anybody broke fifty minutes for ten miles in Ireland they were looked at as being tremendous. I suddenly brought it down to forty-six minutes and then I realised that this was what I was best at. It was the sheer frustration of lack of opportunity on track that switched me to marathon running. I realised then that I could run at a very fast cruising speed relentlessly over ten miles.

At that time I was running so well I could do what few can do now, I could live with the present crop of Kenyans over ten miles then. And I took it from there and ran my Dublin City Marathon in 1982, where for eighteen miles I was inside world record pace and cruising. But I began to cramp as I hadn't done the training for the distance and probably started off too fast. Eventually I was nearly walking the last five or six miles, but the time still stands as the fastest time ever for the Dublin City Marathon, two hours, thirteen minutes and thirty-five seconds. I won the Cork City Marathon as well on a very difficult course. The marathon wins now include Dublin twice, Cork twice, Belfast twice, Stamford, New Jersey, my biggest win, third in Houston, ninth in the Los Angeles Olympics, third in Columbus, Ohio.

I won the Olympic trials in Cork in 1984 and I was chosen for the Olympic Marathon in Los Angeles with John Treacy and Dick Hooper. It was run on 12 August 1984 at 5.15 pm. I was in such good shape that I reckon that I could have won a medal in the 10k. We ran the opening two laps in the Santa Monica Stadium and we ran from there and went through Santa Monica. I recall doing the first two laps, which was a half mile, in two minutes thirty seconds which was five minute miling pace and that is what I wanted to run even though it was ninety degrees, but it felt easy. I remember exiting the stadium, running at the pace I wanted to run at. I went through ten miles in fifty minutes and twenty miles in one hour forty minutes. I was comfortable. I was sure at twenty miles I had the race won. As sure as you can be.

There is a photograph at eighteen miles of all the great marathon runners in the world. Unfortunately, I hadn't joined the group and was just an image in the background at that point. Everybody was there and it was the greatest marathon field ever assembled. There was Decastella, he was the world record holder at the time; the great white hope, Alberto Salazar from the US; you had the Kenyans and the other Africans; the Mexicans, people who were expected not to be inconve-

nienced by the heat; Carlos Lopez from Portugal, who to my mind was
the greatest distance runner of all time; Seiko, the great Japanese runner; Charlie Spedding and others. It was the pantheon of all the great
marathon runners. I was looking around all these fellows about a head
taller than everybody else and I was with them and briefly led.

Seiko wasn't even sweating and he looked to be going easier than
everybody else. At about twenty miles he took off his peaked cap and
threw it away as if to say it is starting now. But in actual fact when the
pressure came, he was the first beaten. But he looked great at that
point. Brendan O'Shea my coach, also a Listowel man, reckons that I
should have gone for it at twenty miles, but when we got to twenty-one
miles we came to a water station. We all queued up for the water. When
we came to the station, Spedding took off and did a four-forty mile. As
I was about to respond, a big burly official stepped out with a container
of water to give it to somebody beyond me and I cannoned into him
and there was a major pile-up.

I got the first signs of cramp at about seventeen miles. I joined them
at eighteen and a half and I was going to see if I could hang on until
twenty-four and then go. So here I was in a dilemma: will I go with
Spedding and Treacy and de Castella? Or would I remain content with
being in the top ten? If you told me before the race that I would finish
in the top ten, I would have been very pleased with that. Would I cut
my losses and be happy with being in the top ten? I had a history of
cramping and I knew if I got one major cramp I would not make it to
the finish. The cramps were in both legs and you knew if they got
severe they would stop you. You would have to stop to massage your
legs, you would lose momentum, you would lose heart, you would
lose everything. So I was able to back off to five minutes fifteen seconds
pace and still maintain my position. So that was the way.

When I finished the marathon there was hardly a brack on me. I was
hardly out of breath. I ran two hours, twelve minutes and nineteen seconds. I was surprised that I was only a minute behind the fourth finish-
er. It was coming down into the stadium in a steep hill that I got my
severest cramp. I stopped for about forty seconds. I was almost a
minute stuck there as I didn't want to enter the stadium hobbling and

having people concerned about me. And people at home wondering if I was going to collapse.

I wanted to run my final 500 metres in dignity and not stagger all over the place. I finished in my own time in ninth. And afterwards I was assailed by a feeling of what could have been if I wasn't cramping. Or maybe if my training had been slightly different. My cramping could be caused by my physical architecture. I am a bit big for running marathons. Most others are a bit more compact. I would have gone close to the world record in the Dublin City Marathon in 1982, but for cramping.

I had never run in that kind of heat and competition before Los Angeles. And I proved conclusively that I could run with anybody in the world. I had run in the Olympics. The dream in Lizzie's kitchen was fulfilled.

Brendan O'Shea, whose father taught in St Michael's just before my time, was a great coach. He was not just an influential figure, but a very good friend and still is. If I had listened to Brendan properly, really listened, I would have run better in Los Angeles. I think all my life I have trained too hard. Extremely hard. That is the way I am.

After the Olympics I was back teaching within two weeks. When I ran in the Olympics I was up against full-time runners and I was a full-time teacher. I have to say at no stage did I get sponsorship or help from anybody in this country and that is a severe indictment of the system. I believe it goes back to the old ethos that lots of people in this country attribute sport to gaelic football and hurling. And anything outside of these games is not really sport. And they never took time to nurture other sport.

I have no interest in gaelic football and, as you've asked me to elaborate, I'll explain. I'm not doing so to be controversial. It is taking away from the pool of young people we could have for sports such as athletics and other international sports if it wasn't so powerful. If you look at last weekend. To most people the major happening was Ireland winning against England at Twickenham at rugby. For me that meant nothing. That weekend Caitríona McKiernan won a Grand Prix in Portugal against the best in the world; Eamon Coghlan became the first man over forty years of age to run a sub-four minute mile and TJ Kearns won a silver medal in the British Indoor Championships. What did it merit in the newspapers? Most people don't even know they achieved these things, perhaps Coghlan yes. We read over and over again Ireland beating England, to the point that it became a pain.

To me the only sports worth talking about are the true international sports, soccer and running. They are truly international and when you go out into the world and you run, you are running against everybody. And if you make the top ten, then you can say, as I could in 1984, 'I am in the top ten in the world'. Rugby is only quasi-international. There are only a handful of countries playing it seriously and only a handful of other countries half playing it seriously.

If I was in any other country I would never have to work. In 1984 I got a sheaf of telegrams after Telecom had those special well-wishers telegrams for those in the Olympics. I have bundles of them. The expectations of the Irish people are very high. If I had not been working and had been full-time in athletics, maybe I could have brought back the gold. But what was I supposed to live on? I had been up against fellows who had never worked and had been in training camps at altitude.

Nowadays things are beginning to change and Cospóir are giving out grants. But to my mind what you need is to identify the talented people and put them on what would be considered a salary. It goes back to the parochial ethos in that they consider excellence to be what they see in Croke Park in September. To me I see a gang of thirty fellows running around who are only ten per cent fit and yet they think themselves fit. I don't see international calibre athletes. I see people who are very moderately fit.

I train twice a day, seven days a week, all year round. At the moment I am injured, but I have already biked 50k this morning and I have done a gym session and it is now shortly before noon. It is my aim now to be the top over forty distance runner in the world. There are very few people in the world who, I feel, could beat me over the long distance if I am fit.

LOUISE McDONOUGH

(COUNTY REGISTRAR)

I was appointed Kerry County Registrar in 1976. My predecessor, the late Tom Clarke, had been ill for some months and I acted in a deputy capacity for six months. A woman colleague was appointed in County Meath in August, 1976, and I was not formally appointed until September, although I had been acting County Registrar from June. We were the first women County Registrars. There was no particular wonder attached to the fact that a woman was taking up the position of County Registrar. The only qualification you needed was to have been eight years qualified as a solicitor. Within a year I was into a general election and that was the first big trauma in my career as County Registrar.

The fact that I was a woman, working in a mainly male preserve, had ceased to faze me a long time before taking up my appointment as I had qualified as a solicitor sixteen years previously when few women went into the Law.

When I became County Registrar my immediate difficulty was working with a staff who did not know me and who would, I suppose, have preferred somebody from Tralee rather than Listowel. I remember when I went to the courthouse in Tralee on the first day in the job, I didn't even know how to get into the office. Having got over the initial reservations that the staff might have had we never looked back and it has been a great experience.

The County Registrar has a number of different hats. Responsibility for the administration of the Circuit Court sittings in Kerry; District Probate Registrar; local Registrar of Titles; County Sheriff and Returning Officer at all elections, other than local elections. The administration of the Circuit Court forms the major part of my duties. I do not have a judicial function in most aspects of the Circuit Court but I have a quasi-judicial function in some minor matters. We have all administrative work done for the Circuit Court Judge when he comes around four times a year for sittings in Tralee, Killarney and Listowel. As District Probate Registrar I issue grants of probate and administration for people with a residence within Kerry. I have a branch of the Land Registry where people can get a copy of their title.

The County Sheriff title sounds the most romantic, but it is the least pleasant aspect of my duties. It means that I execute court orders and entails collecting money on foot of court orders and, unfortunately, I have quite a number of possession orders to execute also. This means taking possession of houses, occasionally for private individuals, but mostly for building societies. It's reasonably commonplace and I would have a number of possession orders lodged in my office every month as Sheriff. These possession orders are, however, very often settled on the doorstep. I have two court messengers who actually physically execute the order. But if there is the prospect of trouble of any kind I attend with the court messengers.

On occasions, when news of my impending arrival got around, I have been met by a coterie of neighbours to try and prevent me. We try to avoid actual ejectment and we write to the people involved and sometimes we get the help of the local priest. We do everything we can to avoid coming with a carpenter, the police and the paraphernalia to forcibly evict somebody. The word eviction is emotive and we try every other means possible before embarking on one. But you will find the person who has no merits whatsoever and just sits there and sort of says to you when you arrive that we are going back to Penal times and you can't evict. But the law says you can.

The Revenue Sheriff executes tax certificates and, strangely, if he isn't able to execute, it can go back into court and if a court order is issued, then I am asked to execute. We go for cash if we can get it, but we seize property as well. I remember one occasion when I went to seize a lot of furniture from a hotel. The place was locked up and I was formally dressed, having been in court earlier that day. I can break in forcibly, but I don't like doing so if it can be avoided. We discovered a small window which was open. My court messenger was with me and he helped me up onto a barrel which we found and I got partly in through the window. I was stuck half-in and half-out, with pink shoes looking out from under my long dark skirt. My court messenger was politely trying to get me in and politely trying not to look at me at the same time. Eventually he gave me a good shove and I fell in on top of a carpet and I let him in through the front door.

There is nothing romantic about being the Sheriff; even the expression, 'sheriff's posse'. A posse is just a sheet of paper, 'posse comitatus', the document I send to the police to get a police escort if I am expecting trouble, which I do when carrying out an eviction. It requests the police to attend and sets out the number of police I want and they come with me. They do not have to intervene unless there is violence threatened. The Returning Officer at elections is the role I like best. I had a pretty traumatic first election in 1977 because I didn't really know much about it. My father was very involved in local politics and knew an awful lot about the system, but I didn't.

The administrative part I could cope with, but I had a very hassle-ridden count in the old Ashe Memorial Hall. I had to put up with a lot of recriminations at the time. However, once I had done the next election and everything went well, I had by then worked out my own system. It gives me the most tremendous buzz. It is terribly hard work with weeks of eighteen-hour days for me and my staff preparing for the poll. I have two constituencies, Kerry South and Kerry North. I do the administrative work for both, but when it comes to the count, I look after Kerry North and I appoint the County Secretary to be the Deputy Returning Officer for the count in Kerry South.

I have to organise two hundred and sixty polling stations throughout the whole county, which have to be manned with a presiding officer and a polling clerk. They have to be equipped with all the necessary items like voting booths, ballot boxes, stationery. Every single article comes from the one spot, my office. And the necessary manpower to operate the system must be provided by the Returning Officer.

One of the most traumatic nights of my life was the famous count in the general election of February, 1987, when Dick Spring held on to his seat by four votes. When we finished the count initially, there were five votes separating Dick Spring, Labour, from Tom McEllistrim, Fianna Fáil. A recount was immediately called for. With hindsight and the experience I now have, I would have postponed the recount until the next day. I would never again start a recount at twelve o'clock at night. I had the late Donie Browne with me as my legal adviser. He had no official title as such, and he never accepted a penny for all the work he did to assist me down the years. He just loved it and he was brilliant and knew Proportional Representation better than anybody I have ever known.

The initial count finished around midnight. Donie left the count hall thinking I would leave the recount until the following day. There was a very practical reason why I wanted to press on and not postpone until the following day. I had taken a calculated risk which did not come off in that the count centre, the CYMS hall, was not available the day after the count as it had been booked for a furniture display. I would have had to remove everything to a different counting centre. I discussed it with the staff and the candidates and we decided to go on. But Donie had left. My son Desmond was helping out and I sent him off to find Donie and he duly arrived back with Donie within half an hour and Donie stayed by my side all through that long, wearisome night.

We had to go through all the thirty-four thousand votes again. The way a first recount is done is that you don't disturb the bundles, although you go through the ballot papers one by one. You open them out so that the candidates and their agents can see them. If a significant error is discovered the papers are then replaced in the mixing box and you start all over again.

The result of the recount was a one vote change. That would not have been one single voting paper; that would have been fractions of votes here and there, discovered in the transfers of various surpluses. It is usually on the transfer of a surplus you will find the tiny errors, because that is the most difficult part of the whole operation, the transfer of a surplus. After the recount the calculation came out with a difference of four votes instead of five. At one point the difference had gone up as far as seven and come down to four during the course of the recount. We have a very good count staff of about thirty with two supervisors and a manager, Eamonn O'Mahony.

It was nearly five in the morning when the recount concluded. There was a national focus on it as it involved the leader of the Labour Party, the pressure was unreal that night. You could have cut the atmosphere with a knife and an awful lot of people stayed until five in the morning as there was an air abroad that there would be political blood spilt on one side or the other. Tom McEllistrim of Fianna Fáil, who lost out, was amazingly gracious about the whole thing, I must say. He was very gentlemanly. Everybody was exhausted and tempers were frayed. It was a tribute to the count staff that there were so few minor errors. A serious error is unlikely because of the way we do the count.

Our very first operation in an election count is to go through every ballot paper looking for two markings, the official stamp of the presiding officer and a clear number one. If you get the first count right, you have a very good chance of getting every other count right. If you are more than one or two votes out in your first count, you've had it, because your subsequent counts cannot be right then.

The quota is worked out by the number of valid votes, divided by the number of candidates plus one and you add one to the result of that calculation. If anybody exceeds the quota on the first count, he or she is deemed to be elected. They are not declared elected until after the final count. If that elected person has a sizable surplus, you may have to distribute that surplus as the second count. And this can take a long time. On a surplus which arises on foot of a first count, you have to recount all of the elected candidate's ballot papers seeking the number two votes on these ballot papers.

However, if a person had a very small surplus, you wouldn't necessarily have to distribute the surplus at that stage. But if, as happened with Dick Spring's vote in the last election in 1992 where he had about three thousand of a surplus, it's necessary to go through all his number ones and find how many were transferable. All transferable votes can't be transferred, so you work out the fraction that goes to the others. On any subsequent count, when distributing a surplus you only recount the last parcel, as they call it. These votes are the votes that each candidate would have got in the transfers in the previous count. This all sounds very complicated, but it is much easier to do it than to explain.

While all my election staff know the mechanics of counting votes, Donie Browne came into his own when interpreting the *Electoral Acts*. There are sections which give the impression that a situation can be addressed in a number of different ways. Donie would be there with his copy of the Act. Election agents would come along and say, for instance, that the next procedure should not be an elimination, but the distribution of a small surplus. They would point to a section of the Act which would seem to support that argument. Donie would never dismiss an argument out of hand, he would always consider what they had to say, and he would always come up with the right answer and know the right way to go about it. It took a tremendous load off me as I would be involved in the mechanics of running the count.

He was regarded very highly by all as they respected him as the soul of integrity and, as I said, he was there because he liked the count and we were great friends. He had been there in Tom Clarke's time as well. I learned more from Donie Browne than I would if I had been a year studying the *Electoral Acts.*

I get my brother, Michael, who is a lawyer, to attend at the Killarney count centre. All the election agents are now lawyers and if the political parties are represented by lawyers, I like to ensure that my deputy returning officer can also have a lawyer to call on. In general our politicians here are a grand bunch. I am not just saying that. I have had one minor unfortunate experience in that a candidate was totally graceless after being defeated. At the end they all usually thank the staff. But this one deliberately excluded my staff and myself, but that happened only once.

There are certain polling stations in Kerry where I find it impossible to get staff to man them for elections. To read about the unemployment situation and what is called 'disgraceful double-jobbing of teachers and other persons in employment', one would imagine there were queues for these jobs. In some areas there are, but in other areas I can never get anybody. The Gardaí have often helped me get dependable staff in these areas. They also escort the ballot boxes from the polling stations and provide security for the polling stations and the count centres.

My interest in elections provided me with a great experience earlier this year when I went to Malawi in Central Africa for three months. I was an election administration adviser to that country's Electoral Commission.

The Commission did not always take my advice as they sometimes felt they could do it better themselves and did so. My main task was writing a book of instructions for the polling station staffs for the whole country in the lead-up to the Malawi general and presidential elections. We also had to go into the bush doing hands-on training of election staff throughout the whole of Malawi which has a population of seven million. It is very poor and over-populated.

I was asked to become part of a United Nations team helping the Malawian Electoral Commission as a result of speaking at a conference in Budapest three years earlier. While there I became involved with an American organisation called the International Foundation of Electoral Systems (IFES). They cover elections all over the world, concentrating on countries which strive for democracy. In Budapest I spoke on our system of Proportional Representation and managed to confuse every-body who was there, I would say. However, my talk provoked interest in our system and, as a result, I was invited to speak at other confer-ences in the UK and at one in Orlando, Florida. But I had never previ-ously been requested by IFES to do any practical work until I was asked, just before Christmas, to go to Malawi for three months as they were having their first multi-party elections there.

Dr Hastings Banda, the Malawi President for Life, had ruled the country with a rod of iron for thirty years. The Catholic bishops in Malawi had initiated a movement towards multi-party elections through a pastoral letter issued in 1993, which forced Banda into a Referendum in June, 1993. By almost two to one the people voted for multi-party elections. It is not easy to vote there as they have to walk through the bush for eight or ten miles, sometimes a woman with a baby strapped on her back. There was a lot of intimidation at the time of the Referendum. Elections were held in May 1994 and Dr Banda's party was defeated. My term in Malawi was a truly unique experience as I like electoral work and I like to travel and this gave me the opportunity to do both. I have travelled extensively, mainly in the East, and I hope to travel a lot more while still mobile.

My father, Louis O'Connell, was a well known figure in Listowel. I am the eldest of the family, then my sister, Pat McManus, who is now in Australia; Michael is the senior partner in Gerald Baily & Co, Solicitors, Tralee; my youngest sister is Jacqueline who lives in Dublin. We were all educated in Listowel and none of us went out of Listowel for our education until Michael and I went to university. I attended the Presentation Convent right up to Leaving Cert.

My father was the biggest influence on my life. I was very fond of him and close to him. When he suggested that I do law it was unusual for a woman to do so. I had no particular feelings on the matter and I went along with it. In those days you did what you were told anyway. At that time in UCD we used to do the law course at the Four Courts and the university course at UCD at one and the same time which caused problems of bilocation at times when there was a clash of lectures. We all had bikes and we knew all the short cuts through the lanes between Earlsfort Terrace and the Four Courts.

I was a student in the first year of the new BCL, Bachelor of Civil Law degree. There had been no specific degree course for law students until this BCL degree was introduced. And I was there at the start of that. I managed to get the BCL and the following year I got my parchment as a qualified solicitor and I started working immediately in Listowel with my father who was a one-man show.

I feel now I should have got experience elsewhere, but he was waiting with bated breath for me to come back. He often said he did not know how I stuck it out with him, as he was a very strong-willed man with very definite notions on how he ran his office which did not always coincide with mine. He just refused to change and we often had battles about that. On a general level we got on well. He loved to hear himself talk and he used to love court work and he would do all the District Court stuff and had a great rapport with the late Cyril Maguire, the District Court Justice at that time.

As a result I didn't get much court experience. I did the conveyancing, probate and that kind of stuff. He used to depend on me a lot. It was he who suggested that I might go for the County Registrar's vacancy when it turned up and it really surprised me as he depended a lot on me. I did not think he would ever be keen on me leaving the office, but I think he felt it was an opportunity for me and as a result he encouraged me to apply for it. He got in various assistants after I left and then my son, Louis, qualified and he now runs the practice by himself.

In hindsight I should have done a year or so in some other practice after qualifying and got into advocacy. My father should have encouraged me to do so. I used to attend the High Court in Dublin, as he hated travel, but there was no advocacy involved there as barristers are the advocates in the High Court. I regret that I wasn't into advocacy, because I feel I would have been quite good at it. Another person who had quite an influence on me was the late Seán MacBride who was a very good friend of my father's and very good to me when a student.

My husband Billy is originally from Bettystown, County Meath. I met him at a dance at the old Central Ballroom in Ballybunion and fell in love to the strains of Maurice Mulcahy's band. Billy works for the Department of Agriculture. We have four children, all grown-up. I like living and working in Kerry and have never really wanted to live anywhere else.

JOHNNY WALSH

(FOOTBALLING GREAT)

I was born in a public house in Ballylongford, on 11 February, 1911. My father David Walsh was a Corkman who came to Kerry working with the creamery. My mother was Mary O'Brien who came from a mile outside Ballylongford. She was a farmer's daughter and my father came up here from Clonakilty. He married into the pub which my mother's people had and they settled down here in Ballylongford. There were five of us in the family and I was the second. My brother Mick is the eldest and David, the youngest, a priest, died over two years ago. The two girls became nuns. Mary, a Holy Rosary nun, spent over thirty years in Nigeria and is now in Raheny in Dublin. The other sister, Sr Theresa, taught in Great Yarmouth in England and is still active in the St Louis Convent community there.

Growing up here in Ballylongford, my earliest memory is of the Black and Tans and the problems they caused in the village. I remember them well and I can also recall the military passing through the village on their way to patrol along the Shannon Estuary. It would have been during the Great War and I suppose they were watching out. There was a Colonel Hickey billeted near Carrigafoyle. The Tans were in a barracks in the village. There would have been about twenty of them. I remember them coming into our public house throwing their rifles around the place. You couldn't refuse them drink. My father was under observation by them as he had three brothers involved in the republican movement in West Cork. Two Tans were shot here in Ballylongford.

I went to the national school here and we had Paddy O'Brien as principal and a local farmer, Tim Brassil, was the assistant teacher.

Later on a second assistant came, Eoin Moriarty. The Irish language came into the schools and became popular and they used go away to brush up in the Irish. I left the national school when I was about twelve for St Brendan's, Killarney. It was a tough place that time, and a lot of bullying went on with the young lads coming in. I started playing football there. I didn't know anybody in St Brendan's and I had nothing to do in my spare time but to go out and kick a ball every spare minute I had. I got into it there and I got fairly good at it. I was playing with lads who were much older than I was.

Football in the schools was not organised when I began there and it was while I was in my third year that a league for schools was started by Dr Eamonn O'Sullivan. He was a doctor in the mental hospital and he had been at St Brendan's and was a friend of Canon Breen who was president of the college. His brother Paddy taught in Listowel at the same time. I was three years on the senior side in Killarney. There were boys three years older than me on the team. I played corner forward and I played three years legally under-age for St Brendan's and then I went on to Rockwell College and played three more years there. My older brother was in Rockwell and I didn't like Killarney.

I suppose they weren't too happy with my progress either at home and that was a factor in me being sent to Rockwell. There was no gaelic football in Rockwell and my father felt I would have to apply myself to the books a bit more if I didn't have football to turn to. But I had to play some game and I got into the rugby there straightaway. I got there in September and got into the college side after Christmas. I played in the forwards as I was a useful man to fight for the ball and get possession. I remember we had a match with Roscrea in Roscrea and we went on to Blackrock and played them the following day. We won the Munster Senior Colleges Cup in that first year. We won it three years, but I missed out the middle year because I fractured my elbow before the final. I had to get it wired up in the Mater Hospital.

After Rockwell I went to Waterford to train to be a national teacher. We won the Waterford County Championship in gaelic football and I played my first Senior Inter-County Football with Waterford in 1931/32. That was in the National League and we won a few games. I then made the senior Kerry team later in 1932 and we won the All-Ireland that year. That All-Ireland Final was the first championship match I played for the Kerry team and I played midfield. We beat Mayo in the Final.

That was the last of a great Kerry team and that was their four-in-a-row. You had Jack Walsh, Con Brosnan, Robbie Stack, the Landers, Miko Doyle, Paul Russell, Jackie Lyne. I was the youngest on the team at twenty-one. I was in a dream. We went by train from Listowel with Jack Walsh, Con Brosnan and Robbie Stack. We went up on the Saturday and we stayed at Barry's Hotel. I won my next All-Ireland in 1937 and in the 1938 we lost a controversial Final to Galway, and I was on the winning sides on 1939, 1940 and 1941.

I was teaching in Ballylongford from 1934 as I had been a while sub-teaching in Dublin and I also studied at UCD at night. I didn't finish the degree course, because I got the teaching job in Ballylongford.

I remember coming home in 1933 for the Easter holidays, and some people came to our bar with whitewash and I asked why they picked on us? They had marched out in military formation and they got the order to charge and I levelled two of them. Another strong Fine Gael man was with me and he hit a few of them with an iron bar and they scattered.

We had a trip to New York in 1933 and a New York player came on to mark me in the last match. This was Kerry against New York. He said to me, 'You are an effing Blue Shirt. I will send you back in a coffin'. I was handy at the boxing at the time. I told him he had an hour to do it and let the best man jump the fence. The first ball that came in he drew a clout at me, but I side-stepped him and caught him. I staggered him and he began to get very quiet. He was going for me on the quiet. I beat him for another ball and I pretended that I didn't see him coming and as he approached I picked the ball and met him and he was carried off. That sorted him out. A sub came in and said he didn't like dirty play and I told him I didn't like it either. I was only twenty-one. When I came home I lost my place on the team over politics. I was dropped in my prime, and the message I got was that I was finished.

I joined Garryowen Rugby Club in Limerick after being dropped by

Kerry. Garryowen put me on straightaway in 1933. The Garryowen chairman was Dermot O'Donovan, the solicitor. I knew him from Rockwell. A few matches brought me back into it and we played at the Markets Field. I told some of the Kerry players at the time I would never again play gaelic football. None of the players broke with me. When I started playing rugby I was banned by the GAA. I used to get a bus every Saturday morning for the matches and when we came to the Munster Senior Cup they hired a car to bring me down to Limerick to train four evenings a week.

Dave Ringrose and Dan Langan were on the team. I got on the Junior Munster side the first year and the Senior Munster side the second season. That was in 1934 and 1935. I started to play wing-forward and then they played me in the backs. I played in all of the Inter-Provincial series one year. I finished playing rugby in March 1936. I went to two Munster Senior Cup Finals with Garryowen and some maintained that I would have got on the Irish side if I stayed at that game. However, I felt that I wasn't big enough for the forwards and that I didn't have enough pace for the backs.

Miko Doyle approached me to go back playing football for Kerry. I had to do six months' suspension after finishing up playing rugby in March 1936. I came back playing with Kerry and I had one of my early games in Listowel in a National League game. I got a great welcome and *The Kerryman* was full of it.

I was lonely leaving the rugby because I made some great friends down in Limerick. Mick Mackey, the great Limerick hurler, and myself became great friends. He used to be a vigilante. The GAA had vigilantes at the matches watching out for members who might be there as spectators or playing. That entitled Mackey to go and we would meet and have a drink after the games. We became lifelong friends and we would meet in Limerick and regularly at Railway Cup matches when hurlers and footballers would travel together along with Paddy Leahy, the Tipperary hurler. The three of us would be staying at Barry's Hotel.

In 1936 the Kerry team was rebuilding. Paddy Kennedy and myself were put in midfield and you had Seán Brosnan, Joe Keohane, Tadhg Healy. Politics did not come into the team. There used to be a bit of a

needle over it in club matches. I said when I was looking for reinstate-
ment if I did not get back straightaway I wouldn't pursue my application. There was great disunity in the county at the time and there was
great disorganisation. Con Brosnan was fighting my cause and I was
allowed play in North Kerry during the six months suspension period.

The county team had what we called then 'combined training'. That
took place in Tralee and then it switched to Killarney. We used to stay
over when we were training. In 1937 we trained in Tralee and from
1942 on they switched to Killarney where Dr Eamonn was training. If
you were working they would put in a man in your place. I was teaching and would be on holidays, so I did not have to avail of this.

One match sticks out in my mind. It was the Semi-Final of 1937.
Laois had a good team at the time. One of my great friends who comes
to Listowel Races every year, Bill Delaney, was one of four brothers
playing for Laois. They were fine footballers and they all played
around the middle of the field. The first match was down in Cork. It
was the Semi-Final.

I was very fond of shooting and the shooting season opened on the
Friday before the match. I was out on Cnoc an Óir all day near
Ballybunion, from dawn to dark travelling after grouse. We didn't get a
shot until about eight o'clock in the evening. Between that and dark we
shot about twelve grouse. I was flattened after it. My father nearly
closed the door on me when I came home and he said I wouldn't be
able to move on Sunday for the Semi-Final. So I went back to the sea-
weed baths in Maggie Daly's in Ballybunion to try and sort myself out
on the Saturday. I was sorted out for the match, but the last quarter of
an hour caught me and my legs were bending under me. I got a few
hefty knocks and the game was a draw. I could do nothing for the last
quarter of an hour.

The replay was fixed for Waterford, two weeks later, and for that
game I trained like I never trained before. I used love saving hay and I
always felt it was great training. It would be like weight training nowadays. Out with a pike and walking around the meadow. I did a lot of
rowing at Saleen Point. I was always keen on that. I trained like a devil
saving hay. It would be a tough day's work and I would finish up the

day with a swim at Saleen Pier and wash all the seeds out of my hair. I got my own back in the replay down in Waterford and we barely won. Laois were very strong. The Delaneys were like a strong diamond in the midfield, centre back and centre forward positions.

The last Kerry four-in-a-row team you could see it coming. I used to be training the under twenty-ones and we won three under twenty-one championships and so there was great material. It was always the big thing in Kerry to be an Inter-County man. Soccer now has taken over. Some young lads now wouldn't kick a gaelic football at all.

I kept up my interest in rugby. I used to attend matches during the Ban years on the sly. I have been to Garryowen and saw some of the All-Ireland League games.

Young lads don't have pride in gaelic football anymore. The pride is gone. That is modern youth. They are out for a good time and won't make the sacrifice. On a night before a match we wouldn't take a drink, but today they could be out all night. I didn't drink alcohol until I was thirty years of age. And that came about from somebody daring me. I hadn't any mind for it. We were after winning a County Championship and one of the lads blackguarding said, 'Drink a pint'. I said, 'Try me out,' and I finished it for a bet. I started Shannon Rangers and we were the first to bring a County Championship here to North Kerry in 1932. The Shannon Rangers were drawn from Ballylongford, Tarbert and Ballydonoghue. Actually, Ballydonoghue didn't come in the first year. Con Brosnan was organising North Kerry, as I wasn't very popular for breaking away.

I am worried about the state of football in the county. There isn't the same loyalty to the clubs. Some lads will play with outside teams and won't play with their own local club. They won't train enough. Mick O'Connell stands out in my mind. He was the best exhibitionist I have ever seen. Jack O'Shea also stands out. In my own days Paddy Kennedy was very good. So were Seán Brosnan and Con Brosnan in the old team.

I always look back to the height Seán Walsh could go for a ball. He could go higher than anybody I know. I remember one night a crowd of

Dubs came into the bar on the night of the Listowel Races. One said that the super sub (as Seán Walsh became known) couldn't field a ball with Mullins. I produced that great photograph of Walsh soaring over Brian Mullins. It captured Walsh way over Mullins. He could go up straight. O'Connell could go high, but Walsh was the best to go up from a standing position.

One of the most extraordinary scores I saw was made by Charlie O'Sullivan in an All-Ireland Final. He was knocked on the ground and from the flat of his back he kicked the ball over for a point.

Once I got a goal which I couldn't remember getting. It was against Meath in an All-Ireland Final. I used suffer a lot from loss of memory, probably from an old boxing injury. I often played and could not remember parts of the game.

OGIE MORAN

(MANAGER KERRY TEAM)

MY earliest memories are being on the beach in Ballybunion having six or seven swims a day during fine summer days. The weather of childhood always seems fine. Going to the Black Rocks in the morning and then playing soccer on the beach in the afternoon. The beach was central to my childhood in Ballybunion. I was the youngest of eight children. My father was from Sussa, near Ballinskelligs. My mother was Bridie Tangney from Castleisland. She was from a big family, there were fourteen of them in all. They met in Castleisland when my mother was working in Hannon's Drapery Shop. My father was Denis and I was Denis Óg, hence Ogie. I was never called anything else. I was only nine when he died on July 23rd, 1965, in Ballybunion. My dad was always in the drapery business and we lived in Killorglin for a time. He had served his time in Duggan's Munster Warehouse in Kilkenny. He was in Charleville first.

I was in Croke Park in 1960 for the first time and in 1962 I was fortunate to be the mascot for the Kerry team. I walked in the parade with Seán Óg Sheehy who captained Kerry that day. I remember that parade in the 1962 Final. I went back to the stand to my father to watch the game after the parade. Kerry beat Roscommon; Gary MacMahon, the Newcastle West solicitor and son of Bryan MacMahon, got a goal that day. I became mascot through the long friendship between the Morans and the Sheehys. My father and John Joe Sheehy, father of Sean Óg, were lifelong friends. My father was very much involved with Kerry teams. He travelled every Sunday to games all over the country and there was a great tradition of my father supplying the playing kit for the team.

He and Fr Paddy Mahon of Galway were great friends and they

used have a bet on an annual tournament game between Kerry and Galway where the winner would get a suit length and the loser a shirt and tie. I went to the games with my cousin Mick who lived with us. My dad was very traditionalist in his views and was very much in the anti-soccer mould. He would have been old style Republican. Mick, my first cousin, was a great influence in my life.

Mick was from Sussa as well and he came to work in my father's shop in Caherciveen one summer for the holidays. He was aged about twelve then. He decided to stay with us and became one of the family. I never knew the house without Mick. My father and Mick were very similar. They went to the matches every Sunday. He would have gone to all the games when I was growing up and would have seen me progress at under age.

My entry into competitive football was in under-fourteens with Bally-bunion when I would have played with Donal Liston, the Griffins, Joe Casey, Tom Griffin, Joe Diggin, Owen Liston, Pádraig Liston, Tim Tiger Griffin and Tom Allen. We were trained by Niall Horgan and John Francis Ahern, Willie Casey, Mikey Diggin and Dan Ahern would have been the main men in the club then, bringing us to all our games in the car.

School teams can run in cycles and at that time in Gormanstown College, where I received my secondary education, we had a good team in the Leinster Colleges. There were lots of good players such as Paul McGettigan, and Mickey Martin. We won the under-fourteen Leinster Colleges and then the Junior and Senior Leinster Colleges. We then went on to eventually win the All-Ireland Senior Colleges in 1973. I played midfield with Paul McGettigan and Mickey Martin was captain. Fr James Grourke and Joe Lennon looked after the team. Fr Grourke was from Achill and he was with us from under fourteen all the way up. The two of them worked together with Fr Grourke doing most of the spade work.

My first time playing for Kerry was a minor game in Emly against Tipperary. That was in 1972. I was sixteen at the time. We were beaten by Cork in the Munster Final. Mikey Sheehy, Pat Spillane and Paudie O'Shea were on the team. We lost three minor finals in a row. No minor medal. Cork beat us in three Munster Finals. Jimmy Barry Murphy was on the Cork minors then. In November 1972 I won a Senior County Championship medal with Shannon Rangers. I was wing back and lucky to have people like Jackie Walsh, Paudie and Eamon O'Donoghue and Brian McCarthy to mind me. Shannon Rangers was an amalgamation of Ballylongford, Beale, Ballydonoghue and Ballyduff. There was a very good club side in Ballylongford at the time. It was one of the best in the county. There would have been only four or five players on the team from outside Ballylongford.

Mick O'Connell would have been my idol. I remember one occasion when I was about six years of age, after the games in Killarney when I was with my cousin Mick, meeting Mick O'Connell in the Park Place Hotel, and Mick produced a tape and measured Mick O'Connell for his suit. It was a great thrill to be there alongside Mick O'Connell. They were great friends and when they met it was football talk. It was one of those occasions that I saw Mick O'Connell close up. It was like seeing the Pope. I was able to name the Kerry team backwards at that time.

My first senior game with Kerry was in 1974 against Offaly in Tullamore. It was a very new look Kerry team. Mick O'Dwyer came in then with new selectors and new players were brought in. On that new look team was Pat Spillane and Tim Kennelly. It was basically the 1970 minor side which played against Galway – Jim Deenihan, Ger O'Keeffe and John O'Keeffe. At midfield you would have Paudie Lynch. Johnny Bunyon played full-forward that day in Tullamore. I was wing-forward and Brendan Lynch was inside me. Mickey Sullivan was on the forty. John Egan was also playing. But it would not have been their first game with Kerry. I remember going up to Tullamore with my cousin Mick. My brother James was also there. I played OK and I was kept for the next day. I marked a fellow called Grogan. It was very tough and physical. Offaly had a lot of tough guys – they were very physical. Two weeks later we played Dublin in Killarney. Dick Spring had his first game for Kerry that day in Killarney and it was my second. Dublin were All-Ireland champions. Brian Mullins, Alan Larkin – all those players were there.

Then we faced into my first championship. We were up against Tipperary in Clonmel in the first round and that was a close game for a long time. John Egan came out to the forty and turned the game. I was in midfield with Pat McCarthy.

There were two high points in my career with Kerry. The 1975 Final, beating Dublin. That was the year Mickey Sullivan was stretchered off. We were all very young, all in our early twenties and there was no-one married on the team. I was nineteen. We were the outsiders and Dublin hot favourites. Reminiscent of the 1955 Final. And the other highlight was of course captaining the team in 1978. The captain's role is not a very onerous one but it's a great honour.

The day I was captain in 1978 we were well ahead and with a few minutes to go I remember thinking of my speech and in the final minutes of the game I was thinking out what I might say. We were fifteen points up and I said to myself, 'We're going to win this'. Con Murphy presented the cup to me. It was great to put your hands on that cup for yourself, your family and, of course, your county.

In 1975 we won it against the odds out of the blue and in 1976 we lost it. We might have got carried away with ourselves after '75. Mick O'Dwyer said that if we had not won in 1975 we might have won six or seven finals in a row. In 1976 we didn't make the same sacrifices and we might not have trained as hard as in 1975. In 1977 we lost in a classic game in the Semi-Final.

Dublin were going for a three-in-a-row in 1978. It was a tremendous occasion that Final. It's always great playing Dublin, especially in an All-Ireland Final. The whole country outside of Dublin were behind us. There was tremendous buzz about the games, the training, the media, the whole atmosphere leading up to the game and the game itself. The whole country was caught up in those games.

Mick O'Dwyer was a huge influence on my career. He took over Kerry when I joined the Kerry panel – the same day. I was there from day one. His greatest attribute is his ability to handle people. It's a great achievement to win an All-Ireland, but to keep winning them is an even bigger trick. He was able to keep fellows on their toes even when they had six and seven All-Ireland medals, looking for an eighth one or a sixth one. He was able to steer them away from getting carried away with themselves. He was able to handle them individually and keep getting the best out of them.

The players had a great passion for the game. There was a great bond between the players and that still exists. There is a great comraderie and respect which is still very strong. We still have a great affinity for each other. Most of the lads trained all year round and as a group we trained especially hard from March to September. We were away on trips together in Australia, Hawaii, England and the United States. The squad got on well and within that bigger group you would have your own mates, a closer circle that you would get to know better.

I togged out for my last time for Kerry when I was sub in the 1988 Munster Final down in Cork – I was thirty-two.

After graduating from UCD I taught for two years before joining Shannon Development in 1980. They were long days with a lot of travelling to and from Shannon for training. The social loss for training was never an issue for me. I was always busy with football. I don't ever remember having thought what I was missing because of the demands of football. Ballybunion was a lively spot during the summer and being part of a big family there was always plenty of night life, but you just didn't have late nights. You were conscious of the fact that you had to keep your place on the team. If you were out 'til three or four in the morning, you wouldn't survive. It was a very competitive scene that time. There was also the other issue of letting down the squad. That Kerry team had a certain esteem and people expected a certain standard from it. After Munster Finals we used to have four or five days back in Dingle when you might never see the bed. It was always a ritual and if you won the All-Ireland, celebrations would last till Christmas.

The thing I liked best about the whole scene was that journey from the hotel to Croke Park on All-Ireland Final day. There was a great feeling and it was tremendous to look out of the bus and see someone you knew from Ballybunion or Ballylongford. It was great to see those familiar faces at that hour in Jones Road. That's the part of the day I enjoyed most, getting close to Croke Park.

I have been asked from time to time to pick out one player of that team. They were all great players. And if you were to ask me to single out one, then I would have to choose Pat Spillane as being outstanding.

Owen Liston was the most valuable player. When he was going well the whole full-forward line benefited. He brought the best out of those around him. He is the player I would have hated to lose most before a game. Pat Spillane was a tremendous footballer. He had a tremendous hunger and a great desire to be the best. Pat Spillane always played a great game.

The 1982 Final, the five-in-a-row, which we lost to Offaly; Jimmy Deenihan was a tremendous loss that day. He might not have been as celebrated a player as people like Pat Spillane or Jack O'Shea or Mikey Sheehy. He broke his leg that summer in training. It was a great first half in that game with great scores from both sides. We missed a penalty. We came back and went a few points up, the referee gave some soft frees. We were playing out time, four points up with three minutes to go. Then we were only two points ahead and then the goal came. It was shattering.

Football is such a serious aspect of Kerry life – like work; the satisfaction is in the achievement. You never thought of enjoying football. There was a job to be done, an All-Ireland to win. If you won, it was fantastic. The game was never there to be enjoyed. If you won the All-Ireland you enjoyed it. If you didn't win the All-Ireland, you didn't enjoy it. You enjoyed success; you didn't enjoy defeat. It's much the same now. It was a relief not to lose. You were expected to win and it was great then to have won. The relief and satisfaction not to have lost!

I now work with Shannon Development in North Kerry; most of my work is in the tourism side. It's a good time with Structural Fund money from the EU. We are trying to maximise the potential of North Kerry for the good of Kerry. I was always keen to come back and work in Kerry. I never saw myself living anywhere else. I wouldn't live anywhere else. I think Kerry people are prouder of their county than most other folk. I think it has to be connected with the football and the beauty of the county and the Irish language. Kerry is very proud of its education. There has always been a great meas on education in Kerry. We rejoice in the success of other people and are proud of the success of people like Dick Spring, Denis Brosnan, Con Houlihan, Brendan Kennelly, Moss Keane and so many others.

MARGARET GEANEY

(BUSINESS WOMAN)

CRAG Cave was discovered near Castleisland in 1983 and it opened as a tourist amenity in 1989. I had been abroad and had seen that caves had been very successful in attracting tourists in Britain, Spain and France. I went to Yugoslavia first on holiday and it was almost by accident that I found that nearly everybody was visiting the local caves as they had an appeal to people of all ages.

Castleisland is at the gateway to Kerry and for decades tourists had been passing through on their way to Killarney, Dingle and the Ring of Kerry and we felt we had the product – Crag Cave – to hold tourists in Castleisland. So tourists are now coming to Castleisland and not just passing through. Since we opened in 1989 we have had about a half a million visitors.

When we were deciding what we would do, there were many sleepless nights as we knew it would involve a huge investment. But we got tremendous encouragement. For instance, the people from the Marble Arch Cave in Fermanagh were very encouraging. They came and visited Crag Cave and they felt it was right for development for tourism. They put us in touch with geologists and engineers and consultants.

We contacted Bórd Fáilte in 1986 and Michael Gowran came and he told us that we had a Rolls Royce product and that we should develop it accordingly. That was before Structural Funding. Shannon Development gave us every encouragement. Brendan Russell and Tom O'Donnell and John Leonard were very helpful. They organised financial help. North Kerry was switched from Bórd Fáilte to Shannon Development as far as tourism promotion was concerned.

Crag Cave has cost us about a million pounds to develop. Most of it was our own capital. We had to sell off some of our assets and we formed a Business Expansion Scheme and mortgaged our farm. It was a great risk, but we decided to spare nothing.

Our accountant, Andrew Kelliher, organised us with a BES scheme and that took a lot of financial worries off our shoulders. Before we got any grant aid we had to raise our own money. You may not believe it, but we had a very friendly bank manager, Pat O'Sullivan, in the AIB. The whiz-kids from AIB in Cork came down and they saw the potential.

We were ready to commence work in 1987 and the machinery moved in early in January. Brian Judd, an Englishman, a very enthusiastic speleologist with experience in cave development, promised to develop the cave for us. For instance, they had to decide where to make the entrance as the cave is sixty feet under the ground. There was a quarry going down about thirty feet and they decided to build a shaft in there.

For the supervision of the building of the shaft we had Dan Walsh from Castleisland. He had been a contractor in England digging tunnels and is now retired in Castleisland. He was the ideal man to take on this work. They had to start building down rather than building up. That was a major job. There were about fifteen men working on that. It was built by direct labour with Dan and Brian Judd. It was a venture into the unknown.

I remember the first day, they brought in the big machines. Brian remarked, 'This is a big adventure'. And it surely was. And it has been a most enjoyable adventure ever since.

Brian loved every inch of the cave and these formations had been developing for millions of years. This 'natural wonderland', he called it. He was meticulous and would allow only three people to work in the cave at any one time, because he didn't want to disturb the formations. He laid a narrow gauge railway inside the cave. He got glass cases made to protect the formations. We got Michael Scott, the theatrical designer with the Tivoli Theatre in Dublin, and he did the lighting for us. He enjoyed this challenge and the delight of presenting this gift of nature to its best effect.

People from all over the world are absolutely fascinated at what we have achieved under a field in Castleisland. One man remarked to me recently that we were all so insignificant when you think of the time that it has taken for these formations to come about.

We opened on the 20th of May, 1989. The first year we had about fifty-five thousand visitors and the numbers are increasing every year. It is a family business and I am a director with my husband, Donal, who is a retired GP.

He was born on a farm in Firies. A man of the land, he always had an ambition to buy a farm. He bought the land to farm it and he put it in my name. I felt very privileged to have been chosen to be the guardian of the cave and we all do as a family. We are all very conscious of the privilege of having this wonder of nature under our feet. The cave was discovered after Professor John Gunn went looking for the source of the local river Maine and went into old muddy caves in front of the farmhouse. These old caves had always been a source of adventure for children, and animals sheltered in them.

In these old caves he came to a well or a sump and got the idea that there was something beyond that. He got cave-divers to come from England. They dived into the well and swam twenty feet through flooded passages and came up in another sump in these caverns that had never any form of life. No animals or human had ever entered them. Martin Farr, a Welshman, was the first man to enter the cave. John Cooper came after him. There were so many passages that they were going about with their flashlights for about two hours before they met each other. They were thrilled. They mapped the different passages and named them from the book *Lord of the Rings* and the marvellous underworld.

We really didn't know what was there until they came up with some beautiful photographs that showed the treasure we had under our feet. We realised the potential for tourist development as I had been to Yugoslavia and to Aillwee Cave in County Clare.

I was one of the first to go down into the cave. This was before the shaft was built. I managed to get in with the help of Brian Judd and saw it for myself. My husband and I travelled extensively then to see what they had done with caves in other countries. We have developed it to the extent that people can go through it in about half an hour.

People are now beginning to think tourism in Castleisland, and this is great. It won a prize in the National Tidy Towns Competition last year and since the cave was developed, three other tourist products have been developed in the area. And in the town local souvenir shops have opened, restaurants are staying open for dinner and a forty bed-room hotel is being built in the Main Street. I am a member of the Castleisland Sliabh Luachra Leader Group and plans are under way in Scartaglin for a centre of traditional Irish music, song, dance and folk-lore. This will create jobs and economic growth.

I find the Regional Technical College in Tralee a great help. A lot of the staff we are employing in the cave have been trained there. We have six guides and at peak season employ about eighteen people. Our plan is to stay open all year and we are marketing with the new groups in Killarney, Tralee and Kerry Airport. They are giving a very good deal. This will make a big difference with all the new all-weather tourist attractions in Kerry.

When the cave was discovered, Pádraig Kennelly, who is editor of *Kerry's Eye*, couldn't believe one family could take on this project. He said in an article that with the cave, Kerry has everything now. We are only fifteen miles from Killarney, the capital of tourism in Ireland. Guest houses and hotels appreciate the cave as it can add an extra bed-night for them.

The cave has a constant ten degrees centigrade temperature, winter and summer. We have lots of ideas about further developments. Gerry Daly of the RTE gardening programme has done a park plan for us. The farm itself is in a beautiful setting and the visitors love it. We have a dining-room which serves lunches and we may go in for evening entertainment as well in time. The possibilities are endless. What is needed in Kerry is well presented, sophisticated, Irish music shows.

I enjoy a challenge and I get a great kick out of going out there and marketing the cave. For the past three years I have attended the world travel market. For the first few years we had about seventy per cent Irish visitors, but last year it was about fifty per cent Irish and fifty per cent foreign. Crag Cave has been a great asset to Kerry. It is an all-weather tourist attraction. There are three areas in Kerry which merit a two star rating in the Michelin Guide and Map of Ireland – Killarney, the Ring of Kerry and Crag Cave. The late Eamon Keane, John B's brother, wanted RTE to film part of the programme of his life in Crag Cave. He wrote in the visitor's book, 'Crag Cave is a prelude to eternity's wonders'.

The wet day is definitely better than the fine day. And some people who don't like it too hot come to the cave when it gets very warm. We try to get university students with a knowledge of geology as guides.

I have always been conscious of my freedom. My father gave us this appreciation of being free and my husband who adored my father realised this. I have had a freedom that most women of my age didn't have. I have travelled a lot and this influenced me. It broadens your horizons. My husband has great courage and is an adventurer, as I am.

We work as a team and we encourage our family and the young people who work with us at the cave to do the same. I always tell my children that the sky is the limit and I have told my daughters to go out and get professions, because I think it is very important for women to stand on their own two feet. Education is very important. That is where freedom is to be found, along with travel. Two of my children have done world tours.

Women have always been the underdogs and the scales can be balanced through education. I don't like the phrase 'Women's Lib', but I believe in equality.

The support and encouragement from all the family was crucial in a project of this scale. It was a Geaney project, more than anything else. I have met people who have started new projects around the county and they tell me that they got the encouragement from what I have done. It has encouraged women around the county to think of setting up their own enterprises.

There isn't a place in the world to touch Kerry with the beauty and the quality of life. I feel very proud of the young people who work in the cave. They are proud of the cave and they are proud of their country. They can speak several languages and are so confident.

I feel we should be getting a lot more tourists into Ireland. We have to manage our marketing budget better. I like what is happening in Kerry now. I think we have to package holidays better and Kerry is ideally suited to this packaging. We must try and open for twelve months of the year. The airport at Farranfore is very important. That will be a winner and we are only seven miles from it. Tourism has shown its capacity to create jobs.

Our nearest market is in England. On a television programme recently they said seventeen million visit Blackpool every year. We must go over there and see what they are doing and what makes them successful and imitate them. I think we should be using the marketing money from the Structural Funds very carefully. This is our opportunity. The roads are in very bad condition. The coach operators are concerned about the damage the roads are causing their vehicles after they travel through the country.

Flying into Ireland is very expensive as is ferry travel, especially at high season. Car hire is also very expensive. There is an external and internal transport problem. The product is right. People are just simply amazed when they get here at the variety of things that they can do. Even getting baby-sitters in hotels and guest houses. Abroad this is impossible. But here in Ireland the industry responds to the people's needs. Self-catering is also getting very important. But in Kerry we have the trump card. We are only an hour from London, through Farranfore. English people are coming back in big numbers to Ireland and they just love it. The weather does not bother them.

My father, Jack Shanahan, was a chemist in Castleisland. My mother was Lil Reidy. My father was shot by the British in 1921 and he almost died. He was so badly injured that, in effect, it spared him from being executed and he was exchanged for a captured British officer. He thought that he was going to die, and ever after he had a great love and appreciation of life and that came through to us. He was a wonderful father. I never heard him say a bad word about any person. His brother Richard was killed by the British in 1921.

I spent many happy hours in my grandmother's public house. I went to school in Castleisland and to the Loretto in Dublin. After secondary school I decided I had enough of study and did a commercial course and I went as a receptionist to the Southern Lake Hotel in Waterville. It was owned by the Meldons and it's now Club Med. While working there as a receptionist, Donal Geaney was doing locum for the local doctor, Dr O'Byrne. He called into the hotel one day to see a patient and I asked him if he was Con Geaney's brother. Con Geaney was the famous Kerry footballer who was married to my step-aunt. Anyway we started courting and we were married in a year.

He is twelve years older than me and he had gone to Africa after qualifying. We settled in Castleisland. He wanted me to move to Tarbert, because he could get a dispensary there. But I wouldn't leave Castleisland as I love it here. I think it is a great place to live. We settled in private practice in Castleisland and he got the dispensary in Brosna.

We lived over the Medical Hall, my father's chemist shop, for about five years after we got married. We have seven children. Bernadette is a psychiatrist in London. She is married to Mike Finnerty from Athenry. Then there are twin girls – Marie is married to an Italian vet Gitano D'Urso and living in Donegal, and Margaret is married to a Scotsman, Vincent Durkin, and they are now helping us to run the cave. John did medicine and another son, David, farms and works at the cave. Then there is Donal who is also a farmer. Finally, we have Lisa who was born with brain damage and when we realised she was handicapped we were very sad, but she also has brought great joy into our lives. Through her we have met the most wonderful people. People who work with the handicapped are the salt of the earth. God bless them.

Business was bred into me. All before me were shopkeepers and I am a shopkeeper. I was able to take the whole Crag development in my stride and I suppose it came naturally to me. I had great support from my husband who has retired and from our son David. I did a market-ing course in the Regional Technical College in Tralee.

I suppose I was always involved in community projects in Castleisland. We have a Community Centre. And I would say the idea for that was formed at our fireside with Fr Michael Leahy, who is now a canon and parish priest in Listowel. It cost eighty-five thousand pounds about thirty years ago. It was a great development. We helped raise a lot of money to pay off the bills with Tops of the Town competitions in Castleisland that went on for about ten years. That was great fun. Every street in Castleisland had their own show.

We also got involved in settling the Travellers. Castleisland was to the fore in Kerry in the settlement of Travellers. I am a director of the Parents and Friends of the Mentally Handicapped. In days past there was very little support for parents. I found it very lonely. Now there are pre-school clinics and the Kerry Parents and Friends of the Mentally Handicapped have funded a workshop for the moderately and severely handicapped.

I am a very enthusiastic person and I enjoy life. I love all kinds of music. When we were growing up my mother played the piano and there was an old singsong very often. We had great fun. I have as my philosophy of life a motto my mother had hanging on the wall when we were children, 'I shall pass through this world but once. Any good deed I can do, let me do it now. For I shall not pass this way again'.

HUGH O'FLAHERTY

(SUPREME COURT JUDGE)

I was appointed to the Supreme Court in March 1990 straight from the Bar and I did not have the advantage of spending some time in the High Court. In the ordinary way appointments are made from the High Court to the Supreme Court which is something I would favour. It happened in my case that I was asked to go straight to the Supreme Court.

We are five in number, the Chief Justice and four associate judges. And then we have the President of the High Court, who ranks next to the Chief Justice in seniority, and is also ex-officio a judge of the Supreme Court. But most of his time is spent running the High Court where there are a total of seventeen judges. There is a right of appeal of nearly every kind of case from the High Court to the Supreme Court. As well as that we have to provide a judge to preside in the Court of Criminal Appeal which hears appeals from the Circuit Court and the Central Criminal Court which is the criminal division of the High Court.

When I was first starting off at the bar, the judges would not have read the transcripts of the evidence in advance at all. Therefore, a great deal of time was spent going through the transcripts of the actual hearing. Of course, that was a more leisurely age! Nowadays we spend a great deal of time in advance reading long transcripts of trials that may have taken twenty or forty days and there is even an appeal where the case lasted a year in the High Court.

We have only one kind of original jurisdiction and that is only where the President refers a Bill to us to test its constitutionality. The last occasion that this happened was in relation to the Matrimonial Homes (Protection) Bill which we declared to be repugnant to the Constitution.

However, once such a Bill is referred to us and is pronounced constitutional it can never be challenged again. That is regarded as a drawback because circumstances may become apparent later that were not apparent when the Bill was first referred. Therefore, in my view, the reference procedure should be used sparingly and where there is a set topic for resolution. Suitable Bills that were referred in the past included one that asked the question whether non citizens were entitled to vote at Dáil elections (answer : no) and another where the question was whether legitimate children could be adopted (answer: yes).

The one thing a judge needs is as much experience as he can get. You learn as an advocate. But I think you also learn a lot as a trial judge, hearing witnesses and summing up cases. Mind you, I am eligible to sit as a High Court Judge and have done a stint or two there. But our work load in the Supreme Court does not allow for much of that and while I would like to do more trial work, I do not get the chance. I would like to have the opportunity of meeting human beings in the courts, witnesses and litigants, more often, instead of having to deal with the dry pages of transcripts of evidence.

You ask how much in touch judges are with everyday matters? I suppose if you are married with children, as I am, you are immediately in touch with a great deal that is going on in all walks of life. So I don't think judges are removed from the realities of life. We read newspapers and watch television and we go to sporting events and we have certain favourites in the sporting field; in my case they tend to play in green and gold. But you are removed from a number of very simple things such as if you felt strongly about a political development or an environmental issue you would not be able to add your voice to what is being said or to demonstrate. You are really precluded from doing that because you cannot take sides. That would be wrong. In a way that is a curtailment of one's freedom of action. One might like to speak up or write to the newspapers or take some stance, but you should not. If, as it says in the Constitution, a judge must be independent in the exercise of his judicial function, there is the necessary corollary to that, that he should stay outside the political arena and areas of controversy. He is given great independence under the Constitution; his position is per-

manent during good behaviour and he cannot be removed save by resolution of each House of the Oireachtas.

The *quid pro quo* is that he has to stand back and not get involved. And just as I think the politicians and the Government are generally very scrupulous in never invading the judicial domain – not doing it consciously anyway – an Act may be passed which as it happens transgresses the Constitution – so a judge must respect the sphere of influence of the legislature and the government and exercise judicial restraint, as we call it. This is part of the doctrine of the Separation of Powers which is enshrined in the Constitution.

On the question of dress in court, the wig and gowns which you ask about, I think sitting in the Supreme Court, if everybody, including the judges, was in their ordinary suits, providing they were respectably attired, I don't think it would affect our proceedings in the least. I don't see wigs and gowns as having any great relevance as far as the Supreme Court is concerned, because we deal only with legal arguments and we do not hear witnesses.

At courts of trial the argument for a special garb, and I put it forward for what it is worth – I do not say I subscribe to it – having people garbed in a gown at least introduces a certain anonymity to the individual barrister, be it a man or a woman, young or old. Thus age and appearance all get subsumed. And that is a good thing, because the advocate has to present a case neutrally. As an advocate it does not matter whether he or she believes in the guilt or innocence of a person. None of that is relevant. The job of the advocate is to do the best job that he can for the client. Whether the wig is necessary I do not know. I think not, but that is a personal view. I would do away with the wig but I would not feel sufficiently strong about the matter to campaign one way or the other. If people feel strongly about it, I would abide by the democratic wish of the profession. But I think most professions have a certain amount of ceremony. Take academic circles or the church, even in the operating theatre there is a certain garb appropriate for it and I notice that the Russian and German constitutional courts, for example, are very richly gowned and, in the German case, with a very interesting head gear. I do not think it is a big deal and I do not think people are intimidated or put off. That is certainly not the intention and if I thought for a moment this garb had that effect, I would be four square in abolishing it.

Mind you I was reading something John Mortimer, the creator of Rumpole, said the other day and that was that he felt the criminals were in favour of being sentenced by a man in wig and gown; it would be one thing to get twelve years from such a person, but they would feel very upset if it was handed down by someone wearing a shirt and jeans.

The history of this is interesting. The first Chief Justice, Hugh Kennedy in 1922, was opposed to the wig and he used to come out on the bench and solemnly take the wig off. He was anxious that it should be abolished. The other judges wished to retain it, not through having any great love for it, but there was a move at the time to design a new set of garb for the judges. This task was entrusted to the poet WB Yeats, not the artist Jack Yeats, who, it might seem, would have been more appropriate. I think it was the fear of the possibility of the introduction of multi-coloured garb that drove the judges to believe that the devil they knew was better than the devil they did not know. That may be part of legal folklore, however. A judge has to obey the rules of court like everybody else and the wig and gown is the garb prescribed by the present rules. We can relax them, of course. For example, in hot weather we can doff the wig.

My freedom, I suppose, has been curbed since my appointment to the Supreme Court. I think the thing I miss out of my previous existence is my contact with people with problems and helping them solve them, hopefully, on most occasions. That has gone. It is an isolated existence in that way and one that you are committed to and there is no place else to go, I think. You can get out of most things nowadays. But being a judge you can never go back to practice, for example.

I was born in 1938 in Killarney. My mother died when I was four and after that I was moved to Caherciveen where I was brought up by an aunt who did not have any family of her own. She was Mrs Bridie Sheehan. She lived to be a good age. I went to the Christian Brothers in Caherciveen and have the happiest memories imaginable of my time with them. And I have still a great friend from then, Brother Dineen. He is retired in Dublin and I still see him quite often. There was also Brother Rogers, a true Dubliner, who is still to the good. There was a fine secondary school there, but it was thought that I might need the discipline of a boarding school so I was sent to St Brendan's from 1950 to 1955.

It was a tough regime after the War. Food rationing was still in place. I had a very good friend there, Gerald Courtney, who has just retired as a Superintendent of the Gardaí in Dublin and we have kept up the friendship over the years. Similarly, Paddy Culligan, the Garda Commissioner, was there in my time. Niall Mulvihill, the orthopaedic surgeon, was another. There was a great emphasis in those days that many would go on to the church from St Brendan's. I did not have any great ambition to do anything in particular. I had thought I might be a clerk in the Dickensian sense. I was a great reader of Dickens in those days. My aunt was a bit more ambitious for me and she thought I might do something in the way of getting a degree. I thought I might take the more conventional side of the Law and become a solicitor. But my aunt Bridie decreed that I should go in at the deep end and do the Bar although we did not have any connections in the Law at all.

I went to UCD and got into the debating societies fairly rapidly. Some women began to show their worth at about that time, people like Maeve Binchy spectacularly so. She was a wonderful character. Her father was William Binchy, a very successful barrister on the South Western Circuit. I did a BCL which had just been inaugurated and I was one of the first to do it. Tony O'Reilly was in that class too. We have regular class reunions. The last was our thirty-fifth and the next will be the fortieth. I was qualified very young after four years study. I was just twenty-one.

I think every experience you have counts as an advocate. You must know everything of everybody's work if you can. If you were of a mechanical bent, which I am not, and a good man to strip a car, then that would help you in a case involving a defective car. Signs on, in the Law at the moment we have a lot of people with all sorts of qualifications, who began life as engineers, accountants, scientists, doctors and some alchemy has drawn them into the Law. And of course their other discipline will be called into use at some stage or other.

I was then beginning to do my first few cases in the District Court and there was a District Court registrar who was very kind to me. I eventually approached him and asked him why he treated me so well in his court and he said that he used to attend the Literary and Historical Society, that was the old debating society in UCD, and he used to climb up in the back of the lecture theatre with the hundreds who milled around. He said he had great time for me, not that I was much of a debater, but it was the amount of punishment I would take in the way of heckling and jeering!

We cut our teeth in the District Court in those days, I don't know if young barristers still do so. We were very glad to get work of any description. I can remember the first trial I did. I defended a man who was charged with receiving stolen sacks. It was a jury trial and I took it over from somebody who got a more lucrative drunk-driving case. In those days we had all male juries. Middle-aged and middle-class. It was all very paternalistic. I remember standing up to make a speech for this fellow and I went completely blank. An eternity seemed to go by and I looked at the dock and I said to myself, 'You poor devil, to be defended by somebody so inexperienced'. Whereupon, I got sufficiently angry with myself, and something got unleashed. Anyway, he got off. That was in the old historic Green Street where Robert Emmet stood at the Bar.

I didn't go on Circuit, I stayed in Dublin. There was a very strong Bar going to Kerry. You had William Binchy, whom I mentioned, followed by the great Maurice Danaher who was one of the greatest lawyers that ever was. A hero of us all. He had taught in China and had that Oriental calmness about him. He was a wonderful writer of opinions and a wonderful lawyer. There was William Roche and Dermot Kinlen. And then Richard Johnson coming up on the rails. Both are now judges, too. So I proceeded to make as much of my fortune as I could in Dublin, but made the odd foray to Kerry. The Kerry Circuit was as strong as you could get.

Phil Clarke from Ballybunion was a great champion of mine. He had qualified a long time ago as a solicitor at a very young age and afterwards had a very full career culminating as County Registrar in Monaghan. He had been abroad many years and then resumed practice in Dublin. It was what would be called in America almost a *pro bono* practice in that he took on every manner of case. He once acted for a woman who had been treated badly by her husband in that he had run off with all the funds of the business. The tax legislation, nonetheless, had originally provided that she should be the 'accountable person' as the business was registered in her name. But by virtue of an amendment of the legislation – which was designed to give extra protection to the revenue authorities – the law was changed so that the actual person who held the money should be deemed to be the 'accountable person'. Phil spotted this opening and got the wayward spouse to write a confession statement which was then put before the Appeal Commissioner. He instructed me, but the case was won before we started and it showed what a superb tactician Phil was. He gave many young barristers, who are now in the front rank, their first cases and he was a most astute lawyer.

My great hero was Desmond Bell, a leading Senior Counsel in those days. He could do any kind of case, a murder case or the most complicated company law matter. A wonderful brain and a marvellous man. There was also Ernest Wood who was the quintessential advocate, marvellously cutting and brilliant. Coming up fast in those days was the present Chief Justice, Tom Finlay. He was cut off in his prime by being made a judge quite young. Of course I 'devilled' – that is a form of apprenticeship – with Tony Hederman and I afterwards joined him as a colleague on the Supreme Court.

I was also doing a bit of journalism at night. After I would finish in the Court in the afternoon I would have a short break and would work in the *Irish Press* a few nights a week subediting. That entailed writing headings and reducing the length of stories so that they would fit into the page. It was still the old hot metal system. The deputy editor, my great patron, was Fintan Faulkner, a County Louth man. I did every form of journalism but sport. I did feature writing and leader writing. I loved it and it was marvellous training.

But the difference was that in the newspaper world you were putting on a fresh production with each edition and your reputation was only as good as the last edition whereas, at the Law, with each successful case, a brick was added to the building and it remained there and it is not ephemeral. So that was why I eventually decided to opt for the Law. I enjoyed my three years in the *Irish Press*. The Editor at the time was Joe Walsh, whose son Harry is now writing the history of that newspaper.

I think the media in Ireland are very good. There has been some very good investigative journalism over the past number of years. I do not want to be too particular in case they come before me in another capacity. I think the very fact that so many papers continue to exist and that the provincial papers are very strong is a very healthy state of affairs. I think they do their work with a great deal of courage and conviction. The thing any journalist has to guard against is getting too pally with anyone in government in the broadest sense. He has to be a bit like us, a bit detached on occasions.

With regard to the Law, I know of some advocates who are fierce cross-examiners and reading some of the transcripts of their cross-examinations they appear very tendentious. But when they come before us in the Supreme Court they are as gentle as lambs, because if they began to get cross with us, it would not work. So what I am saying is that different styles are required for different courts. The modern advocate is so better equipped than when we were setting out. A huge amount of research has been done and there are a great number of legal textbooks now available. There are four or five books on the Constitution alone. MacMahon and Binchy on the Law of Torts (that is the legal word for *wrongs*) would hold its place with any comparable book in the world. Bryan MacMahon is the son of the author Bryan MacMahon and William Binchy is the son of the great barrister that I mentioned to you a moment ago.

I became a Senior Counsel in 1976. The work as a Junior Counsel got so heavy that it became necessary to move on. When you become a Senior Counsel, in theory at least, you get less cases, but probably get paid more and on you go. You must be aware as a Counsel how a judge should be handled and what his likes and dislikes are. If you waste too much time, you begin to lose him and that will apply with most judges, even the most patient. The judge is there basically, no matter what your good or bad qualities as an advocate are, to do justice to the litigant. So that is his paramount aim, but you naturally, as a Counsel, want to assist him in that direction. You look out occasionally for a judge's foible: I remember having a client who had sustained a number of injuries including an injury to the finger of his right hand which did not seem too severe in the sense of being terribly disabling. However, in the course of a consultation in advance of the case, it emerged that he was very keen on the guitar and could not play it anymore. The judge who was to hear our case was very musically minded and so we made sure to highlight this inability to play the guitar and the judge was very horrified to find that this man's musical career was being curtailed in this way. That would be a bit of inside knowledge, yes.

Judicial independence is very strongly enshrined in the Constitution. I was at a conference recently in Germany where the various jurisdictions were asked to outline the state of the judiciary and the consensus of opinion was that the Irish regime was better than any. I am not making comment adverse to the British system, only that it is a fact that many of their judges are part-time judges and not permanent. There is also a power to remove judges from some of the lower courts which is not applicable here. I am just saying this by way of contrast. The thing a person wants is to get a good hearing. Even if he loses. If he gets a good hearing and a chance to put his case, he will come out reasonably content even though he naturally would have preferred to have won. I think that is a big thing in the Irish character – getting a fair hearing. I think there is nothing more likely to cause a sense of resentment than a person feeling they are being cut off. I think there is a very strong feeling in the courts in this country that people should always be given a hearing and this also applies in tribunals.

I think the more experience you have the better. I think the suggestion is made about the tradition of selecting judges in England that they tended to come from the Oxbridge tradition. That is that they had been at either Oxford or Cambridge. But, nevertheless, they rendered some great judgements in their day. Whereas if you had somebody exclusively from a working-class background, could the people from the Oxbridge background say he did not understand them? Surely the whole tradition in this country is more egalitarian and we are all originally from peasant stock.

Some of the great judges of all time have Irish ancestry. For example, Lord Atkin, who formulated the 'duty of care' which has prevailed all over the world since 1932, his father was from County Cork and his mother was Welsh. Lord Devlin, once again an outstanding judge who retired from the bench in his fifties, was of Northern Ireland stock. He died within the last two years, having become reconciled at the end to the rites of the Catholic church. Then, of course, the outstanding American constitutional lawyer of the last fifty years was undoubtedly Justice Brennan whose parents came from Kilkenny. At the present time six of the seven judges on the Australian High Court (which is their Supreme Court) have Irish ancestry.

You ask about going back to Kerry. I give a big cheer when I am down in Iveragh each time I go into the sea for a swim at Coos Crom or off Valentia Island. I holiday there and we have a premises there. I go down as often as I can get out of Dublin. There is always some new mountain to be climbed or some fresh discovery to be made. My idyllic day in Kerry would be a day out on the sea with my pals, Mick O'Connell and Ned Fitzgerald, heading for the Skelligs or the Blaskets. That would rank high. Another would be to climb Carrauntoohil or Mount Brandon or our holy mountain of Caherciveen, Cnoc na dTobar. The third idyllic day would be to attend the Munster Final in Killarney with Kerry having a comfortable lead with ten minutes to go so that there would be time to take in the scenery; another would be a day at Ballybunion Golf Course and to have the privilege of having a birdie at any hole there!

You ask if I am a religious person. I would hope that I am reasonably religious. When the last day comes, I will probably be in the back row, but if I get inside the gate I'll settle for that. Archbishop McQuaid who had the reputation of being on the strict side, nevertheless used say that if you were a married man you had *ipso facto* done enough for the church. I am putting a lot of store by that. Now if it came from one of the more liberal theologians I might have my doubts. My sister, Mrs Pearl Dineen, lives in Caherciveen. Her husband, Con, is the príomh-oide in the Caherciveen Vocational School which is named after Daniel O'Connell. Pearl was one of the first graduates of the Shannon School of Hotel Management and she trained in Germany and Switzerland. To say there have been no particular incidents that have profoundly affect-ed the way things turned out for me might sound smug. However, I have had no brush with death, for example, which people say is the thing which concentrates the mind most of all.

My wife, Kathleen, is from Cloonacool, near Tubbercurrey, Co Sligo. We met at the Mater Hospital where she was a staff nurse. We have two sons and two daughters. Hugh is twenty-eight, an accountant, the next is Catherine and she is in the film world having played a role in the movie 'In the Name of the Father'. She is a production assistant. Rory is a stockbroker in Wall Street and our youngest, Brid, is following in my footsteps and is doing law in UCD. We spend a lot of time together as a family. Our house is fairly centrally situated so all the children's friends seem to gravitate on all sorts of occasions and at all sorts of hours of the day and night. And we have one of those rooms which has an Aga fire which is a great centre of attention and everybody seems to congregate there.

There is a special pride in Kerry. But you find it in all counties. In the Kerry Association in Dublin we are sub-divided once more; there are Listowel people, Ballybunion people and Killarney people and we are not Kerry people at all. We are getting more parochial in the best sense of that term, I think. And maybe it is no harm to take pride in the local heartland. All the trades have gone. In my boyhood there were four blacksmiths in Caherciveen and, of course, several harnessmakers, shoemakers and all types of tailors. All those trades which were there from the dawn of time were swept away almost overnight. It is sad, but there is nothing you can do about that. As against that there is an industrial estate in Caherciveen which is employing a good few people. So I think there is hope for that and the big thing is that we are produc-ing a generation of people who are hugely educated. I believe at the moment we are sending out a most articulate, highly educated group of young people; in the old days you think of the young people who went out with no education and who did so many stirring deeds; but nowadays the Irish *diaspora* is highly influential not only in political but in business circles throughout the world. What everybody should be doing is trying to find work for our young people.

I would move back to Kerry. If I got the chance in the morning I'd be off. I would love to retire to Kerry. It has a great grip on me. The days would not be long enough for me there.

JOHN COOLAHAN

(PROFESSOR OF EDUCATION)

WHEN I was growing up in Tarbert I was very aware of the variety of the landscape with woodlands, hills, boglands and, of course, the Shannon Estuary. Physically it was a very pleasant area and it was an interesting one in that it was inter-denominational. There were Methodists, Catholics and members of the Church of Ireland and we all went to post-primary school together, just as the farmers worked together. My father had a small farm and my aunt, Mina Coolahan, had a pub in the village. She died recently aged ninety-five years. There was tremendous intermingling in the pub and I agree with John B Keane when he says that a pub is a great place to be associated with when growing up. There was tremendous richness in the personalities and the variety of chat and banter.

The pub had a great tradition of music and song and there was a great respect for the individual and his song or story. My aunt was an extraordinary woman who kept a close interest in international affairs. She was educated in England and returned home and became a bit of a legend. She was constantly in touch with emigrants who wished to trace relatives.

One of the strengths of North Kerry is this respect for individuality and, indeed, eccentricity. Even as a young lad I was conscious of it and I feel very privileged to have grown up in that kind of community and landscape.

There was a deep-rooted tradition of schooling and, at secondary school level, we were very fortunate in having a small secondary school in Tarbert, just on the hill outside the village. It was called St Ita's College and was run by a very remarkable woman, Miss Jane A

McKenna and her team of teachers, who included Mr and Mrs Pat Carey. It was fired by people with a belief in the importance of education and who wanted to share this belief with the young people attending the school. Miss McKenna had a feeling for French and English literature which was stunning; that was an inspiration to me and to others. The school was co-educational and multi-denominational. With small numbers, there was a great sense of intimacy about it.

The quality of the teachers was such that it encouraged a liking for, rather than a resistance to, education. Jane A McKenna was a woman before her time. She had studied in Eccles Street in Dublin and the Sorbonne in Paris. She came from Loughill in West Limerick. She had a strength of tradition and a regard for learning which was a reflection of that whole area where education was so deep rooted. She was a leader by nature. In modern times she would have been a university lecturer. She had great courage and set up first of all a secondary school in Glin, where my older sisters went to school. My father bought the house on the hill overlooking the estuary from Major Leslie, the local landlord. There had been a school attached to it going back to the seventeenth century.

About 1938 Miss McKenna approached my father about setting up a school in Tarbert. The original intention was to have a girls' school in Glin and a boys' school in Tarbert. My father rented her the house for about thirty years. I did my Leaving Cert in 1959, just as the jobs scene began to improve. I had six job choices and the question was which way to go. My own instinct was to go into teaching and I went to St Patrick's Training College, Drumcondra. I have no regrets and ever since I have stayed in teaching in different areas of education.

One of my interests is the history of education and I have a tremendous respect for the earlier tradition of education within the Irish heritage. I see myself as an inheritor of that tradition, doing what I can to assist in the process and leading it forward in response to contemporary and likely future needs. That linkage gives a great sense of unity to my life and I think I am fortunate in that I find myself in a job that I always wanted to be in. I am thirty-three years in it, in one form or another.

After St Patrick's, I stayed in primary teaching from 1961 to 1965, in

Bray mainly. Being near Dublin was an advantage as it enabled me to do a night degree course in UCD. Teaching turned me on and I then proceeded to do a Higher Diploma. This confirmed that I was in an arena that suited me. I then went secondary teaching in Blackrock College, as I wanted to get a feedback from older kids on literature and other subjects. While at Blackrock I studied for an MA in English.

Towards the end of the sixties, a Masters in Education course was started at Trinity by a Kerryman, Professor Val Rice from Abbeydorney. This attracted me straightaway. It was full-time and I applied for it and was in the first group. I enjoyed it and came out with first class honours. I then went to work in Carysfort College in 1971 in teacher training. It was an exciting time of great change. I did a PhD in Trinity. I was anxious to widen my experience in education and at night taught in the vocational sector in Dublin. This gave me an introduction to students from different backgrounds. In 1974 I joined the Education Department in UCD and we got into a rebuilding process in education studies. I spent from 1974 to 1987 in UCD and did a lot of work on text-books and research.

The Professorship of Education in Maynooth then became vacant, I applied and that is where I am today. Maynooth is a very busy and interesting campus. The scale of it permits closer relationships than you get in much bigger university settings and it has a very warm tradition. This position gives me a certain authority in the arena of education at a time of great change in policies. The past few years have been extraordinary. The OECD was doing a study of Irish education and the Department of Education asked me to do a policy paper for the OECD, which I did. It influenced the OECD report on Irish education, published in 1991.

Momentum gathered as the then Minister for Education, Mary O'Rourke, decided on comprehensive restructuring and a reform of Irish education. For many reasons the agenda for change grew and she asked me to help the Department of Education as a special adviser on the preparation for the Green Paper. I worked with her and her senior officials very closely up to December 1991, besides doing my own work in Maynooth. Minister Brennan then came into the Department and changes took place on the Green Paper in which I had no role. It was issued in June of 1992.

The agenda for change has given rise to tremendous debate over the past two years. These two years have been of extraordinary importance for Irish society, for Irish democracy and Irish education, because of this remarkable debate on Irish education policies. It has been a very rich process and I am delighted it has gone so well. Of course, there are different opinions about different aspects of it, but the main thing is that people are interested, informed and trying to improve the proposals in question.

In May, 1993, the Minister, Niamh Breathnach, asked to meet me. There had been about a thousand submissions on the Green Paper with many conferences held around the country and she wanted it all co-ordinated. She asked me if I would act as Secretary General to plan and organise a National Education Convention, which she intended to establish as a key stage in the consultative process. In such situations you don't say 'no', you just get stuck in. I knew it would be another summer gone, but so what!

In July she announced she would have a National Education Convention where all the key partners would be brought together. It hadn't happened anywhere else in the world, and there were no precedents. There was immense interest, as all sectors were brought together in Dublin Castle in October, 1993. I was Secretary General of the Convention and I picked a team of academics to assist me. We did a lot of planning and it has been generally recognised as having been a success.

A lot of people were sceptical and caustic about it working out. I can understand that, because it was risky and tricky. It worked, and created a remarkable new climate between the various partners in regard to the education process. A remarkable dynamic emerged during the course of those meetings and, then, following the Convention, it was my job to prepare a report. To maintain the momentum, this report was produced in January, 1994. Such documents can run into trouble, but this document was met with great warmth in that the Convention had done the job of pulling the threads together, establishing the framework, posing the key issues and the key options.

The government had plans for intermediate education structures, regional structures to act as an intermediary between the Department and individual schools. This was mentioned in the Programme for Government in January, 1993. People felt there wasn't enough clarity about what the Department had in mind and the Minister undertook to produce a position paper setting out her plans more carefully; this she did on 11th of March, 1994. She then asked me to reconvene some of the key bodies from the Convention and to lead the debate forward on the specific matter of regional education councils.

I agreed, and we convened, in what were termed 'round table discussions' in Dublin Castle which have just concluded; I am now preparing a report for the Minister. The report is being presented in early June, 1994.

All this is leading into a White Paper which will convey government decisions on future policy on administration, curriculum, and a wide range of issues in relation to Irish education for future generations. From that White Paper, new legislation will result. It has been a very privileged period in which to have been involved. It has been demanding, with a lot of hard work, but satisfying also in that one is participating in the reshaping of the education tradition to which one is so attached; and trying to bring it into line with contemporary and future needs. One is also trying to see what developments need to be put in place to ensure that Irish education is in a position to cope internationally.

I have had a very privileged career from teaching and all aspects of teacher training and into key national policy level, helping the Department from an academically neutral position. The strength of Irish education is the ongoing awareness of its importance. The attitude of the people has been its great strength, and when Irish people have been given a chance of education they have availed of it at every opportunity. When Donogh O'Malley introduced free education, the people rose to it and availed of it. The school bus, travelling down the boreens, is one of the most important symbols of the State taking care of its children, bringing the children warm and without charge to the schools. It is a tangible symbol of a caring state.

We now have a situation, which is tremendous, bearing in mind our resources, where seventy-five per cent of all young Irish people complete the Leaving Certificate – and forty-three per cent now go on to some form of higher education. The targets are that by the end of this decade, nine out of ten children will complete the second level, which will be six years long, and fifty per cent will go on to some form of higher education. These are stunning educational achievements and aims.

The key strength is the realisation of education's value and the importance for Ireland of what we call nowadays, 'the knowledge base'. In an island country the knowledge base is crucial with changing patterns of employment. We need to invest and keep investing so that our children are equipped to find jobs wherever they go. In the fifties they had to leave, but the education level then was not good.

Our weakness is a tendency towards fragmentation. In one sense, it is a good thing to have so many agencies and associations and so many groups reflecting on education. The danger is that too many will get wed into their own tradition and work to defend their own corner without looking at the wider common good. We have five different types of post-primary school and I think it is time to bring more coherence to bear and to plan for more co-operation and interchange in the interest of the common good.

The Green Paper says that all post-primary schools should be called secondary and that, by and large, they should be much the same. There are still great inequalities in the system linked with the inequalities in society. The school can't solve all equality problems, but nevertheless, it has a role to play and a lot of casualties occur between individual schools. You need, it appears to me, a structure which keeps a greater overview.

The system has grown very fast and expanded very well, but the older administrative arrangements are no longer sufficient to respond to the needs. There has to be a realignment and restructuring of the administrative framework and of the roles played by the various agencies. That becomes crucial at post-primary level.

To take one tangible instance, we are facing a situation of declining demographic numbers. From 1997 onwards the numbers in post-primary schools will be declining. Two things will happen: as we go into the new century you will have a very significant decline in pupil numbers in the regions. Changing curricular policies require more options at senior cycle for the fifteen to eighteen age groups. You will need schools of a certain size to give all these students their curricular options and to have their rights facilitated and responded to. The very real danger is that schools will go into a free-for-all market scramble for pupils. The children most likely to suffer will be children from weak socio-economic backgrounds.

I believe we need to put into place a framework which will bring schools together, facilitating the amalgamation of some and, if they can't be amalgamated, facilitating much more co-operation and sharing of resources. Another fundamental weakness, one we are addressing at the moment, is that of a very highly centralised system. You have the Department of Education and the individual schools, except for the Vocational Education system. The Department, controlling so much, has become very clogged at the centre. Where you have a clogged centre, it is not doing the work it should be doing and not giving the service it should be giving. So we need to break this highly centralised system, which has also encouraged a strong dependency culture.

The key administrative change required is departmental reform, something which is long overdue. The Department accepts this needs to be done to enable it to concentrate on the things it should be doing such as strategic policy planning, ensuring that standards are maintained, budgetary controls, and helping the weakest in society. It also needs to devolve a great deal of its other responsibilities down to another authority and to the schools, to encourage the schools to be more self-reliant, encouraging boards of management to be genuine boards of management and liaising more with their community and building from 'the bottom up'.

A key question being discussed at the moment is whether we should have Regional Educational Councils and, if so, how many? The Ministry is saying eight; the vocational education sector is anxious to have a lot more. I don't know what the final decision will be. All the talk about structures is important in itself, but it is still secondary to the quality of the system. But, at times like this, we must look at the administrative restructuring.

We are working very well on curricular change and the teachers are redrafting the curriculum. We will have a new curriculum for primary schools in 1996. It won't be a grassroot newness, but a development of the existing one, which is a good curriculum. That is a very healthy thing to do, periodically. The present curriculum has been in place for about twenty-five years. There is also tremendous restructuring of the senior cycle programmes happening, in which the teachers have had a great part. But the implementation of the change is difficult as many teachers require in-service training and resources have to be found.

You have to ensure that what they are doing in schools is meaningful to pupils and linked into their world. All children cannot be expected to fit an elite system or one which is geared for high flyers who will be going on to university. We can't have them fitting what is convenient for us; we have to ensure that programmes are geared so that they can link with students; that the students just don't become failures of out-of-date programmes. Schooling should become an area which builds self-confidence and self-image; of achievement, not failure. That doesn't mean you won't have grades of performance, but, at the moment, programmes are 'out of kilter'; they are highly academic, their modes of assessment are highly academic, there is not enough variety on how we assess. But we are working hard and it is a difficult process. It is being addressed responsibly, which is encouraging. It is an enrichment process, one of not throwing out the baby with the bathwater.

If I was asked to make certain changes, I would put my main emphasis on the in-service training of teachers. Unless teachers are committed and skilled in relation to the new changes, very little will happen. Unless teachers are retrained, are comfortable with, and drive forward changes in their own classrooms, then change will not occur in a thorough and sustained way.

Another improvement I would like to see is in the examination process which needs to become more varied and flexible. The kids go into exams and everything is packed into a couple of hours in a highly pressurised competitive context. Exams haven't changed much since they were established in 1878. I would see more scope for continuous assessment of practical work during the year. I would like to see more encouragement of project activity, more assessment of science practicals, woodwork practicals, technical practicals and art practicals. Art practicals do take place and there is progress in modern languages. I would be inclined to go gradually and have practical subjects assessed in an appropriate manner.

The transition is extraordinary. At one level it is very challenging and at another it is very exciting. I think we are doing a lot in the right direction and what we end up with will be worthy of our people which is very important, for education has to be of service to our people, both young and old.

I am not impressed by the approach they have taken with education in England. It has gone the wrong way. We have approached it through consultation. This has given the partners in education an opportunity to respond and contribute to government policy, with the Minister adapting and changing. It is a very healthy relationship. There are occasional tensions, but it is tremendously democratic. The exact opposite is taking place in England and the tensions there are much greater.

Denmark has a great deal of interesting development, as have some of the Nordic countries. I am happy that we are not isolated; there is a great internationalisation of ideas.

We are not looking on our policy changes from an insular perspective. Our windows are open to what is happening elsewhere. Other countries are very interested in Ireland's approach to education change. Education is a conservative force everywhere and there can be a lot of inertia built into it. Sometimes, the forces of inertia and the *status quo* can be a bit too strong. I am a bit uneasy that people may not be stretching enough at the moment.

Education is a bonding of the generations. We need to build on the achievements and traditions of the past in putting in place an education system in line with the individual and social needs of a challenging future. As in the past, Kerry people are likely to be active participants in the education system of the future.

DONAL O'DONOGHUE

(COUNTY MANAGER)

AS Galway County Manager I have a simple goal. It is to make County Galway a better place in which to live than it was when I first came here. I have had a very rewarding career in local government, that is government at county level and people level.

I was born in Droumduhig, about three miles north of Killarney in 1942. My father and mother, Daniel and Mary, are now dead. I went to national school in Ballinilane and then I went on to St Brendan's College where I did my Leaving in 1961. From there I went to work as a clerical officer with Tralee Urban Distict Council for two years. In 1964 I went to Listowel Urban District Council where I spent three years as Town Clerk. I have very happy memories of staying with the O'Flaherty family in Church Street.

At the time, the Council was successful in acquiring the Cows Lawn, now the Town Park. I look back with great pride on that development. There were about thirty acres and twenty people in the town, each had the right to graze a cow there. The Council secured ownership for a total of four thousand pounds or two hundred pounds a cow. It has turned out to be a fine amenity for Listowel. It was my first major job in local government and a great training ground for me. Louis O'Connell was chairman of the UDC when I came and after him Patsy Walsh and Gerard Lynch chaired the Council. Others on the UDC then were Barney Hanley, Toss Stack, and Captain Thomas Shanahan. They were very happy days. From there I went to Limerick as a staff officer with the Corporation and I also worked with the old Limerick Health Authority.

I returned to Tralee in 1970 as Accountant to the Tralee Urban

District Council and I spent three years there, one of which was as Acting Town Clerk. We bought a lot of land at that time for housing and industrial development. From there I moved to Roscommon in 1974 as County Acountant for the next five years. The seventies were very active years for local authorities, particularly in relation to industrial development where we co-operated with the IDA in acquiring land in Castlerea, Roscommon and other towns. From Roscommon I moved back to Limerick as Finance Officer in 1979 and I spent eight years there. These were very productive years as the designated area scheme came in and I was appointed liaison officer. I was involved with the major developments at Patrick Street and Arthur's Quay in Limerick and also the City Hall complex.

I take a lot of satisfaction at having been involved in the very initial stages of planning of these developments. I also acted as City Manager in Limerick in 1987 when Tom Rice left to become Cork City Manager and before the present Limerick City Manager, Jack Higgins, took up office. It was a very important period in the development of Limerick.

In January 1988 I came to Galway as Assistant City and County Manager. A designated area scheme had just commenced and for five years I was very involved in the refurbishment of Middle Street, St Augustine Street and other streets which have been changed out of all recognition. There was great dynamism by the Corporation in leading the whole pace of urban development in Galway in co-operation with the developers. We helped put together site packages and outside the designated area we assisted Roches Stores in their development. This was a very exciting period. The designated areas scheme worked very well and over one hundred million pounds worth of developments have been completed in Galway through that scheme. It was a very significant input into the whole economic life of the city. The type of development that has taken place has respected the heritage and the archaeology of Galway. The development has been very kind from that point of view and the narrow streets have been retained.

In January, 1993, I went to Meath as County Manager and remained there for fifteen months before returning to Galway as County Manager. In Meath we came up with a very innovative scheme to col-

lect service charges. We had a lot of outstanding money from water charges and we offered those who paid by February tickets for a free World Cup draw which included flights, hotels and match tickets for three games. It was very successful. From one year the collection went up from sixty-nine thousand pounds to four hundred and eighty-nine thousand pounds. It more than repaid itself and, just as important, it showed the human face of the County Council.

I came back to Galway in April, 1994, as County Manager. We are now working on short-term and long-term plans for the social, economic and cultural development of the county. As resources are scarce, it is important that they are spent effectively. What we are trying to do is involve communities, because we have many communities who are anxious to do things for their own locality. I think it is vital that they are encouraged so they can contribute in their own way to the development of their own localities. The County Council can inspire and co-ordinate that kind of development.

We are very much in a changing environment with more and more regulations coming from Brussels. Change must be managed in the most effective way possible. In relation to planning and the environment, there is going to be more public input into these areas and it is important that this input is co-ordinated in a way to ensure that the county grows in a proper way and that the Council is the main development body providing the infrastructure. We want to see to it that the county is in good shape to avail of any investment opportunities that come its way. It's like a race in which the fittest win. The county in the best shape will win the best investment opportunities.

I have a number of core values in local government. We must provide quality service and that means having satisfied customers. I see our clients as customers to whom we provide services and it is important that we think in that way in local government. We also need an effective relationship between the executive and the county councillors. We must work as a team rather than against one another. Unity is strength. Councillors need information and we use area meetings between councillors and officials to improve the channels of communication. The Manager carries out the day-to-day management of the local authority and the Councillors are responsible for the formulation of policy and adopting the budget. Each side has legal responsibilities, but in practice it works like a board of directors.

There are only two democratic systems in this country, the Dáil and the local government system. I like the local authority system and it has played an important role in the development of the country. That is why one of my core values is the effective relationship between the executive and the elected members. In my time I have not had any great difficulties with my relationship with the Councillors in all the authorities in which I have worked. I feel that where you have unity and teamwork, you have a very progressive Council.

Over the past number of years the Minister for the Environment has devolved additional functions to the local authorities. We now have new regulations on planning, environment and pollution. This is to be encouraged and something I like. It is a very democratic system. Power should be devolved to its lowest level of competence and, from that point of view, I consider the local government system to be a very important arm of government. If we look at other countries, particularly Denmark where seventy per cent of all public expenditure is spent by local authorities, I think we have a long way to go, but progress is being made. In the past year, we have seen the advent of the new regional authorities and this is an important arm in the whole local government process. These authorities will be responsible for the co-ordination of local government services at regional level. However, I believe that certain services are better co-ordinated from central level, as we are a small country.

In 1977 rates were removed and service charges were introduced later and they play an important role in local government finance. They bring in thirty-two million pounds and if that money was not there, local authorities would be in a difficult situation. The service charges play an important role in the financing of local government and it looks as if they will continue to do so.

Our budget in County Galway works out at about a million pounds a week. We have over two thousand people on our payroll, with about thirteen hundred directly employed. We must at all times respond to the changing times, and find more innovative ways of doing things. We must never be happy with the *status quo.* We must be more innovative today than we were yesterday. Local authorities have sufficient room to look at different ways of doing things and to be more efficient in the discharge of their business. This is something which we are always looking at.

I believe in forward planning and we are now reviewing our five year plans for the infrastructure. We must have plans to avail of funds which become available. The roads are now a big issue. The roads in some areas have become bad because the whole pattern of traffic has changed over the past twenty years. Farming has come a long way from the pony and trap and there is huge machinery now moving along small country roads which were not built for that type of traffic. The local authorities are working on these roads and it will take a few years to complete. Farming has changed for the better economically, but it has brought these incidental problems in relation to the roads.

Another area which poses problems for some local authorities is the whole issue of refuse collection and disposal. I think the future will involve waste minimisation to a greater extent and that will involve a number of different activities such as recycling. The whole object will be to reduce drastically the amount of refuse being carried to landfill sites and I think that will be the broad strategy that will have to be adopted.

With new legislation coming from Brussels, landfill sites will have to be maintained to a very high standard in the future and that is going to involve local authorities in substantial costs, not alone in providing the sites, but in maintaining them. The landfill site developed by Kerry County Council near Tralee has been developed to a very high standard with Cohesion funding from the EU.

My goal is that by the time I leave Galway County Council, the county will be a better place in which to live, with better services. I have worked in different local authorities with a variety of people and I have always tried to keep learning. In our job there is an emphasis on training, and I require training myself to ensure that I am as innovative as possible. Our people respond to the challenge which I give them to make Galway County Council the best local authority in Ireland, so that people from outside who look in can say, 'Yes, they are doing a good job there'. I have been a lecturer with the Institute of Public Administration and that helps me in the theory side as I lecture to the students who do the BA course in Dublin in Public Administration. I visit other Councils in other countries and learn from those. Our staff are continuously being retrained. Recently all our senior staff underwent a course in communications.

The development of staff is very important and they have responded to initiatives I have introduced. We are out there as part of the government of the country at county level, at people level. We are acting as a development organ and I want to remove as much bureaucracy as possible from the system.

I am married to Anne Collery from Newcastle West whom I met while we were both working with the Limerick Health Authority. We have two children, Don and Shirley Anne. They are both attending Coláiste Iognáid in Galway. My brother, Jerry, and sister, Eileen, live in Killarney where they work for the Southern Health Board. Another sister, Bridie, lives in Dublin where she works for the National Rehabilitation Board. My sister-in-law, Mary, resides in the family home at Droumduhig.

MARGARET DWYER

(FESTIVAL OF KERRY DIRECTOR)

I became the first woman President of the Festival of Kerry in 1971 after having been involved with the festival from the early days. I held that office for three years and it was a memorable experience. I am still a director of the Festival of Kerry and it is a most exhilarating organisation to be part of. The festival is always looking for new ways forward to improve on what already is there. I would like to think that I have played my part in this great Irish success story. Tralee embraced me many years ago and I feel very much at home here with my family, friends and relations.

The festival was initiated in 1959 at a time when Tralee was depressed and had a lot of people emigrating. A lot of shops had closed. The idea of the Rose of Tralee was thought up by a group of men who met in Roger Harty's public house. These included Florence O'Connor, Dan Nolan, Ned Nolan and Joe Grace. A committee was formed and I was on it. Dan Nolan, publisher of *The Kerryman*, had tremendous contacts and with these and the backing of *The Kerryman* the idea worked. He was the president of the committee and ran it in a very business-like manner.

I was on the accommodation sub-committee and we had to go around the town and find out if people would be prepared to take in guests during the festival. We got a marvellous feedback with people prepared to open their homes to complete strangers for the festival. Dan Nolan and Roger Harty went to the United States in different years and organised two Roses from Boston and New York. I think we had six Roses in that first Festival of Kerry.

The first festival cost about £800 to run and the first Rose of Tralee was Alice O'Sullivan. At that time a Rose finalist had to have Tralee connections, at least one parent had to be from Tralee. Alice still comes back to the Festival. In 1960 we decided to go out and look for sponsors. Guinness had a representative in Tralee at the time, Percy Begley. He lived in Killarney and he managed to get the brewery interested. They came in small and built and built their sponsorship. Aer Lingus and Bord Fáilte came in later and I am still on the sponsorship.

Dan Nolan was our worldwide contact. He was the first President and he was very strict. We had to have our business completed when we got to a meeting. He never addressed us by our first name. There were no excuses and he set the tone of getting on with the job without any excuses.

The media really took to the event and forged our way for us. We had great support from people like Terry O'Sullivan of the Dubliner's Diary column in the *Evening Press*, Tom Hennigan of the *Evening Herald*, Noel Smith of the *Irish Independent*, his brother Gus Smith of the *Sunday Independent* and many others who were marvellous to us.

Frank McManus, a photographer with *The Irish Times*, got some marvellous pictures and these were of immense help in giving the festival invaluable publicity. He got some dramatic settings in which to picture the Rose of Tralee. On one occasion I remember, we had to have the Rose out at Fenit at six in the morning so that he could get the ideal effect from the early morning light. That made it to the front page of *The Irish Times*, a wonderful picture.

Florence O'Connor, who succeeded Dan Nolan as president, had an ability to see around corners. This was well demonstrated on one particular occasion. Bórd Fáilte, instead of giving a grant, had a scheme for festivals where they would guarantee a festival for any loss. Florence would not let us take it. He said the festival would not succeed if we spent money without caring where it came from. He wanted a bottom line and not to have this handout mentality brought in. And he was right, because so many of the festivals which accepted the Bórd Fáilte guarantee against loss are now gone.

The festival is very grassroots and very Kerry. It's a quiet festival with nice girls. There is no 'Miss Universe' type vital statistics thing.

They have to be pretty, with personality and intelligence. There have been great romances out of it. Even my own family experienced this wonderful aspect of the Rose of Tralee. Geraldine Healy, who came originally from Spa, was selected as the Limerick Rose in 1967 having moved to work in Shannon. My son Seán was home from University in the States. Seán had known Geraldine as children, as both families were very friendly. But they went their separate ways, going to different schools growing up. Seán went up with Florence O'Connor to meet the Roses coming in on the Friday and he met Geraldine. He said he would like to escort Geraldine and by the next festival they were married and now live in the US.

In 1971 I succeeded Florence O'Connor as president. I wasn't a unanimous choice when I was elected the first lady president. One member said women were far too bitchy, but after my first year that same man came up to me and told me that I had brought dignity to the office.

Denis Reen, like Florence O'Connor, was another with a capacity to see around corners. There was a suggestion that we should have a working chairman as well as the president. Denis Reen came on as chairman in my third year as president. He was very young and vibrant. He has made tremendous contributions to many major developments in Tralee.

I wish I was thirty years younger as Tralee is so vibrant with places like the Aquadome open and other new developments coming on stream. We in the festival have engaged a consultant to help us project to the year 2000. We don't go along with the adage 'if it ain't broke, don't fix it'. We are at a plateau now. There is nothing wrong with it, but we need a change, and we don't know what that change should entail. We will have a report by the end of September after the 1994 festival is over.

We have a very close association down the years with Guinness. The first Managing Director we met was Robert Green. He was a charmer, pure gorgeous, a businessman, and truly a gentleman. He married his childhood sweetheart who was an Italian Contessa and he brought her to the festival. Then we had the late Guy Jackson, who was tragically killed in the air disaster near London. He was a businessman first, but when we got to know him he was tremendous to us. Bobby Howick was a wonderful guiding star for many years.

I came to Tralee to live in 1948 from New York. My mother was from Tralee and her maiden name was Ryle. My husband, John Dwyer, was a lieutenant and was killed in January, 1945, after the Battle of the Bulge. He was in the Third Army and they had been called on to relieve the First Army. My younger son Seán was born after the death of my husband and there was just ten and a half months between Seán and my older son, Ryle.

I worked for AT&T in the United States. It was the parent company of all the Bell systems. After the death of my husband, I went back to work and got a job with TWA. My husband's people had been friends of Howard Hughes and they helped me get this job which I enjoyed. It was in customer service. I was there on duty the day the first passenger plane left Le Guardia for Rineanna which is now Shannon.

At that time I found it hard to settle. I had been to Ireland in 1936 as a child. The Olympic Games were in Berlin and we travelled with some of the American team. My mother brought my sister and myself on a Cunard liner and we sailed into Cobh. My mother was one of eight children, seven girls and one boy. Three had remained on in Tralee.

My decision to return was made while attending Mass on St Patrick's Day, 1948. I just thought of going to Ireland. My late husband was very keen on photography and he had built up a considerable collection of equipment. I took them into a camera store in New York and sold them and this paid for the fare to Ireland. I travelled over on the *Mauritania* with the two boys. We came for a holiday, but we stayed on. My aunty Anne was married to the town clerk in Tralee at the time, Con Kennedy. They lived in Castle Countess and they had eleven children. So my children had lots of cousins in Tralee. Nora Relihan is another first cousin of mine as her father, Tom Ryle, was my mother's only brother. We were embraced by the entire family, the O'Connors, the Kennedys and the McLaughlins. My mother and her sisters and brother had kept up contact always through their lives, no matter where they were. One sister was in Australia and another in South

Africa and my mother spent most of her life in the USA. This was great.

I returned to America to close up my house and to move my furniture here in 1949 when I moved here permanently. I had an American widow's pension and in 1949 you could live very well on that here in Ireland in comparison to the United States. That was one of the reasons why I went back to work after my husband's death. And when I had to give that up, my mother had to pay the rent. I was dependent on my family which was crazy. But I could live on my pension here in Ireland, and live well. Behind my back they used call me the 'merry widow' in Tralee. I took to Tralee as I am a town person, rather than a big city person.

Tralee is a fun town and a great social place. I never remarried, because I never met anybody I wanted to. And also my father died when I was ten years old and my mother never remarried. My father-in-law had remarried after my husband's mother had died. And my husband had a difficult time which I only learned of when we were married. I was independent and my children were independent and I couldn't afford to give up what I had.

One of the first things I found hard to get used to when I came to live in Tralee was what I thought was the absence of a social life for women. I always went out on a Saturday night in the United States. I remember one of my first Saturday nights here, my uncle and his brother went out and I said to my aunt Gertie were we going out and she said women didn't go out on Saturday night. She said that on Saturday night the children had to have their bath, and we had to get ready for Mass in the morning.

For many years the social life of Tralee revolved around Benners Hotel where there was a fantastic manageress, Molly Johnson. She ran a great hotel, wonderful food, the fires were always glowing and the copper pieces displayed around the hotel were always shining. It was a real old coaching inn and you could never miss a Saturday night in Benners. It was lovely, fun and great conversation. You would have Florence and Sheila O'Connor, Norrie and Harry Laide, Jimmy Caball and Masie, Gertie Sullivan and Storeen. Then you would have Donie and Jean Browne, Joe and Maeve Grace. It was just fun. Benners was special. You could afford to go out to eat quite often in those days, it wasn't that expensive.

One of the great attractions of Tralee for me was the fact that you have both sea and mountains. I love them both and to have them near you together is just marvellous. And then it must be the people first, last and always the people.

JOE O'TOOLE

(GENERAL SECRETARY, INTO)

I was born on the day of the Kerry County Football Final on Sunday, July 20, 1947. It caused its own problems as West Kerry were playing John Mitchell's in the Final. The lads were waiting at the bridge for the second of the two taxis to take them to Tralee, but it was commandeered to rush my mother to hospital and, as a result, they were late for the match. And to make matters worse West Kerry were beaten. The following year West Kerry had their day of glory when the same two teams met in the Final. And they didn't win the County Championship again until their win a few years ago.

My father, Miko, was a Garda in Tralee for about twenty years until 1965 when he went back to Dublin. He had been a Garda in Dublin when, one night during the Emergency, he transgressed some curfew rule and there was a scuffle on the way back to the depot with a friend. The following morning he was on his way to Dingle and his buddy was on his way to Donegal.

He is from Lettermore in Connemara. My mother, Teresa, was one of the Moriarty family in Dingle. My mother's family are very strongly Fine Gael and my father's family were very strong Fianna Fáil. They never discuss politics during elections, but at all other times politics were discussed and argued every day and night and it's no wonder that I'm an Independent.

My father bravely carried the Fianna Fáil line to the Moriarty family, whose comfortable and cosy Fine Gael consensus was considerably unsettled when Hilda, my mother's first cousin, married Donogh O'Malley. Much as they loved Donogh personally, accepting his political affiliation took a major swallow. Both the Moriartys and the

O'Tooles are extrovert and gregarious. Both are tightly knit and family loyalty is considered to be a premium. My mother will be less than pleased to see this kind of family detail in the public domain. The Dingle and Lettermore roots are still vitally important to me. In fact they are me. My first cousin in Lettermore, Peadar Ó Tuathail, is an Independent County Councillor in Galway.

My mother had a shop in Dingle and all my aunts and uncles had businesses there. One aunt owns O'Flaherty's pub which was the first traditional music pub in Dingle. My cousin Fergus now runs it. My uncle, Paddy Moriarty, has a butcher's shop. Another uncle was the celebrated Foxy John who was the first man to rent bicycles in Dingle. My mother had a shop in the Mall. There is a unique feature about the four houses in the Mall in that they are built across a stream which still runs underneath them. I was reared in the one with the gable facing towards the harbour. I still miss the sound of the running stream which was a constant element of my childhood.

We sold general groceries and fruit in the shop and I was reared in business. Even to this day I could stick my nose into a box of oranges and I would know if there was a rotten one at the bottom of the box. I think if you buy and sell fruit at a young age you learn a lot. And I used to help my uncle, the butcher, kill and skin sheep while I was involved in undertaking, bicycle repairs and furniture delivery for the other. It is a very unusual background for a trade unionist, but it has been of great benefit in that there is very little at the other side of the counter that I don't know about. During my late teens I would have been in charge of some of these businesses while on school holidays.

All my education was in Dingle and I can safely say that though in the meantime I have picked up degrees and qualifications, and even a title, I have not learned anything new about people since the day I left Dingle. I am the eldest of five and have four sisters.

One of my sisters, Sabrina, married an American called Bruce Antoniotti. They live in Dublin and they are both barristers. She was a teacher and decided to follow her husband into law. My next sister Anita is personnel manager with Primark or Penneys. She spends much of her working life on the far side of the table from trade union negotiators. She is highly skilled and we learn a lot from each other about our respective roles. Another sister, Phyllis Cunningham, is the National Kidney Transplant Co-ordinator. She has the extraordinary job of moving from the tragedy of a family in one room who have lost a loved one, to the joy of a family in the next room through the giving and the receiving of body organs. She is based in Beaumont Hospital. My youngest sister, Grace, worked in the import-export area, based in London. She is fluent in a number of languages and had an exciting job which took her around the world. She eventually opted for more regular hours and now teaches German and French. She is married with two children and works in the inner London area.

My father was stationed only briefly in Dingle, but in all my time growing up, he was stationed in Tralee and went in and out every day. He was a founder member of the Garda Representative Association and when he went back to Dublin he was in B branch and he worked there until retirement. On retirement from the force he was employed by the Garda Representative Association and he only retired from the GRA in 1993. He has always had a great commitment to the organisation of workers and the need to be organised, articulate and able to put forward a point of view.

Dingle had an unusual thing like most Munster towns, where there was a hangover from the early part of the century, in that there was a regulation that men could not teach children under the age of seven years. It is quite significant in the light of the current debate on incest and child abuse.

In Dingle that tradition lived on and we started off with the nuns and Sister Rose was my first teacher. That first day I kicked her in the knee and ran down the road to my grandmother's shop.

I told that story on radio recently. I thought Sister Rose had long gone, but I got a lovely note from her on the 19th of March, asking did I ever expect to get roses? The cover of the card had roses on it. She was delighted at the mention. I went from Sister Rose to Sister Kevin who was a Tralee woman. And then to Sister Evangelist who prepared us for First Communion. First Communion Day in Dingle was extraordinary in providing three unique experiences. Firstly, we traversed the tunnel which connected the nuns' convent to the church. It was the only time that we were allowed enter it. Secondly, we got breakfast in the convent and thirdly, Sister Evangelist, of whom all were normally in constant fear and dread, stole the first kiss from every communicant as we came back into the tunnel, much to the chagrin of parents. People in Kerry attach a lot to the first kiss of a First Communicant.

Then I went across to the Christian Brothers School, the monastery, which in fact was across the road from my own house. I really enjoyed post-primary school, although I was a disaster in many ways. I was a poor footballer. I was probably the worst footballer ever to leave West Kerry. If the team were really stuck they would put me in goal with Tom O'Shea, Paudie's brother, in front of me as a solid full-back. In the school band my talents were soon exposed and I was given the job of carrying the flag. On a few rare occasions I graduated to the triangle. It was an unusual school in that it encouraged debate and argument in English and Irish. The captain of the debating team was Brendan MacGearailt who is currently a County Councillor. I alternated between first sub and fourth in the team. I didn't think much of it at the time, but it was afterwards I realised the significance of the emphasis on articulation, argument and debate. That tradition lives on there today.

My best friend at school and growing up was Pat Neligan. His home was like a second home to me. Pat went to the College of Education a year before me. He was best man at my wedding as I was at his. Pat is now back in Dingle teaching in the CBS post-primary school. Ruairí O'Connor, the third person in my childhood friendship group, was the priest who officiated at both our weddings. He is currently a Holy Ghost priest in Kenya.

Tom Lundon from County Limerick, one of the lay teachers, had a great influence. He encouraged my innate scepticism and challenging attitude. He taught me all through secondary school. For the final few weeks before the Leaving I was suspended from maths and physics as a disciplinary measure and that annoyed me. But I got a very broad education there. It was an extraordinary thing when I look back to think we did Latin through Irish from an English textbook. My only regret was that we didn't do a continental language.

After that I went to St Patrick's Training College, Drumcondra. I got a good Leaving and the options were Aer Lingus, Civil Service, teaching. The bank was out as my grandmother didn't want me counting other people's money. The only thing I was asked not to consider was medicine. My mother was less than enamoured at my decision to pursue a career in national teaching, though I fully recall her most prescient of remarks around the time I qualified, 'Maybe you could go and become General Secretary of the INTO and a Senator like that nice Mr Brosnan'. It was many years before either prospect even vaguely crossed my mind!

I gave a commitment to an uncle at an early stage never to drink whiskey or never to do medicine. The attitude was that everybody drinks, but be careful of whiskey. In fact on the day of my Confirmation I took the pledge, but when I came home showing off the badge to my mother, she looked disdainfully and said, 'You'll take a drink like your father and uncles when you are seventeen'.

When I arrived in Dublin I was cocky and argumentative. I went to St Patrick's without a vocation for teaching. But I felt that a person is fit to do many jobs in a lifetime. And the reason I went to teach was that friends had gone there and I was attracted by the long holidays in teaching. I make no apologies for that. I wanted something that would give me space and time. And it is ironic that I have not taken a long holiday for twenty years. I have never taken holidays for holidays' sake. More significantly, I loved every minute of teaching. I still miss the classroom today.

I found the two years in St Patrick's very useful. It is a course which gives a grounding which a university degree won't give. There were thirty-two curricular areas. I was the first president of one of the St Vincent de Paul conferences in the college. Visiting hospitals and homes got me interested in the whole area of disadvantage and this has stayed with me ever since. It also gave me a respect for the St Vincent de Paul Society which I still hold in the highest regard although I am no longer involved with them.

During my second year I was on the student representative committee. That was my first elected position. In July, 1967, I got a job teaching in Blanchardstown. I taught there with Joe Dillon, a relation from

Dingle. Paddy Murray, who was a shot-putter in his day, was my principal. He got me involved in school sports and taught me a lot about teaching and running a school.

I moved to Rolestown about five miles west of Swords where I taught from 1971 and I live near the school in Kilsallaghan where Tom Dreaper trained Arkle. Jim, his son, trains there now and his wife is on the school board of management. At that time there was no middle-class in the area; you were either an owner, farmer, trainer or jockey, a groom or a farm labourer and kids in that part of County Dublin would have lesser experience of Dublin City than I would have had at the same age from Dingle. I would have been in Dublin more times at their age than they would have been when I taught them. They would talk about going to Dublin which I found extraordinary. My wife, Joan Lynam, is from that area. We have lived there since 1971.

Joan is a PE teacher. Her father had moved from Longford to North Dublin in the forties. He farmed successfully, mixing dairying, cereals and dry stock. He was generous enough to give Joan and myself a lovely site to build our home. On Joan's first trip to Dingle in 1970 I introduced her to my grandfather, Sean the Grove, who was a very successful businessman and who also had a small farm. 'Tell me now, are ye in business or in farming?' he said. Joan laughed and said, 'We have a farm, but I am the youngest in a family of eight.' 'It doesn't matter, you'll be all right,' he replied. Dingle people love that story. Whereas Joan does not like the razzmatazz of politics, she is a superb organiser and campaigner at election time.

In Rolestown my principal, Bob Doyle, was the INTO branch secretary and I got involved in the North County Dublin branch. I was involved as chairman and was active in various issues in the mid seventies. In the 1977 election for general secretary I supported Gerry Quigley. He won. I became a member of the central executive council and moved on from there.

I became General Secretary of the INTO on January 1, 1992, and effectively I am the chief executive. It is the largest and most widespread organisation in this State covering the thirty-two counties and covers every part of the island. It is more widespread than the GAA,

the Catholic church, the postal service, the Gardaí, and the political parties. It is closer to the pulse of the people than any other group and has
been dealing with education longer than any of the parental bodies.
And it has given a huge amount to the development of the State. There
isn't a political organisation which doesn't depend on primary teachers.
We have three members in Cabinet at present. There are twenty thousand members in the Republic working in more than three and a half
thousand schools and a further five thousand in Northern Ireland.

You ask about the attitude of the public to change in education.
Change frightens most people. You can build a wall around yourself, your
profession or your job and keep the whole world out. You can ignore the
fact that there are no longer two-person buses, that there are no longer
bank closings in the middle of the day, that stores open on Sunday, that
there is greater transparency in society and that there are greater needs.

I have a very simple view on this. I don't think teachers should be
running away from change or be afraid of it or building walls to keep
change out. I think we should be leading, directing and pointing to
where change could bring us; that we should be bringing forward the
proposals; that change should come from us. And that has been my aim
as general secretary. Our duty is not to the parents or the State, or the
churches, it is simply to give the best possible opportunity to the generation of kids that are at school at the moment and make sure they are
better than our generation.

In terms of excellence, I believe Irish primary teachers are at the
highest level globally and we have made a huge intellectual investment
in primary teachers in this country. That is what has kept the system
going, highly intellectual people with a lot to offer, and getting the best
out of it despite overcrowded classes and despite having the least funded primary school system in the developed world.

Culturally, we are very strong in Ireland. I know this from my own
travels. Irish people tend to come forward as being gregarious, articulate, noisy, loud and influential. I am never worried about us being
over-run by the cultures of other countries. Irish culture will learn, gain
and feed off other cultures. Europeanisation will do nothing to damage
Irish education, it will enhance it.

On the Irish language, I am a Gaeilgeoir to my finger tips. All my education was through Irish and I love the language. I use Irish every day, whether it is dealing with people or giving interviews. The thing that bothers me is pushing it on people. It is a beautiful, most expressive language and it is a language people should feel comfortable with. I resent that INTO members are shouldering the responsibility for the revival of Irish and that is unfair when too few others are bothering. Irish deserves support, the communities that use it deserve support.

Living in Dublin has upset the purity of my Kerry canúint. One of my friends, Donal Ó Loinsigh from Kilfountain outside Dingle is a native speaker. On one trip home he was accused of 'ag labhairt le accent Blea Cliath' because he had slipped into the dreaded caighdeán. I know how he felt. I remember after doing an Irish language TV interview receiving a letter from Dingle, 'Cuir uait an Ghaeilge sin and labhair Gaeluinn as seo amach'. Gaeluinn is the actual canúint spoken in West Kerry. We are fiercely proud of it but it does become diluted and polluted away from home.

I went to school with the last generation who lived on the Blaskets and I saw those people struggling with language. I saw people who were brought up with Irish only and were badly treated when they went outside the Gaeltacht, not in their home areas. They were not allowed develop their English and people in the Gaeltacht know they have to have English skills. There is a sort of zoo approach to the Gaeltacht in some parts of Ireland. I remember a debate in the Oireachtas about setting up a national park on the Blaskets which I supported. Somebody put in a proposal that no transistor radios be allowed on the island. So we were saying to the people of Dunquin that you can't go across to the islands on a Sunday afternoon and turn on to hear the Munster Final on the radio. Is there any understanding of the culture of our people down there, keeping them away from technology? I say load in the technology and support the language. Give them all the support they need. They are not getting half enough. I think that the Gaeltacht people are great, dignified people. They don't whinge. I will always support them.

MOSS KEANE

(RUGBY PLAYER)

I have made some great friendships through rugby. I recall being down in Killorglin three years ago when my uncle, Canon Matt Keane, was celebrating fifty years in the priesthood and who walked in the door but my friend Peter Wheeler, the former England international. He found out where I was and would not pass the door without meeting me. He was on a golfing tour of Ireland at the time and used to play hooker against us.

I enjoyed the company and the few pints after matches. The thing about me drinking the pints is a bit exaggerated. If you get the reputation of getting up early, you can stay in bed until lunchtime. My social life didn't cut across my rugby. Everybody else treated the game the same way. There was no sponsorship involved then. When sponsors came in and players started looking for money, it got serious.

For the last four years when I played for Ireland we trained a minimum four days a week. When we trained, we trained hard; but the period was shorter from October to March, whereas nowadays they do it from July to May. I wouldn't for a moment accept that players nowadays are anything the better for it.

In 1978 in the first round of the Leinster Senior Cup, Lansdowne were beaten by Terenure at the end of March, and I never took the boots out of the bag until the middle of August. There was mould on them. And still we were fit enough to beat the All Blacks in Limerick at 3.45 pm on the 31st of October at Thomond Park. We started to train in the middle of August and trained hard from there on in, but nothing in April, May, June and July. I didn't get too overweight. I had a very good tapeworm at the time, and my playing weight was seventeen and a half stone.

I remember in the All Blacks game, towards the end, there was a bit of dust up and Andy Haden was going to draw on me and I just said: 'Don't, don't. Please don't. You are going to lose the frigging fight as well?' Obviously, someone in the back of the crowd heard me.

When I was training there were no programmes scientifically set out as there are now. We trained the traditional way which, in the long run, is probably better for you in later life. You just went out and ran around. I used to go out to Belfield with Paudie Lynch the Kerry footballer. He would have been preparing for the All-Ireland Semi-Final. We would race against each other. I won't say who won those races – in deference to Paudie. We'd go for a run first and then a pint. The benefits of the run might be cancelled out by the number of pints afterwards.

I don't think I would enjoy playing international rugby nowadays. I start to sweat in the chair just watching it on television. We went out to Australia in 1979, the famous tour when Wardie was dropped, and we beat Australia in the two tests in their home ground. That would be unthinkable now. The intensity has increased immensely in rugby at international level with big sponsorship. We don't have the numbers of players in this country to sustain competition of this intense kind. If you lose one or two players, there is no-one there to replace them. I enjoyed myself, that was the whole name of the game. I was talking to Barry McGann recently and he said we were the last eejits who played international rugby; it cost us money. They are all being paid now.

I am a native of Currow, four miles outside Castleisland, pure absolute GAA territory. I went to Currow National School and then to St Brendan's. My father, William, died two years ago and my mother, an O'Mahony, is from Bullock Field outside Castleisland. She always wondered how she survived at all because they were surrounded at home by the Lyons, Savages and Woulfes. I have two brothers and I was the eldest. Brian was next and then Matt who is at home. I was too big and awkward growing up to be any use at football. In my class the best known would be Micheál Ó Sé who played for Kerry. There was Liam Lynch from Ballybunion, who is now a doctor in Rathkeale, Co Limerick, and there was John Shanahan from Kilflynn. There were two lads who are now headmasters in schools in Mayo, James Fogarty and James Lundon. There was Tom Keane who came after us, one of the fish people from Dingle.

The lifestyle in St Brendan's was pretty heavy going. A lot of people came out of it well. I came out of it probably the least well. A few years ahead of me was Denis Brosnan and Michael Dowling and they have gone as far as they want to go. Of course, they are still relatively young men.

In St Brendan's I was young enough for the Dunloe Cup the last year I was there. I was a sub on different teams. In my last year I went in to study seriously and even on Saturdays I studied hard. I gave the study the full whack the last year. I gave up playing and I said I might as well stick to what could be good and I got on OK in the exams. I didn't cut it at St Brendan's at football. I went to the Salesians in Pallaskenry for a year, the agriculture school, because it was deemed that I was too young to go to university at that stage. I spent a year in good, rustic conditions. I enjoyed Pallaskenry, to a degree. When you are growing fairly fast at that stage you need a lot to eat. Food was always a problem with me. Savage. The staple diet was good enough for everybody else, so it had to be good enough for me too. I don't think there was enough for anybody. I played football in Pallaskenry. We had a funny situation in that the majority of people there were from Kerry. They had about sixty students and more than thirty were from Kerry. A lot of the guys had been to St Brendan's.

There was a Limerick gaelic football competition for *The Kerryman* Cup. We won it. We were only young lads aged seventeen or eighteen. And we beat a crowd called St Patrick's from Limerick in this junior final. It was an experience as you had to be fairly sharp avoiding the stray elbow. They substituted finesse with a few other things. It was my first time playing outside of a secondary school situation. *The Kerryman* Cup was my first success. I remember I was full-back and I was marking a fella who was old enough to be my father.

I went on to UCC and did Dairy Science. In my first year I played in a special competition for under-nineteens. The following year I played senior and had the great thrill of being full-back in front of Billy

Morgan who was in goal. I don't know if it was that big a thrill for Billy. That was the Sigerson Cup. We won three Sigerson Cups and I captained the winning team in 1970. I played full-back all the time. I would never judge a player in his teens. You have to wait until he reaches his early twenties. We won the Sigerson in 1969 in the Mardyke, in 1970 in Newry and 1972 in O'Toole Park in Dublin. Brendan Lynch scored a goal with the last kick of the game when we were two points down. It went in off John O'Keeffe's hands. I became captain of the side in 1970 because two very eminent members of the team, Brendan Lynch and Jim Coughlan, were going for the captaincy and I was moved in as a compromise captain. Jim Coughlan was a great minor and was a sub for the senior side when still a minor. Paudie Lynch and Dan Kavanagh were on those sides. John O'Keeffe was with UCD. From North Kerry they go to UCD, you know. The first Sigerson winning side I was on was captained by Christy O'Sullivan from Finuge.

The Ban was lifted on Easter Sunday, 1971. Billy O'Mahony from Abbeyfeale, who got a final trial for Ireland, was captain of UCC and he came to me. He said they were a bit small in the pack. He said they would help me along and I agreed. I played with UCC rugby team virtually every Saturday and when the gaelic team had a game on a Sunday I would play on the Sunday as well. Naturally the performance on the Sunday mightn't be that great after the Saturday.

I picked up some technique from watching rugby on the television. The amount of technique you need in the second row is not an awful feckin' lot. I played a bit of junior rugby the first year. Rugby wasn't as organised as it is now. It's gone desperately serious now. I don't know if a lot of the fellows I played with could have played at the level it is now played. Maybe there is something in it for them now. Even if there was something we wouldn't have bothered our arse. We enjoyed it and everyone was the same. The English were fierce cavalier about the whole thing; the Welsh got serious and won four Triple Crowns on the trot. It was in the late eighties it got serious as sponsors began to come in. I played for UCC the first year, 1971/72; played for Munster 1972/73 and played for Ireland 1973/74. It just happened like that. That was because there was nobody else there. The tradition of rugby in

Castleisland goes back a long way with the Doyles and Joe O'Connor who played for Ireland in the 1930s. Then there was a fellow from Knocknagoshel; there was also a fellow from Valentia Island, Bob Graves, who played for Ireland. I was capped fifty-one times for Ireland. They said I got fifty more than I should have. I last played for Ireland against Scotland in Lansdowne Road in 1984. The funny thing: I was dropped by Munster twice and never dropped by Ireland. I was on the 1966 Castleisland side which won the County Minor Championship that year. They always had big minors in Castleisland.

I was banished to Dublin from Cork in 1972 and I have been in Dublin ever since. I played gaelic with Civil Service in Dublin. I always kept my Munster connection after coming to Dublin. I refused to declare for Leinster. And that's it. I ignored the pressure to declare for Leinster. I had nothing against Leinster, but I didn't see why I should play for Leinster.

I go to Kerry still once every three weeks. I stay in the home place. I don't think it would be practical to move back to Kerry as I am employed in Dublin. I have moved forty-five miles back in the direction of Kerry since I moved to Portarlington. My wife Anne is from Portarlington. We have two girls, Sarah, aged twelve, and Annemarie who is ten. I commute to Dublin three or four days a week and do a bit of travelling as well in the job with the Department of Agriculture.

The Kerry spirit would have been epitomised by the great Kerry teams. When you are on the perimeter of Ireland you have only one way to go. There are some parts of Ireland where they have been spoon-fed from the day they were born. They might be more talented, but don't have the same will. The small bit of hardship doesn't do any harm. There is pride and this grows with distance.

There were some great characters in rugby in my time, people like Phil O'Callaghan of Dolphin. Players are now more robot like and their personality is coached out of them. There were some great days in the Shelbourne Hotel, where we are talking now. When we won the Triple Crown in 1982, all the forwards were married and all the backs were single. I took a very broad view of sport. It was a surprise to do what I did because it was never intended. I never set out to do it. It just happened. When it began to happen I got more serious and that's the way it unfolded. We went through bad patches in the international side. The one moment I remember was the genius of Ollie Campbell and Gerry McLoughlin going over for a famous try at Twickenham. Ollie converted and we won 15-16. The other moment was the win against the All Blacks.

We had great days, bad days and all sorts of days. As you get older, you only want to remember the good ones. I love going back to Kerry. There is an enigma there, something extra-terrestrial. It's the people and the beauty of the place. If you had the Mediterranean climate, there would be millionaires all over the place.

BRIDGET GLEESON

(INTERNATIONAL GOLFER)

MY father, John, was the head greenkeeper at Killarney Golf Club and we lived in a lodge near the fifteenth green at the O'Mahony's Point Course. Apparently he used to take my mother out for golf lessons and they would bring me along as I was only a toddler. It ended up with me learning golf and not my mother.

Dad, who was then a scratch golfer, used to take me onto the course when he was working and I am told that I actually was knocking golf balls around at two years of age. My father was born in what was the old clubhouse in Killarney. His mother and father worked and lived there. My mother was from Castlemaine and didn't know much about golf until she came into the midst of it.

When I was about three, Frank Hall's television programme, *Newsbeat*, featured me in a report. By the time I was five I was spending time out on the course every day. In 1967, when I was about four, the BBC were filming in the area. The programme presenter, Cliff Mitchelmore, was out for a round of golf when he spotted me chipping goodo onto the fifteenth green practising. As a result I appeared on BBC. I was then invited onto the *Late Late Show*. I suppose with few, if any, other four year olds playing golf, if you are any way good, you obviously become a bit of a media attraction. At that stage I was able to chip and putt, and get out of bunkers. I couldn't hit the ball very far, but when I hit them they went in a straight line and there were no fresh-air shots.

I attended Fossa National School, and after school I would either put in some practice or play a round of golf. My father would have a bucket of balls for me to hit. I was something of a ghost-like figure in and around the fifteenth green as anytime people would pass, I was there pitching and putting. I was second in the Lady Captain's prize when I was aged nine and I was runner up in the club championship that year also. I played a lot of golf with the men members at Killarney. I had more freedom than junior members would have now.

When I got older I had some others playing with me, lads like Eoghan O'Connell who is now a professional playing on the tour, and Tomas Kelleher. I played golf with Eoghan's sister, Noreen, who was a fine golfer also. I won the club championship several times and I was nine when I played in the Irish Close Championship in Mullingar and won my first round. Mary Governey beat me in the second round.

When I went on to the Vocational School in Killarney there was a problem in that many of the major senior ladies' events are played early summer when schools are still open. This meant getting time off in April and May, but the school was very good to me in this regard. I was fourteen when I was capped for the Senior Munster Team and that was my entry into serious senior golf. On that team were Ann Heskin, Claire Keating and others. I was also capped for the Junior Irish Team.

I got my first cap in Southport. I halved the one match I played. I then went on to play number one on the Junior International side. The junior events did not impinge on my education, as they took place during the summer holidays. I had no coach as such. My dad gave me all the tuition through my career. We had sessions in the Senior International Team, but they could be described more as bonding rather than coaching. At times to get more practice, he would bring my bike into the school in the back of the car and I would cycle home, getting there well ahead of the school bus which I caught in the morning. It was golf first and study later.

Another person who had a big influence on my golfing career was Andrew Shields. He saw me one day when he was out playing golf in Killarney and he spotted me chipping near the fifteenth green. He was from the North of Ireland where he had a hotel. I was about seven years old when we met and he became known to me as Uncle Andrew. He used bring our family up every summer to the North to stay in his hotel and to play the courses there. We continued travelling up there until the Troubles got bad. We stayed in his hotel in Portstewart, the

Carraig na Cuaill. He became very close to our family. One summer he introduced me to Fred Daly, the only Irishman to win the British Open, and to John Letters who gave me a set of clubs. They were made specially in his factory for me and I had them for many a year. I used to give exhibitions in the North, like playing out of a bunker with just one hand on the club when I was only seven or eight years old. Andrew became ill and retired and he used come down to Killarney. He died about fifteen years ago. On his death Andrew left me a fund which covered my expenses for the next couple of years. Golf is a very expensive sport because of the travel and due to his generosity I was able to play in events which I might otherwise not have played in. He did not have any children and I was like an adopted niece.

Before I left school I got my first Senior International cap in 1980. I won the Munster Senior Championships in Muskerry, beating Ann Heskin in the Final. It was my first senior win and I had been doing well in scratch cups. I went with the Irish team to Cruden Bay in Scotland and the team won the Home International. I didn't actually get to play, but my name was put top of the Irish players on the trophy as it was done alphabetically, even though I didn't hit a ball. It can happen that the newest player might not get to play, but it was tremendous experience at sixteen being on an International side with players like Mary McKenna and Claire Hourihan.

I played my first game as a Senior International for Ireland the following year in Burnham in Berrow in England. I got one game and I halved it. There was a lot of debate in women's golf as to why I was not capped between 1981 and 1987 as I had won the Munster Championships in 1983, and normally if you win in Munster you walk onto the Irish team. But I didn't get on and there was a lot of hype about it. I felt a bit hard done by as I was in the peak of my game at that time. For instance in 1984 and 1985 my handicap was plus two. I would have been among the three lowest handicapped women golfers in the country, but they still would not put me on the team. When I sought some explanations, the reason I was given was that I did not hit the ball far enough. It didn't seem to matter that I was good around the greens.

I won the Munster Championship again in 1987 and I was having tremendous problems with a thumb injury in my left hand. It was caused basically by wear and tear on my hand. When I was recalled to the Irish side that year I wasn't physically fit because of the hand problem and it seemed strange that they decided to put me back on the side when I was on a downward spiral. I couldn't travel because of the injury. I felt that I would be unable to do myself and the team justice and it might do more harm than good.

After having my hand examined by many doctors, I eventually went to a specialist in Dublin, Mr John Curtin, and by X-raying my hand in a different position, he noticed that it was growing differently from the other thumb. He said that if I could put up with the pain, it would not cause any further harm. Knowing this I was able to get out and play. It is still quite painful to this day, but I was concerned at that time that I was doing damage. I have got used to it and I do exercises before playing and it doesn't bother me.

In 1991 I did well and I became first reserve on the senior side. At the Interprovincials I had won five of my six matches and things were looking good and unfortunately in the middle of the 1992 season I had a bad car crash which put paid to everything again. It happened in July and I missed all the big tournaments. Golf requires a lot of driving and the last thing I wanted to do for some time was to get into a car.

If you miss the Interprovincials you miss the Irish team, unless you win the Irish Close. In 1993 things went reasonably well, but there is newer and younger competition coming along all the time. I have three full caps to date. I have won the Munster Senior Title three times, the Irish Junior Title two times. As well as that I have played interprovincial golf.

I got married in 1985 to Liam Healy, a bank official with AIB. We joined the bank together in 1981 and we met again when he was posted to Killorglin and I was in Tralee. We have spent the past eight years in Clonakilty from where I travel every week to Killarney to play. I was transferred to Cork city when Liam was transferred to Clonakilty. I was doing relief work and it necessitated a lot of travel. This was very difficult. Although the money was good, life in general wasn't. After six months I resigned in 1987 and I returned in 1993 as a temporary official.

During that spell off work, things didn't work out in that when I had all the time in the world to play, the hand injury came against me. I kept trying to play but it was a constant battle. I was playing off three handicap, and had recovered from the accident. This 1994 season began to take-off well with the Cork Scratch Cup in April. I ended up joint second, only a shot out. I began to feel that things might begin to go well and then, unfortunately, I had a miscarriage in May. That put me out of it. I was neither physically nor mentally capable of playing serious golf.

Kerry has some magnificent courses. In the north of the county there is Ballybunion, ranked among the top five courses in the world by all the major golf magazines. I have a great love for Ballybunion. One of my first Irish Senior Close Championships was in Ballybunion in 1977. I just qualified and I was up against Mary McKenna, the top Irish golfer in the first round. I was thirteen at the time. I remember saying to my father before I went out that I would be lucky if I managed to make it past the tenth hole. I played very well and a lot of people still talk about that match. She beat me on the eighteenth. It was a tremendous tussle and there was a huge gallery. Without doubt that must have been one of the most memorable matches of my career. Mary McKenna won the Irish Close that year.

When I entered the bank afterwards we met on many occasions, as Mary played number one for Bank of Ireland and I played number one for AIB. We had some major struggles in the inter-bank competition. I remember one year in Rosslare it all hung on our game and it went to the twentieth and I eventually holed a ten foot putt to win. Mary O'Connor from Mallow was another very good golfer in the banks' teams. She played for the Ulster Bank. The three of us often ended up battling it out and these Inter-Bank Championships were every bit as exciting as the Interprovincials. I always looked up to Mary McKenna. Clarie Hourihan was another super player I admired.

Coming from Killarney, I am more a parklands rather than a links player, so I have a love-hate relationship with places like Ballybunion. But it is a fine course. The hole I love there is the eighth, a short par three. It has broken my heart many a time. It is very deceptive. The eighteenth is also a fine hole and it is hard to work out the green. I find

Tralee very long. There is a beautiful par three across the cliff. A fine hole. Dooks is a course I play a lot. It is a very underestimated course. In my opinion it is a super course. I also love Waterville, but my favourite course outside of Killarney is Little Island in Cork. I think it is the most well set-out golf course. Every hole is testing and it is a cross between an inland and a links course. When the wind blows there, you never know what is going to happen.

There is an issue about cheating on the golf course nowadays. I can't understand these people. It's like people trying to hang on to their handicap so they can win the Captain's Prize. Certainly the people who cheat, that is their problem. I couldn't identify with that kind of behaviour on the golf course. I never went out to win as such. For me, getting my handicap down was a big thing, an achievement. I found it good for my morale. People now get so serious about golf, they forget that it is a game. I enjoy my golf and I wouldn't play it otherwise. The day I stop enjoying it is the day I won't play anymore.

I contemplated turning professional in the early eighties when I was getting frustrated about not getting on the International side. I thought about going to America and having a go at the professional circuit. I had looked at basing myself in Florida where I had some friends. I met Liam around the same time and, on thinking about it, I felt I wasn't hard enough for the professional ranks, and looked on golf as a game and something to be enjoyed. I don't think I could get my bread and butter out of it. I wouldn't be able to take it seriously enough.

I enjoy living in Clonakilty and there is a lovely club there. The only drawback is that it is a ninety minute drive to Killarney. I often stay over with my parents when I go to Killarney to practise. Looking ahead, the Irish Close is being held in Little Island in 1995 and I am now preparing myself for that. If I could do well there, I might get myself back on the Irish team. That is my thinking and we have the Curtis Cup in Killarney in 1996. The Curtis Cup is the equivalent of the men's Walker Cup, Great Britain and Ireland against the United States. It would be a real dream come true to play Curtis Cup in Killarney. But you never known, a lot of hard work and a miracle or two. I never give up, not until I have to.

JOHN O'DONOGHUE

(FIANNA FÁIL TD)

I don't believe Republicanism is simply Nationalism, because that would be too narrow a focus for it. It embraces Nationalism, but Republicanism is best defined by Wolfe Tone when he spoke of the unification of Catholic, Protestant and Dissenter. A Republic, to me, tolerates the other point of view, accepts the need for social justice and looks to the day when we have a sovereign government in charge of the entire country. It is a philosophy which embraces an entire people and expresses their ethos in its legislation.

I have said before that I believe that at the heart of Unionist intransigence is the knowledge that as a matter of justice, ultimately, unity must come. You ask where I stand on divorce. I would have reservations about its passage, but I would not take it upon myself to be the guardian of anybody's conscience about his or her marital difficulties. Therefore I would leave it to the people to make their decision on a matter as sensitive as that and accept that decision. I foresee, personally, a considerable amount of difficulties in Irish society leading from the introduction of divorce. I can understand why people, trapped in miserable marriages, want to escape from them. But I really believe in the final analysis the question of whether one should legislate for the minority or legislate for the majority is one of the most difficult tests of any society or of any democracy. In those circumstances I will leave it to the good sense of the Irish people and I will not be campaigning for or against.

With regards to what is euphemistically known as the 'liberal agenda', there are people who would have you believe that there is tremendous support in this country for the introduction of abortion and that there is tremendous support for the decriminalisation of homosexuality. I don't believe there is, that there was or that there will be such support. There is a need for the legislators to reflect the ethos of their people. I do not believe that introducing legislation such as the decriminalisation of homosexuality, or the introduction of legislation for abortion, reflects the ethos of the Irish people.

There was a whip on with regard to the decriminalisation of homosexuality and I adhered to the whip, but I had reservations in relation to it for this reason. In any society minorities have rights. But it is sometimes forgotten that majorities have rights also. Clearly, when these rights conflict, the acid test is this: will you, by legislating for the minority, so interfere, so grossly interfere with the rights of the majority, that they are unable to practise what they consider to be the normal moral code? I believe when that point is reached you legislate for the majority, for the very simple reason that hard cases make very bad law, and anyway, that is what democracy is all about.

I don't have anything against homosexuals, but I want to know if it is the right signal to send down to young people. I was against that as I don't like the idea of a fifty-year-old man going into a bar and it being perfectly legal for him to proposition a seventeen year old boy. I don't think that is a great signal to send to young Irish people. I am not standing on any high moral ground on this. What I am saying is that, as a legislator, one has not just a duty to this generation, but beyond it, to reflect the ethos of society and to do what is best for it and all of the lessons learned in other countries must be brought to bear on these decisions. Let's leave religion aside, and let's deal with the issues of human rights and social justice. If religion happens to coincide with those views, fair enough. In most cases, religion does. But I am not speaking, if you like, from a religious fervour, though I would regard myself as a practising Catholic; I am speaking here from the premise of social justice, human rights and doing the right thing by the Irish people. And however unpopular the right thing is, it must be done.

In the case of the decriminalisation of homosexuality, we were dealing with a peripheral issue to the substantive issue like abortion. But I do not think that Fianna Fáil is set to abandon its substantive position in Irish life. I don't believe the membership will allow that to happen, and I take great issue with certain people who say dismissively of the Fianna Fáil voter, 'Ah, sure they have nowhere else to go. We can do it anyway'. You cannot be dismissive of anybody and in particular you can never be dismissive of the Fianna Fáil voter. There are always places to go. Always.

I would not describe myself as a conservative and I often make the joke that the only liberals left in this country are the conservatives. In every walk of life, you find, unfortunately, like it or lump it, the sheep mentality. And that is true of politics as well. Sometimes when proposals are put forward, rather than speak their minds, some people will say nothing, whilst privately agreeing with you afterwards. I find that one of the most aggravating' things about political life in this country. Invariably, and very often to my cost, I call it as I see it.

In the final analysis, I believe there is a broad mass of the Irish people who would be very deeply concerned about laws not reflecting their ethos. Unfortunately, a considerable amount of legislation in this country is reactive to certain journalists' columns. That has been an unfortunate aspect of Irish political life for some time. Some people saw the success of the Labour party at the last general election as a vote for abortion, as a vote for divorce, as a vote for the decriminalisation of homosexuality. Now I have very little doubt but there is a relatively well-heeled section of Irish society in a tiny minority, but which nonetheless is very opinionated and vocal, which would have voted for Labour for those reasons. But I believe the majority of those who voted for the Labour party, did not vote for it for these reasons. They voted for Labour because they wanted a change of government. That is my personal opinion.

There is a silent majority out there in Irish society and that majority in my humble opinion does not want to radically alter the ethos of this society and change it into another London or another Liverpool or another New York. And that is their right. Here in Leinster House, unfortunately, all too often when these issues have arisen in the past, some people have stayed silent, despite the fact that they knew that their constituents, in the main, were against certain measures.

The big problem is that all too often the silent majority stays silent and only becomes vocal when the event has occurred. In relation to abortion, which I feel very strongly about, I do not believe there is any room for any politician in Leinster House to stay silent in relation to what his or her opinion is. It will be, and is, their duty to act in accordance with what they consider to be the right thing to do and not because some newspaper tells them what to do. I think you will find more of that in Irish politics in the future. The dawning of the so called 'liberal agenda' may well have been the catalyst for that. Pragmatic compromises have had to be reached in this partnership government, but I think when we approach certain core issues conflict may arise, and that may well be the day of the parting of the ways.

I have to say you have some very fine people in journalism and others, unfortunately, who articulate a certain opinion with a view to getting a certain momentum going to achieve what is their own self-opinionated objective. There are certain columnists in certain newspapers who are of that ilk. Within RTE, which is paid for by the taxpayer, you have people who wish to have a certain line pushed or followed. Whether these are opinions gleaned from hectic student days, or whether they are opinions gleaned for a need to be 'modern', or just to be different, it is difficult to tell. But it is extremely difficult to articulate the views of the silent majority, because the minute it is done one finds that a black shawl, to use imagery, is thrown over the person concerned.

One often finds some of those who propagate what they consider to be the liberal agenda, are in fact themselves the most illiberal, intolerant people you could wish to meet. Those with the opposite view, in their eyes, are red-necked, backwoods men, conservatives of inferior intellect, ill-read, uneducated and generally bores to boot. I have rarely been asked by RTE on to a major programme. I wouldn't have a sexy enough image for some of the fellows out in Donnybrook; but if I held different views, you can bet your bottom dollar that I would be on.

I think Fianna Fáil was never suited to coalition. Circumstances have led it into coalition and in relation to certain policies there had to be pragmatic compromises. But the facts are that when the crunch comes, be it in relation to the National question, or in relation to extremely serious issues such as abortion, Fianna Fáil will ultimately, despite the predictions of many, stand by its core principles. That it has to do.

When I spoke in the Dáil in relation to the decriminalisation of homosexuality, I was not speaking against any group of people. I was saying that the practice of homosexuality in society is not in accordance with the natural law. In the same way, the performing of abortions is not in accordance with the natural law. The divorce issue is different from the abortion issue as we are not talking about the very essence of existence but about a social problem, as opposed to the extermination of life at its most innocent.

I was born in Caherciveen in May, 1956, and I was one of a family of seven. My father, Daniel, who had been immersed in the Civil War and joined Fianna Fáil at its foundation, became, ironically, an Independent member of Kerry County Council in 1960. His roots were very much Fianna Fáil and in 1964 when he died, my mother, Mary, was co-opted onto the Council as a Fianna Fáil member. She was expecting her seventh child at that time. She retained that seat on the Council until 1985 and during her term she was Chairman for a year. I entered the Council when she retired from politics. When I went for the County Council in 1985, on the retirement of my mother, I headed the poll. The Dáil election of 1987 saw me once again on the election trail and this time I won a seat and I have been in the Dáil since.

My mother had an enormous influence and I suppose she is the quintessential Kerrywoman. She typifies the resilience of the county, and I don't say that in any boastful way. I would have to look to her as a role model. There she was, a few years after my father's death, with seven young children, facing a local election when it was not fashionable for women to be in politics. She had a little bar and drapery shop on the side of the street in Caherciveen. She also continued on my father's other interests such as insurance, auctioneering and a bit of hackney-car driving in order to raise the family.

She did all that and that is testimony to a person of great determination, tremendous dedication and absolute commitment. Few others have done it, and I suppose that I was imbued with a tremendous respect for women in public life and respect and fondness for young people who find themselves disadvantaged through lack of one or other parent at an early age. I was eight when my father died. The youngest would have been six and then my mother had her seventh child four months after my father's death.

After national school and secondary school at the Christian Brothers, I went on to study law at UCC. In my young days growing up I would have developed a fierce sense of justice and I don't say that in any boastful way. And that would have led me to the Law. Also I had an ambition, even at national school, to one day become a TD for South Kerry and I felt that law would be a good base to begin in politics.

After qualifying in 1978 when I was twenty-one, I went to work with Michael Tynan & Company, solicitors, in Limerick where Greg Tynan was in charge. I stayed there until October, 1980, returning home with the committed purpose of standing for the Dáil at the earliest opportunity. I think I might have been a far wealthier man if I had stayed with Mr Tynan! I opened my practice in Caherciveen. I married Kate Anne Murphy in February, 1982, the day after the election count when I was narrowly defeated for the second time in a Dáil election. She is a solicitor and we met in college. Her father, Michael Pat Murphy, was a Labour TD for more than thirty years and Minister of State in a Labour/Fine Gael coalition government.

I staunchly supported Mr Haughey and when Mr Reynolds became Taoiseach he replaced me as Minister of State in the Finance Department where I had been appointed by Mr Haughey three months earlier. While in Finance I was in charge of the Office of Public Works. I found this absorbing and I was disappointed to lose it. In political life you have to take the rough with the smooth. I had received knocks before and I think I took that one well too.

I admired Mr Haughey greatly and few men of this century were more committed to this country and its people than Charlie Haughey.

There is a song which says, 'follow the fellow who follows a dream', and Mr Haughey had a vision of this country with which I could identify. A lot of people at grassroots Fianna Fáil could identify with it. It was a vision of a Republic, of a just society, of a society which made up its own rules and did not ape and copy the rules of any other country for the sake of doing so – like the *Belgrano* incident.

Haughey expressed a sovereignty and pride in the country which was exceptional in its intensity and which made one feel proud. You knew he would never let you down, and he never did.

You ask if I am worried about the problems facing a place like South Kerry? I am worried. I think that a tremendous injustice was perpetrated on South and West Kerry when the railway lines leading to Dingle and Valentia Harbour were taken up. I recall seeing the last train leave Caherciveen around 1960 and with it went the hopes and dreams not just of that generation, but the subsequent generations as well. It led to depopulation, emigration and migration. The constituency has been picking up the pieces ever since. The challenge is how to replace traditional industries and rebuild the confidence of the people. We have had tremendous success in tourism. But until there is in this country a proper land use policy, I foresee a continuing drift from the land into the centre. Every town in Kerry today sees its population increase and every rural area sees its population decline. If you pay people to leave land idle, then in the next generation, you will see a frightening flight from the land which will be so colossal that it will make the present situation look like a trickle.

Brussels never seriously considered small farmers on small holdings and never appreciated their way of life. It is equally true that a more educated young Irish population has not been prepared to live as frugally as their fathers and mothers did. And that is understandable. But there has to be a system introduced which will again make land productive. I regard it as my duty while I am here to advise my own party leadership and bureaucracy of the problems that exist and that they must be resolved. In certain ways I have had my moments, and these would include roadways, industries, the development of Dingle Harbour and Farranfore Airport etc where I have had an input. Things happen in cycles and there is evidence now that the cycle is beginning to come back in favour of South Kerry, despite the appalling problems caused by European regulations which take little or no account of the small men and women of this world.

AENGUS FANNING

(NEWSPAPER EDITOR)

WHILE I love Kerry I don't know if I would want to live there all year around. At times I hanker for it and say, 'Why am I here at all, why am I not down there ?' And yet I talk to people in Kerry and they say, 'You would go mad if you were living here all year around'. It's a dilemma always. I don't think you ever fully adjust to Dublin. I go down to either West Kerry or Waterville every summer. My brother has a house in Annascaul and I go there when it is vacant. My mother lives in St Brendan's Park, Tralee.

Since moving away from Kerry for so many years I have become very conscious of the difference between Kerry people and other counties. We are a very lively people. You hear people who move to New York tell you that they are energised. Kerry is an energiser. People are active and they stimulate one another. They are actually open people. There is one great myth of the cute Kerryman. I think they are less cute than most and very open. I have often wondered about this and do you know what I put it down to? I say what happens is that somebody comes down to Kerry from Dublin and is dealing with some fellow out in Dingle, say, and yer man is so open and innocent, almost, and then he finds out along the line somewhere that the fellow isn't an eejit at all and then says, 'Isn't that fellow a cute bastard?'

Kerry people are not guarded – they speak very openly, by and large. Again, there are exceptions. People like Brendan Kennelly and John B Keane wear their hearts on their sleeve all of the time. There is a very open culture in West Kerry. The one thing I cannot understand is why unemployment is so high in the county. The standard in schools has always been very high in Kerry. Most of the lads in our time would have skated through this points system.

On the subject of education, one man I like to remember is a teacher, Jim Bailey, who was from Dingle. He was an English teacher in Tralee and I found I related very well to him. He was always encouraging me and was very good that way. He was exceptional and open minded, was away ahead of his time.

I was born in Tralee in 1943 and my father was a school teacher; his name was Arnold P Fanning. He lived in Tralee for upwards of fifty years prior to his death in 1980. He taught mathematics in the Technical School. He was a playwright and one of his plays was put on in the Abbey in 1932 when he was only twenty-seven. It was Cyril Cusack's first Abbey part. My mother, Clara, was from the North of Ireland. Her maiden name was Connell. They met in Newry where my father got his first teaching job after graduating. She was a Presbyterian and became a convert to Catholicism. They married in Dublin and then moved to Tralee. The others in the family are my oldest brother Rio, he lives in London and is a scriptwriter for the TV series Eastenders; then there is Brian in Dublin; and another brother Patrick is in Donegal in the Customs and Excise. I have a sister, Betty McDonnell in Oak Park, Tralee. Her husband died years ago very young of a heart attack. He had a farm outside Tralee and the family had a butcher's shop, in the town. My youngest brother Connell is Economics Professor in UCC.

I started school at Edward Street National School and then went on to the CBS Secondary School. Tony Kennedy, the Senior Counsel, was in my class and so were Dermot Kelly from Strand Street and Seamus Roche – he lived up in Clash – and Tony McMahon. The reason I remember him is that he had the same birthday as myself. I played gaelic football for the Austin Stack's Club and I played for the Kerry Minors for two years, 1960 and 1961. We were beaten in the Munster Final each year by Cork. I played centre-field. Joe Joe Barrett, the *Evening Herald* gaelic games writer, would have been a contemporary of mine. The late Alan Conway was also on the team. The two teams in those two years were almost completely different. The first year there were people like Alan Conway and Pat Dowling, that's Jack Dowling's brother, a good player. John O'Shea from Boherbue was on the team. Wearing the green and gold in Kerry is always something which is highly regarded by the individual and by the sporting public. I played once for the senior side in the *Gaelic Weekly* tournament. We played Fermanagh at Irvinestown and I remember I got a goal and a point. I was at right half-forward. They were short a number of players and they brought on a few minors. Players like Paudie Sheehy and Dave Geaney played that day. Niall Sheehy also played.

I always regret that I didn't keep up my football. You see I went on to College at UCC then and I drifted away from football because I used to go over to England during the summer, working. I played Sigerson Cup football down in UCC during the winter time. I did Commerce in UCC. I liked Cork. If a fellow could bring two hundred pounds back after the summer in England it was a big thing. These would be fellows who worked seven days a week, night shifts all summer. I never really came back with money, but I suppose I supported myself.

I used to spend some summer holidays in Birr where my grand-mother lived when I was young. My grandmother was Annie Fanning and she owned the *Midland Tribune*. Her father founded it. His name was John Powell. Three curates in Birr raised money to launch a news-paper. They wanted to support general agrarian reform and the nation-alism that was going at the time. That would have been 1882, the era of Parnell and Michael Davitt. My great-grandfather was the manager of that enterprise and within a short time he bought it and took it over himself. I don't know how exactly that happened. Within two years of it starting he owned it. The curates raised the money through public subscription. That part of the country was very strongly Unionist. He wrote quite critically of the Unionist establishment and was often in difficulty with them through libel awards. As far as I know he went to jail quite often.

I was influenced by the newspaper unconsciously during those long summer holidays in Birr when I would have been only a small boy. I used to go out with the reporters and go in the vans delivering the paper. I used sit in at the County Council meetings alongside the senior reporter, Buddy Burke. I would have been ten or so then. As it hap-pened, I remember asking my uncle James (Jimmy) Fanning, who was editor and proprietor of the *Midland Tribune*, about going into journalism. He felt I was quite good at it. I wasn't really single-minded about it, but he felt I should go into journalism. He had a vacancy and I started off as a junior reporter with him. I had always been typing since a kid and I was good at that from the start. I was then after getting a degree at UCC and I started off at seven pounds ten shillings a week. I spent about five years in Tullamore. I worked with Buddy Burke and Geoff Oakley. There were only three reporters at the time. We did everything. You would often do four matches of a Sunday. If there was a backlog of fixtures, you might have two senior games and two junior games.

The reason I decided to move to Dublin was that I wanted to get married. My wife, Mary O'Brien, was from near Birr. She worked in the County Council in Tullamore. They were farmers outside Birr and I met her in Dooly's Hotel one night. I was sitting in the bar. I knew her cousin Mary Lyons and they came in with Cyril Dunne, the Galway footballer. I came over and joined them. They introduced me to Mary. Then I wanted to get married a few years later. At this stage I had gone up to fifteen pounds a week but the *Independent* had a job for twenty five pounds a week. A tenner was an awful lot of money in those days. I came to Dublin in May 1969 and got married in the end of June.

When I came to Middle Abbey Street, Louis McRedmond was the Editor of the *Irish Independent* and Aidan Pender was Editor of the *Evening Herald*. A Tarbert man, Bill Shine, was the News Editor of the *Herald*. Brian Barrett was the Chief News Editor of the group. I was on the *Herald* for a good bit and then I worked on the *Sunday Independent*. Then in 1973 I became agriculture correspondent. The EEC was big news at the time. There were a lot of major stories in agriculture from the EEC and great excitement about all the money to be got in Brussels. We were all writing stories about butter prices, milk prices and beef prices. All the figures seemed to be in millions. You had to work it out from both the farmer's point of view and the consumer's point of view. Food prices were a big thing with the rate of inflation in those days. They started to rise sharply when we joined the EEC. So in any given year food was a big factor in the rate of inflation. The Minister for Agriculture was Mark Clinton and he didn't want anything from the consumer's point of view at all. It was complicated and a lot of it unnecessarily so. They wouldn't tell you how much a pound of butter would go up with an increase. There were increases about four times a year. I found a way of working it out and I used always relate these increases for the farmers back to the price paid by the consumers. Bill Shine wanted me out in Brussels nearly all the time. I was Agriculture Editor up to 1982, and then became News Analysis Editor of the *Irish Independent.*

Then I became Editor of the *Sunday Independent* which I thought was quite staid and male dominated. They had Hugh Leonard, one good asset. Trevor Danker was there and John Devine. There weren't many feature columnists. It was done to a formula that failed to take into account the fact that newspapers cannot compete in giving out news instantly in the way that the electronic media can do. The daily papers were also expanding their feature analyses. The one way print can fight back against the electronic media's instant news is to flesh out issues and provide more interpretation pieces. I found the Sunday coverage was very out of date. I was never one to lay down marvellous strategic plans. I go week to week, month to month. I know what I want and what interests me.

The first thing I wanted to do with the *Sunday Independent* was to feminise the paper. I don't really mean that in the gender sense. I mean to brighten it up with regard to entertainment and softer features, things that did not make huge demands on the reader. We have a mix at the moment. It's wrong to compare a newspaper with a current affairs programme on TV. A newspaper, if you are to compare it with TV, should be compared to a whole evening's viewing encompassing sport, politics, entertainment, a mixture of everything. We are trying to achieve a very mass circulation by Irish standards. We are now selling 252,000 copies every Sunday, which is an awful lot of newspapers.

The first critical appointment I made was Ann Harris as Features Editor. I initially recruited her as a writing journalist, but no sooner was she in than she showed an ability to identify people with potential. My style was to go for established names whether it was Eamonn Dunphy or Gene Kerrigan. She was outstanding at identifying people who were not well known. She saw something in them. People like Declan Lynch, Barry Egan, Brighid McLaughlin, Shane Ross. She brought Terry Keane in.

Ann Harris is a motivator and an inspiration to many younger journalists. She rewrites their copy for them. She nurtures them and tutors them and is patient. I am not good that way because I just don't have the patience. She works with those people and they are very grateful to her as they recognise what she has done.

The first thing you have to do in any business is to survive. You've got to make a profit. There is nothing wrong with that; that is where our jobs come from. I make absolutely no apology for that. My job is to maintain advertising and circulation and increase it if possible; that's where we get our jobs from. Without profit there are no jobs anywhere, public or private. I am a mixture of conservative and radical and I am prepared to push the boat out a little bit as I go along in an incremental way. Essentially I am conservative. My bottom line is circulation and profit because that's how we survive and I see no reason to apologise for that. At the same time I do believe that it doesn't exclude good journalism in its various definitions, whether it's political analysis, humour or entertainment or sport or whatever.

I think a lot of newspapers have gone quite dull, very staid. Even jokes seem to be out. There are so many papers out there that are so humourless; they don't seem to want to lighten people's mood at all and I think they are losing out against other media because of a very conservative policy. Politically correct and always taking themselves very seriously. I am certain a couple of nationals and provincials will go. No good having mighty opinions if you have nobody to talk to.

Sunday is a leisure day. I don't slavishly follow market research. In fact we do a lot less of it than people think. In my time as Editor in the past ten years we have done two bits of market research. What surprised me was that most people regarded Sunday as a boring day. Our research showed that. People have the Sunday lunch, go for a drive, visit the mother. If that's the way it is you have to give them a bit of lively stuff and your newspaper becomes more a magazine. Then it is partly forced on you by the fact that Saturday is not a strong news day. Outside of stories we generate ourselves, there is rarely an automatic news lead from a Saturday. I would say that about four times a year you get an obvious spontaneous lead on a Saturday.

Irish journalists can be out of touch and move in a close circle and write for themselves rather than the wider public. I think most journalists write for their peers. They seem more conscious of peer approval than the customer, the paying punter. I can't claim to be perfect, but my main objective is to try and give the customer value for money. It's a fault in Irish journalism. I am not interested in peers; I don't care what my media colleagues think. They may be correct by their own outlook but not by the market. There are exceptions. I try and keep in touch through instinct mostly – I don't think Kerry people lose their instincts.

JIMMY DEENIHAN

(FINE GAEL TD)

IT was September, 1981, when I went up onto the Hogan Stand to accept the Sam Maguire. It was our four-in a-row. I have heard it said that Garret FitzGerald noted me as candidate material when I made the traditional short acceptance speech. Garret may have previously heard my name mentioned as a possibility for North Kerry, as he appeared to take a keen interest. He gave me the impression that he was supporting Kerry on the day. He made comments about some aspects of the game.

I was first approached to run for politics in February, 1982, when the government collapsed on the Budget vote. However, I was not ready and my ambition did not lean towards politics at that time. I was teaching in Tarbert Comprehensive School and I was looking more to a fifth All-Ireland in-a-row. I didn't take the approaches from Fine Gael very seriously, although they were serious. I was also interested in the idea of doing a post graduate course in physical education in the US. I spoke to the authorities in Berkley College in San Francisco and I began making arrangements to go there.

That 1982 election passed and with it came a change of government. However, it was obvious that the new government would not last long. People were disenchanted with the Fianna Fáil government and there were many incidents. It was the infamous GUBU period.

Later that year, on the last day in May, I was injured during training in Killarney. We had completed the usual session of backs on forwards when Mick O'Dwyer called for one more attack. I somehow got entangled with John Egan and my leg was smashed. It was a triple fracture. My whole life changed with that injury. It ended my inter-county career. Some said that the five-in-a-row went with that injury. Certainly my absence from the side took away some of the cohesion since we were a closely knit unit. Pat Spillane had also been injured for that Final. We had developed a very high level of team understanding right throughout the field. We didn't plan things, we went out and did them.

I knew immediately after the accident that it was all up. I will never forget the ambulance journey between Killarney and Cork. My entire football career and future aspirations were running before my mind. The pain was emotional as well as physical. All my aspirations revolved around football, and now I knew it was to be no more. We were getting ready for the first game of the championship against Clare and all the talk was on winning five All-Irelands in-a-row and all the players wanted to be a part of that historic achievement.

After the injury I was hanging around on crutches during the summer of 1982. I met a number of Fine Gael people while they were on holidays in Kerry and they suggested that I should consider declaring myself for politics. Finbar Fitzpatrick, then general secretary of the party, more or less hounded me on the matter over the summer. As there was a lot of internal tension within Fine Gael in North Kerry at that time, I was doubtful about how well I would be received if I got involved. The party had lost the seat it held up to 1977 when Gerard Lynch was narrowly defeated. He had been first elected in 1969 and re-elected in 1973, so there had been no Fine Gael TD in North Kerry since 1977.

Having returned to school in September of 1982, I found it difficult to teach effectively with the handicap of my injury. It became a much tougher job all of a sudden. I began to reconsider where my future lay. I still was not convinced that I should enter politics. One fateful October day, prior to the 1982 November election, Frank Quilter, the Fine Gael organiser in North Kerry, approached me in the gymnasium in Tarbert and told me I would have to run for the party in the election.

That day the government collapsed, following a vote of confidence in the Dáil. Frank had anticipated the outcome and was already on the road looking for a candidate. He orchestrated a campaign to convince me to run, canvassing many of my close friends, people like Jeremiah

Carroll, the great greyhound man, Tom Quilter, Jim Kenny and others, all of whom encouraged me to run.

The convention was in Tralee on a Saturday. By then a real momentum had developed. This was in the middle of the whole Garret FitzGerald wave. There was a huge crowd: the Parklands was packed. There were big screens displaying Garret delivering his message. The amount of enthusiasm was fantastic. I had a feeling that the party was well organised and I began to warm to the idea of being the candidate. John B Keane made a great speech to get things rolling when he proposed me. There were six candidates and it was hotly contested.

Robert Pierse had run in the previous election and he was all set to run again. If I had known him better at that time I wouldn't have contested the nomination with him, because he is a man that I have developed a great respect for. Two candidates were selected at the convention, myself and Mrs Bernie Gannon from Tralee. I found myself facing a church gate meeting the following morning.

The first problem I had to overcome was the perception that I had nothing to offer in politics except the fact that I was a county footballer. That argument indeed was used by some of my opponents in Fianna Fáil at that time.

Actually, on that first Sunday morning, the day after my nomination, not many people outside of Fine Gael were aware that I was a candidate. One individual, a close friend of mine, Joe Halpin, when he saw me on the platform remarked, 'Are you off your head, boy?'

I contested the election and failed to win a seat by one hundred and forty-four votes. Denis Foley of Fianna Fáil edged me out. If I had been on the road in that campaign two weeks longer, I would have been elected. I polled nearly six thousand votes in a very short campaign. While the Fine Gael party was very enthusiastic, I quickly realised that the party wasn't well organised, especially on election day when we were light on the gound in a number of places.

After that 1982 election I had to make up my mind whether I should go full-blooded into politics or remain teaching. A number of people expected that I would return to teaching, and put politics behind me. However, the challenges that politics presented, from trying to win a seat in North Kerry to developing a command of political issues, direct-ed me to politics.

I was disappointed not to win a seat in the Senate, especially since I thought that the Fine Gael public representatives throughout the coun-try would endorse me, given the vacuum the party was faced with in North Kerry. However, Garret FitzGerald nominated me as one of his eleven appointees to the Senate. I was now a working politician.

I found the Dáil a very strange place when I first went up there. Politicians take getting used to. There are a wide range of different per-sonalities. Most politicians rarely show their hand and express their real feelings, although many of them wish they had by the time they have left politics. Dáil Éireann can be a very artificial place, with its own distinctive culture outside of the chamber, sometimes a culture based on insincerity and flattery. I just wish that all the players would be absolutely sincere and straightforward. We need more straight talk-ers in the Dáil. I think too many people have shaped themselves on models designed by PR people.

Everything that I had learned on the football field proved to be invaluable to me as a politician. Being part of the great Kerry four-in-a-row winning team gave me the motivation and the will to win. It also gave me the confidence to face up to this new challenge. The stamina, the endurance, the patience, the motivation, the discipline, all stood to me in my new career.

Initially, I was totally identified in the footballing context. For a peri-od a local journalist referred to me in political articles as the 'footballer from Finuge', or the 'left corner back from Finuge'. After a period of doubt in the minds of some people, I quickly proved that I was capable of dealing with political issues at local and national level. Now the association with the Kerry team is a positive factor. I am always readily identified, not alone in Kerry but throughout the country. It is ironic that the older I get the more significant my football achievements become.

I have been asked on many occasions to give my opinion on Mick O'Dwyer and the influence he exerted on our team. For me personally, Mick O'Dwyer stood out as a man who was very single-minded and focused. He discarded irrelevant issues very quickly. He had a target, and he expected everyone to work as a team to achieve that target. I admired him for his consistency, punctuality and his own personal discipline. He neither smoked nor drank. I respected him as our trainer. There was no arguing or haggling. He laid down the law and we responded. Players respected him more than feared him. He had the capacity to get maximum commitment from everyone. Players often went beyond what could reasonably be called the 'call of duty' to pull out the stops. The pain barrier was often broken under his influence. Nobody ever wanted O'Dwyer to feel that we did not give one hundred per cent at all times. No player was under any illusion as to what was required.

I have often been asked who I think was the best player of that era, excluding myself of course. I would have to name a few players for different reasons. Owen Liston for his unselfishness and his ball-winning ability, along with his ability to create space and his undoubted skill. John O'Keeffe for his great fielding ability and his defensive qualities. He had great natural strength. I must mention Mikey Sheehy for his sheer skill and perfection. Pat Spillane has to be included on any short-list of greats for his tremendous endurance, kicking ability and tenacity. John Egan for his consistency and scoring ability. It is not an easy question to answer since we developed as a team and there was at no time one particular player to whom the whole team looked for inspiration. We never depended on any one player to carry us. You often find that with teams who have one outstanding player, their success or failure will often depend on the performance of one single individual on the day. That was never the case with our Kerry teams. If I was asked to pick my best team of all time, I would opt for the team which won the four-in-a-row.

North Kerry is like most rural constituencies in that TDs must be a part of the community, available to deal with a wide variety of day-to-day problems with which people find difficulty. TDs must support community initiatives by providing information on entitlements, grants and other financial benefits and incentive packages. Reading up on all aspects of entitlements and keeping informed is an important part of a

Dáil Deputy's job. It is important that TDs should not dominate organisations or communities, but should have a supportive rather than a centre-stage role.

Being brought up on a small farm in and around the village of Finuge, I am very concerned about the future of rural Ireland. If rural society is to survive, national government will have to provide a programme of incentives to encourage people to remain in rural areas. EU policy must also be more responsive to the needs of rural communities and the disadvantages they face living away from the main stream of facilities which urban societies take for granted.

Rural society is also the backbone of our tourist industry and tourists come here for a taste of rural life and to meet with ordinary people. Without people in rural Ireland this attraction will not be present. Initiatives like the Leader Programme will have to be developed further and rural communities will have to be given both the financial backing and expert advice to develop projects that will enhance their economy.

DERMOT CLIFFORD

(ARCHBISHOP OF CASHEL)

It is now eight years since I left Kerry for Tipperary Town. On the morning I was leaving St Mary of the Angels, Beaufort, I was on the verge of tears. A Tipperary nurse who worked there reassured me as follows : 'When you go to Tipperary you will find that the people are more friendly and the spuds are better.' 'We'll see,' I replied.

Part of me is still in Kerry. When you leave Kerry, one of the things you miss is the sea. After a few months in Tipperary I went to Dungarvan to do a confirmation and when I got to the top of a hill and saw the sea, my heart lifted. It was then I realised how much I had missed the sea. I am now sixty miles from the nearest beach in Tramore, County Waterford.

I was born in Rathanny, Ballymacelligott, in 1939. My father was from Milltown and my mother from Killorglin parish. My father had emigrated to the United States around 1922. My mother had also been to America; she stayed four or five years. When my father returned he bought the farm in Ballymacelligott and married my mother in 1935. Although my parents came in from outside, the people of Ballymacelligott never made any bones about that and I never heard the word 'blow-in'. In fact, if anything, we got extra respect, because my parents had been in the USA. There were three children, my sister Gertie, a year or two older, and my younger brother John. Gertie, a primary teacher, is married in Australia and John is a Dominican priest in Dublin.

Before I started school I had what could be called a 'pre-school' year. Miss Mary Bridget Baily, a blind woman, was taken each morning to Mass by members of her family. When the youngest, Paddy Joe, had done his year she asked my mother if I would take her as Paddy Joe was starting school. I took her to the church for the year. I used to meet the priests and I got to like them. She would say her prayers out loud when we had the church to ourselves. She taught me to pray by her very direct approach to God. She would go through all the Baily family one by one, praying at length for each. Then I would bring her home and on the way we would occasionally stop at a neighbour's house.

There was Mrs Reidy who was a very strong Fianna Fáil supporter. That was when I first heard the name 'de Valera'. It was sacrosanct in her house, but there were other houses who did not share her admiration for Dev. She would give me a pinch of snuff and taught me to say 'God rest the dead', as I sneezed. Every now and again she would direct her attention from de Valera to me and say, 'Sit down child'. But the bench was too high for me to reach so I had to stay standing. We didn't discuss politics very much in our house and most of the neighbours did not either. The Civil War had its after effects, with casualties on both sides in the parish. We, being from outside, had the advantage of not being linked with either side.

Mary Bridget Baily had lost her sight in an accident as a young girl. I was four when I guided her on the mile walk to the church each morning. It was better than a year at school. It had a profound effect on me at that impressionable age.

A sequel came years later when I went as a priest to a meeting of the National Council for the Blind in Listowel. Nora Relihan and Elsie Healy were there. As tutors of the blind they knew Mary Bridget well. The Council has kept in touch with me since and I still lead their pilgrimage to Knock each year in June.

There were four teachers in Clogher when I started school in 1944. There was Mrs Lizzy McElligott, the infants' teacher, Mrs Catherine Buckley taught the first and second classes, Mrs Alice O'Connor from Farmer's Bridge taught third and fourth. The Master, Jimmy O'Connor, who is still hale and hearty, taught fifth and sixth classes. I still meet some of my school friends. I remember the daily roll-call. Our names were not in alphabetical order but in the order in which we first came to the school. It went like this: Tomás Ó Greabhas, Donal Ó Súilleabháin,

Micheal Ó Brosnachan, Diarmuid Ó Clumhain... Michael Brosnan lives a stone's throw from the old schoolhouse while Tommy Groves is in Melbourne. Many of my classmates emigrated.

Our hillside farm covered about seventy acres. It was a good dairy farm. My father bought it in a run-down condition and he spent years reclaiming it. He was very hard working and his experience in America had trained him for hard work. In our area many of the farmers were easy going. Their conversation was more likely to centre on football, handball or greyhounds than on farming. When I was old enough to milk cows I did so and I worked at the hay, the corn and the turf. I had a very happy childhood. When you hear people talking nowadays of the forties and fifties you always hear about 'the hard times', but things were getting better for us all the time: electric light, a tractor, a milking machine, a radio and a van, all came at yearly intervals from 1947 to 1955.

Clogher school had a tradition at the County Council Scholarships and the preparatory exam for teacher training. Jimmy O'Connor had a seventh class for these candidates. The successful boys would have gone to Ballyvourney and the girls to Coláiste Íde. Many students who otherwise would have finished school at thirteen or fourteen went on to post-primary because they got a scholarship. The Master took these pupils on Saturdays for an extra few hours tuition. I got a scholarship and took it up at St Brendan's, Killarney. A number of the Ballymac lads went to St Brendan's in those years.

Leaving home for St Brendan's was a very difficult experience. It was my own wish to go there so I couldn't very well complain. I had no way out. I found it lonely in the beginning. Suddenly, I was confined in a school with one hundred and forty other boarders. Food was very scarce. Whereas at home you could go to the press at any time and get a slice of bread and butter, in college you got your three meals a day. But there was good camaraderie and we had groups called 'columns'. The Tralee lads had the 'Tralee column'. The columns kept together for recreation. I was in the Firies column. I should have been in the Tralee one and there was a dispute as to which I should belong. In the Firies column there was the late Tim Lyons, the great Kerry footballer. Liam

Chute went with the Tralee column. He was the only other Ballymac lad there in my first year. Later on a number of others came to join us.

When I went to the 'Sem' I had the priesthood in the back of my mind. Then in my final years I decided that I had a vocation. I enjoyed my time at St Brendan's after I settled down. I played with the college teams and I recall a famous set of matches against St Michael's, Listowel. We played four times and eventually beat them by a point. I remember I was marking Jim MacMahon in one of the games. On that Listowel side also were Jimmy Harmon, Ollie Kearns and Jacques Guerin. It was the Kerry Colleges Final. Eventually it was decided on a very wet St Patrick's Day in Castleisland. The Listowel team received medals also because of the true grit they had displayed. I played left full-back. Donal Coghlan was our captain and Pat Dowling our most stylish player. Tim Gunn also starred, as they put it then.

The one player in our class who went on to distinction on the Kerry team was Donie O'Sullivan. But he wasn't on our team as he didn't develop as a footballer until later. It was only when he came to Maynooth that he really blossomed. I was also very interested in music in St Brendan's. Con O'Sullivan from Gneeveguilla had returned from America and was nicknamed 'Con the Yank'. He was a talented fiddle player. He had learned from Denis 'the Weaver' Murphy who in turn was a pupil of Pádraig Ó Caoimh. I took up the fiddle, but with more enthusiasm than success. But it was a very enjoyable pastime. Con is now a medical doctor in the USA. A neighbour of his in Gneeveguilla, Denis Kelleher, was another classmate of mine who was extremely successful in Wall Street.

At that time in St Brendan's there were eight priests and three lay teachers. Their main strength was in the Classics. They concentrated on Latin and Greek. The school wasn't as strong on subjects like mathematics or science then. Classics got prime time. The President, Fr Christopher O'Neill, was an excellent Greek teacher. He would come into study and take the class out for an hour any time when the mood struck him. People who left St Brendan's then did very well at Classics. Strange to say the Classics are coming back in education in America now. Classical learning was central in Oxford and Cambridge up to

World War II. After that, universities became more concerned with science. I had intended, when going to Maynooth, to study Classics, but because of the need to extend science to St Brendan's, Bishop Denis Moynihan requested me to study science. That was October 1957 and Sputnik 1 was crossing the night skies.

Donie O'Sullivan came to Maynooth with me. We shared a room for a year. On the playing field he had an extraordinary will to win. I have never known anybody who was more convinced that he was going to win and as determined to do so. And he often did so against the odds. He missed the 1962 All-Ireland because he was in Maynooth. Footballers then missed All-Irelands, Minor and Senior, as they returned in early September. It was just your lot and I remember a Galway player sitting down listening to a commentary of Kerry and Galway in the All-Ireland of 1959. Galway were being trounced and he was beside himself. Obedience was an important part of the priest's training then.

Compared with life at St Brendan's, things improved when I went to Maynooth. There were more things to do, student societies, plays, an orchestra, a college magazine and so on. Seven Kerry students went to Maynooth that year and six were ordained. These were Bill Radley, Brendan Harrington, John Shanahan, Roger Kelliher, Michael O'Leary and myself. They are all working in the diocese of Kerry. At least a dozen others went to study at different seminaries. One professor in Maynooth, Fr Michael Casey, a Dominican, was very kind to me in the science class. I recall that when he was recovering from a heart attack he used to give six of us chemistry lessons from his bed in the Infirmary as the exams were approaching. He now lives contentedly in retirement there at ninety-one.

There were usually two Kerry students in the Irish College in Rome and I went there again at the request of Bishop Moynihan, in 1960. I was very sad to be leaving Maynooth but, in the event, it was a very exciting time to be in Rome with the Second Vatican Council (1962-1965). I was ordained on February 22nd, 1964, in St John Lateran's Basilica by Cardinal Traglia. There were eight from the Irish College ordained that day. I was the only Kerryman. The Rector of the College then was Dr Donal Herlihy of the Kerry diocese, who became Bishop of Ferns afterwards. My parents and sister attended the ordination, but my brother John, who was studying with the Dominicans at the time, was not allowed to come. I stayed on in Rome until the end of June, 1964 when I did the STL examination.

As I said, it was a most exciting time with the Vatican Council in progress. Rome was full of ferment. It was said beforehand that it would be a quiet affair, that very few changes would be made. At the outset, there was a contest between those who wanted change and those who did not. Pope John XXIII intervened on behalf of those who wanted change. The mood of change was palpable among the students especially.

My first appointment on returning was as science teacher at St Brendan's. I was also Dean of Discipline for eight years. During my second year I did the H Dip at UCC, driving up and down each day. Val Rice from Abbeydorney, now Professor of Education at Trinity College, gave us first-class lectures. Another Kerryman there was the late Con Burns from Rathmore who was extremely helpful.

After eight years in St Brendan's I went to the London School of Economics. I was sent there by Bishop Eamonn Casey as he wanted someone qualified in Social Science. This was another great change for me but it was very stimulating. One famous Professor there, Richard Titmuss, impressed me very much. I did the MSc and came back to Kerry as Secretary of the Diocese in 1974. So I had the advantage of studying the three main disciplines, Classics, Physical Science and Social Science as they came to – and went from – prominence.

During my years as secretary I lived at St Mary of the Angels in Beaufort where I came in contact with a very special community. It was a second home to me.

I was ordained Bishop on March 9th, 1986 and then I was installed here in Thurles on the 12th September, 1988, the feast of St Ailbe, when Dr Thomas Morris retired. While I was Coadjutor I lived in Tipperary town for over two years where I was made to feel very much at home. They rightly pride themselves that Tipperary is 'the home of the stranger'. Being Archbishop is not a lonely life. In fact, it is often difficult to get time for oneself. I tend to go to a lot of different functions, socials, meetings, GAA games and then there are people calling during the day. My daily routine is to get up about 7.30 am and hear the News at eight. Then I say Mass, either in the house or in the Cathedral. Then I deal with correspondence. I get two morning papers. Sometimes I don't have time to read them until the evening. The first thing I look at is the deaths' column. It can involve a funeral later in the day. I read the leading articles and the letters and the sports page, the football and hurling of course. Nowadays, my interest in hurling has outstripped my interest in football.

When I came to Tipperary there was gloom on the hurling front. They envied Kerry's long run of successes in football and longed for the return of hurling glory. They hoped I had brought some of the Kerry luck. I did all I could to encourage the revival. It was particularly happy from my point of view that it was in Killarney that Tipperary won their first Munster title in seventeen years and Richard Stakelum declared, 'The Famine is over'.

When there are Confirmations I usually leave the house around 10 am. It's a very important day for the family, the school and the parish. It is very satisfying as I meet the children and their parents on a very happy occasion. At that age, children are spontaneous and unspoilt. I have a set homily which I prepare before the Confirmation season. I alter it a little as I go along. When speaking to children I try to include a story always. They will remember the story and tell it to others.

A priest has to speak at Mass sixty times a year and to try to vary the homily is quite a challenge. It's easy to make a great impression on a particular subject. I try and apply the readings to what is happening in present day life. It is the most difficult thing I have to do – preparing homilies. I put a lot of work into them, especially at Easter and Christmas and for special occasions.

I get on very well with the local media in Co Tipperary. When I was in Kerry I had very good relations with *The Kerryman* and other local papers. In Co Tipperary the local papers are in private ownership. I think local ownership is vital. The Dublin papers are competing with each other and with the English papers now coming in. The arrival of the cheaper tabloids from the UK has led to a lamentable fall in standards here. It is almost impossible to get a spiritual message into our national media any more. Anything of a spiritual nature is carefully excised from your script. The media tend to confine their interest to political and social messages and they seek a political angle everywhere. I sometimes muse on how the media would present the Beatitudes if they got the exclusive on them from the author Himself!

The national media are continually seeking controversy or conflict. While the plain people of Ireland respect religious values, that is not reflected in the media. Neither is their overall decency and their desire for standards. The national papers ought to aim higher and raise people's intellectual level and morale rather than go down market and downhill after the tabloids.

Carl Bernstein of Watergate fame made a very trenchant criticism of the news media last year when he visited Ireland. He described the media as 'a ravenous sensation and scandal machine which is consuming decent journalism and relegating truth to a new kind of pornography'. His remarks got very little coverage here.

An example was how Pope John Paul II's encyclical *Veritatis Splendor* was treated. The media here picked up the hostility of the media abroad. Long before it came out they had dismissed it. The Holy Father is Christ's Vicar on earth; you would never think so from reading the papers here. As a human being he is superior to most world leaders. He has made an extraordinary contribution to the history of this century. If the leader of any other church or religious grouping were treated like the Holy Father is in the national media there would be a national outcry.

One thing which many people in Thurles will be glad to see is an end to Féile. Féile is an orgy. There is the rock concert in Semple Stadium. In Liberty Square the behaviour of thousands of young people is unacceptable in a civilised town. I should be ashamed if people I respected called to see me while it is in progress. To try and explain to outsiders that this event is run by the GAA of which I am patron puts me in a very embarrassing position.

Young people coming here to Féile will not go home the same

persons. Many of the local people here have been scandalised by the goings on. It was frequently said by parents that some were 'behaving like animals'. Many youngsters who came here drank for the first time and many were lured into taking drugs. A serious outbreak of drugs in a college two hundred miles from here was traced to Féile and six boys in their final year were expelled. Things go on in the streets at Féile for which you would be arrested in any other town at any time and in Thurles at any other time. It would appear that the Gardaí have decided to try and humour the crowds and are happy once there is no violence. I seriously considered my position as patron of the GAA. I decided to stay on because of the enormous influence for good which the games have on our young people generally. Féile has brought shame on the name of the GAA in the town of its birth.

Getting back to my earlier story: The Tipperary nurse in Beaufort married a Castleisland man and I officiated at her wedding in her native parish near Thurles. I recall her promise about the people being more friendly and the spuds being better in Tipperary. 'Mary,' I said, 'you were half right.'

DENIS BROSNAN

(MD OF KERRY PLC)

A lot of the major companies have their own ethos or culture and I suppose Kerry Plc has developed its own over the past twenty years. It's hard to describe. It's a set of standards which are common to everybody in the organisation and we would say those standards are absolute honesty in everything they do and very hard work. We tell everybody, 'Don't join us unless you want to work hard'. And of course that gives great opportunity. It's the excitement, it's the buzz, the keeping of those high standards that brings huge respect everywhere. We have respect among customers, in government, everywhere we go, and that has stood to us over twenty years.

We now have about seven thousand employed, roughly half in Ireland, about two thousand five hundred in the UK and about one thousand five hundred elsewhere.

We started from a caravan outside Listowel in 1972. We rented that for twenty pounds a week. Hugh Friel, myself and others, thirteen in all, we lived in that cramped space for about eighteen months. The organisation has changed, my job has changed. My job now is spending a lot of time with people, all the management in the organisation trying to teach them to do their job better. In the early years I could do it all myself, so I have had to change roles very significantly. But the difficult thing is to keep the excitement there. It's like a winning team going on to win the All-Ireland, trying to keep the buzz and the excitement amongst all the key people. Because if that dies, the organisation stops and things go down. If I can't keep excited I can't keep everybody else excited about their job. There are times when one can get very tired. It's hard to know how you achieve it. I think being Kerry and being a Kerryman helps achieve more because we don't give up easily and we try and set new goals for a number of years down the road. So we have our goals set for the next four or five years and if I don't drive on the organisation to meet them, they certainly won't be met. But it becomes harder to drive oneself as well.

We have production facilities in Ireland, Britain, Germany, Canada, Mexico and the USA. And of course we have sales offices in many countries outside of that. We recently moved into Mexico. We planned it for four or five years by taking Mexicans on board in our own organisation and actually training them to think like Kerrymen.

We have Mexican Kerrypeople or Kerry Mexicans, whatever way you want to put it. But they have all the same set of standards or values as any other Kerry person. And that is what they are carrying to Mexico with them.

Remember when we moved to America back in 1982, we moved in about ten of our top Irish people just to introduce the Kerry way of doing things among the Americans. These Americans are now more Kerry than the Kerry people themselves. That's the culture that binds us all together. We are now getting teams of people together to take on the Pacific Rim from Singapore to Taiwan. We have a few people on board and we will have more Kerry Chinese and Kerry Malaysians shortly.

We feel we have the edge being from Kerry. Maybe we are biased, but that is what we harnessed back in the early 1970s. We harnessed Kerry farmers and people to come together. And right through to 1986 when Kerry Plc, Kerry farmers and workers took shares and they are all as interested in what is taking place in Mexico as perhaps the institutional share holders. So that pride, that togetherness is still there. And long may it remain.

We want our people everywhere to think like Kerry people and to be as much fired up as people going off to win the All-Ireland except in business you have to do it over a long period. To win the All-Ireland it is a one year scene. To be successful in business, you have to do it every year for the next ten.

I would say I haven't changed that much. We have kept our heads all the way through. We have believed in our own ability and that is perhaps myself and other senior managers. We always did it our way. I

think people are always saying about the Kerry organisation is, 'What will they do next?' because we always either come up with the stroke of genius breaking new ground. But we do it our way and we don't do it out of the textbook. We are deeply involved in the training and development of people. But perhaps while others were discovering this elsewhere in the world, we discovered it in Kerry and used it in the full.

Take the hierarchical management systems with layers of management – we decided fifteen years ago that layers of management did not work. We flattened out the whole management structures. They write books about it now. We practised it fifteen years ago. Most of the training is done in-house. I spend a lot of my time just working, training and developing the management.

I read a lot to keep up-to-date with what is happening, there is no great mystique about managing properly. Good management is about doing simple things properly, telling people how not to make mistakes. A lot of it is just to keep playing the game and the ball will eventually end up in your hands in front of the goal. And you have to have somebody there to score at that time. So that's what management is all about. Don't try and make it overelaborate.

We are in the era of legal contracts, but it is more important if you make an agreement with somebody, whether legal, verbal or otherwise, that you stick by it. Too often nowadays somebody makes an agreement and, if something is not written into the fine print, the person may then try and find their way out. Kerry Plc never does that.

We have about six thousand farmers who are both milk suppliers and shareholders and they own through the co-op fifty-four per cent of the Plc and then a lot have Plc shares in their own right. The farmers are very involved there and as management we enjoy that and the farmers do as well. We listen to the farmers at area advisory meetings and have a pint in the pub afterwards and that keeps one's feet on the ground. We work tightly to five-year plans. So we have plans from now to the end of the decade and that plan will take Kerry Plc around the world spread out more internationally.

We wouldn't say that it has gone beyond our wildest dreams. We take every year as it comes and what we are saying is that over the next five years you will see Kerry Plc manufacturing operations in Chile or Argentina, in China, Singapore or Taiwan. That is going to happen and we are preparing the people to make sure it happens. Kerry has two businesses: branded foods which is putting products on the supermarket shelves and the other one is food ingredients which is providing specialist seasoning, spices and other ingredients to food manufacturers. On the food branding we are very much Ireland, UK and Northern Europe orientated and on the ingredients side we are international.

Kerry is going to expand far more in the ingredients sector because of the international opportunities. In food we are confined to Europe, whereas in ingredients we can travel around the world. As a food company, we are about fiftieth in size in Europe. Being large in Ireland does not make you big in the European context. I think it would be wishful thinking to imagine into the future local industries centring around the local creamery making butter or whatever. That has all gone and will never come back. What I am giving a bit of my own time to is trying to keep rural Kerry alive through tourism development. The Kerry Group put a huge amount of money into Kerry Airport to make it a reality and we are putting a lot of money into various tourism projects in Kerry. Rural Kerry will stay alive out of tourism and not out of agriculture.

Kerry Airport will have its new facilities and runway ready by the time these words see the light of day and it will be then a question of marketing. Our sales pitch is that Kerry has the greatest number of hotel beds and tourism facilities in Ireland. So you might as well fly straight in to where they are and be in your hotel room in ten or fifteen minutes. That will give us a major marketing plus and we will use it to the full.

Other airports will fight back but that is good as it will help bring more people to Ireland. The more airports you have in the South West the more tourists you will bring in, and that's good. The airport of which I am chairman is one part of the tourism strategy for Kerry. Fifteen million pounds has been spent on Kerry Airport to date from its green field site. Little of that has come from the State. Half has come from Europe and the other half has come from private shareholders which is a great tribute to Kerry people. Lots of other money has been invested by Shannon Development and the Tourism Board for Water World and in the many hotel rooms and tourist related businesses in Kerry.

The tourism season continues to widen. It isn't just selling a hotel bedroom, it is selling the activities a tourist can avail of when he or she comes to Kerry whether it is playing golf or enjoying the scenery, mountain climbing or whatever. There is lots to do, but it has never been packaged in Kerry. It's a pity. If we were all twenty years younger, and if we were doing Kerry Tourism like we did Kerry Co-op, it would have been a great challenge.

If we are to keep Kerry alive as a county and keep our young people there, it will come from tourism related activity. Not out of farming.

I am chairman of Swing, the golf promotion group. It is not just Kerry, but Limerick and Clare as well. A huge amount of money has been spent over six years by Swing promoting the Swing courses as being the best in the world: Ballybunion, Lahinch, Waterville, Tralee, Killarney, Dooks, Dingle, Shannon and Dromoland. We know they are among the best in the world.

We have stayed out of the national golf partnership which is promoting all Irish golf courses. We think that you can't go out and sell on that basis. It's almost like us trying to sell Denny's Gold Medal sausages and saying if you don't like them, we have a substitute which you can also eat and they will keep you from getting hungry. It would do nothing for the Swing courses. They are known internationally as being among the best in the world and there is no point in packaging poor quality courses with them. The Americans come and want the best and buy the best airline seats, stay in the best hotels and want to play in the best golf courses. And they are big spenders. We couldn't say, 'Would you play a course which would not meet up with the standards of the Swing courses?'.

Kerry people have a passion for sport and we see that through gaelic football and in other sports in which Kerry people are involved, Moss Keane and Mick Doyle and Michael Galwey in rugby. When they play rugby, Kerry people follow them. We also have great support for horse racing. Sport is an integral part of our lives.

Racing generally has been in decline around the world and in Ireland three years ago when I was asked to chair the Racing Board, I was asked to see what needed to be done to reverse the decline in the fortunes of the industry. I came to the conclusion very quickly that racing was overcentralised while at the same time very fragmented. From early on I concluded that, if we were to have any chance, we needed to do two things, firstly to try and bind the industry together under some new authority, and that is what is now happening, and secondly to bring in more money. The government has now voted to double its contribution to the industry.

Young people go to Galway, Listowel, Tralee, Killarney, the festival meetings and Leopardstown. At Leopardstown there has been a huge investment so young people will go if the facilities are attractive. We have to accept that young people are not going to a lot of the tracks and we have to define what the future of every track is. We can't turn every track into a Leopardstown or a Galway festival meeting. But we have to put on a product which will attract the customers and they are the youth of today.

I am cautious about the future of Irish racing. I would be far more optimistic about the future of the Kerry Plc. It's taken three years to get to where we are, which is just the concept of the new authority. If we continue to move at that pace, other events may overtake us and make life far more difficult. We need to speed up and find answers to what is wrong in the industry.

I am a breeder and I have about fifteen brood mares here. They are sent to some of the top stallions such as Sadlers Wells.

I am also involved in other businesses. How do I manage it ? The week can get very stretched. Swing is organised, so is the Airport. Kerry Plc obviously is, as is the Leisure Holdings. The whole racing industry will take a lot of time to get settled down, but that must happen sooner rather than later. And then I might be able to get back to a more normal life.

I would hope I am a good delegator, because the whole place would collapse if they were waiting for me to appear. I will be in the US next week and then back in the office in Tralee in ten days, but that is the norm rather than the exception. Nowadays, I hardly spend fifty per cent of the time in the office. Saturday and Sunday I stay at home and I try to cut away from the outside world. I walk around and look at the horses, play golf or maybe go racing. Croom House is a lovely place with the River Maigue next door.

I married Joan in 1970. I have been travelling around the world since the age of twenty-four. We have become used to it. That doesn't mean it has become any easier. For twenty-five years I have been at this kind of pace, so Joan has to keep the show running at home.

I chose to live in Croom for a number of reasons. We had been looking at the Rathkeale-Croom area in the early 1980s to try and get a stud farm as I had always been involved in horses. I was also trying to choose a place which was close enough to Kerry and close enough to Shannon Airport. This place came along and we bought it in 1986. It has a very interesting history. It was owned by the Lyons family up to the mid 1940s. They were butter merchants in Cork and came here about 1800 and first of all bought some land from the local landlord, Croker. They built the mills on the river and they built Croom House sometime in the 1820s. They lived here until the 1940s when the person who had it was killed in the war and the executors sold the house. It was sold to a man named Stedman, who got killed in the hunt, but who had married a woman named Audrey and she married afterwards a man named King. She is still alive. Last year we started to restore the house to its former state.

I am a native of Kilflynn, about five miles from Tralee. My parents, Dan and Mary are both dead. My brother James is farming at home and my sister, Angela is teaching in Tralee. She is Mrs Angela Nolan. I was the youngest. The farm is at Fahavane on the main Tralee-Listowel road. I went to national school in Kilflynn. We milked about twenty-five cows then on one hundred and thirty acres and nowadays with modern farming it could carry one hundred cows. We used, when we were very young, get a lift in the horse and cart to school when it was on its way to the creamery with milk. It was typical farming in Ireland in those days, extensive farming, with little use of fertilisers.

We started off in the school under Mrs Roche and then it was Mrs Rice and then the Master, Micheal Lynch, who lives in Kilflynn. Interestingly, one of Mrs Rice's sons, Michael, is now head of the whole computer operation in the Kerry group. I remember there was a great stir when the Springs came to school in Kilflynn, when Dan Spring who was the TD sent his children to stay with their grandparents and they went to school in Kilflynn. So you had Arthur Spring and Dick who went to our school. I don't know if Donal came. Arthur was in my class and Dick was a bit younger. I went to St Brendan's. There was a big debate whether I would cycle to Tralee or go boarding to St Brendan's and it was St Brendan's.

Most of those that time ended up in the Civil Service as you had Michael Dowling, now Secretary of the Department of Agriculture, Timmy Dalton, Secretary of the Department of Justice and Paddy Teahon, Secretary of the Department of the Taoiseach. Boarding school was a difficult place for young people as you left home at twelve and you didn't know what was hitting you. It was tough. We survived and came the better out of it. The food was very basic, bread for breakfast and bread for your tea.

I didn't play football because I never had a football growing up. It was all hurling around Kilflynn and Abbeydorney. We were at a huge disadvantage when we went to St Brendan's where they only played football. So any hurling we would play was when we came home at summer. We all played hurling in the hurling field. We never had a football field in Kilflynn only a hurling field. In St Brendan's you had to fend for yourself and make your own way. Whether that stamped us thereafter I do not know. My father died when I was there and I was sixteen, and my mother died when I was twenty-one.

The effect of my parents dying when I was young meant not knowing them that well, because from the age of twelve we moved to St Brendan's and, apart from summer holidays, you missed the whole home life. When they died, I don't think it had that great effect.

The one teacher I admired most was Fr O'Flaherty, he was different. The rest would either beat Latin or Greek or whatever into you. They used the cane in a big way. All Fr O'Flaherty had to do was look at you. He taught English and was a great teacher. And with his looks and voice he had as much control, if not more, of his class as those who walloped you. They were just difficult times back in the 1950s.

I did the Leaving in 1962. It was a total chance that I went to college, because all my friends went into the Civil Service. We were always in the first four or five, myself, Michael Dowling and Paddy Teahon. I was getting first class honours and was not under pressure. I don't know whether I forgot about applying for teaching or if I didn't consider it. My sister had gone to college in Cork and I thought it would be a nice place to go and I had two uncles who had done Dairy Science, Tom Brosnan who was manager of Abbeydorney Creamery and Larry Brosnan with the Dairy Disposal Company in Ardfert. They are both dead now. I went on to UCC and spent four years doing Dairy Science and then another year and a half doing a master's degree.

Life in Cork was fantastic. I wouldn't use the phrase 'getting out of jail', but it was very akin to it. Can you imagine the freedom after being virtually locked up for five years? I stayed in Magazine Road in digs and then a few of us moved off together. Myself and Willie Murphy from Emly in County Limerick. He was doing Arts and he headed on to work in London for Murphy the builder and then he set up on his own and he is still there. In the initial digs you had Dan O'Sullivan who was a doctor and who died about ten years ago. He was from Skibbereen and died very young. You had John Burke, one of the most colourful of the characters who was doing Art. He has done many of the sculpture masterpieces in Ireland such as the famous one with the two men looking up at City Hall in Cork and the piece in front of the Bank of Ireland in Dublin. I met him recently and he told me of his expeditions around Africa. We had John Moloney, an engineer who went to work with one of the Tipperary County Councils.

We split up and I then moved into a flat in my final years with Mick Fleming. He was getting into the Kerry team partnering Mick O'Connell. He joined the Agricultural Institute and he is still in Fermoy. We did the masters together. My masters was into cleaning agents used for industrial use, so I got a job with a Scottish company which produced these agents. That was very interesting and I did the job interview in Belfast, my first time there. I remember it as a very strange place, I probably was in the wrong side of the city.

I got the job and the best about it was that I was asked to start the following week. They gave me a car and a job and I was calling to creameries and one day I happened to call to Golden Vale and I met the late Dave O'Loughlin who was then general manager. He died in 1971. He said to me that I was wasting my time driving around the country and that they were building a new factory and, if I applied for the job, I would get it as the manager.

I was just going on twenty-three and I was with Golden Vale four and a half years. I spent three years in Charleville managing that facility and another one and a half in London as their export sales manager. I was moved from production to selling in my final period with Golden Vale and I went to London to train under Jim Donovan, who was the head of sales and marketing. He is a friend still. In 1971 the world seemed to turn upside down because the view was that they were bringing Jim back to Ireland and I was being trained in London and Dave O'Loughlin died. So it just shows how fate plays a part. In the end of 1971 Eddie Hayes who was the key person in the co-ops in Kerry was organising a factory in Listowel. He left a message for me that they were building in Listowel and he asked if I would apply for the job. I was interviewed in Dublin and got the job. And the rest is history.

Joan is a McNamara from Lisselton. My brother was taking out her sister and it only lasted a short while. Joan happened to come along one night and the other half fell apart and our half kept going. She was eighteen when we started going out together. Joan had gone to the convent in Listowel and her mother was very ill and after she finished in Listowel she stayed at home to nurse her mother for a few years.

Then she moved to work in England after her mother's death. She worked with a building society and so she was working there when I was finishing my time in Charleville. So when Golden Vale asked me to work in London there was an attraction in this for me with Joan already over there.

We married in 1970. Then we set up in London where we lived for a year and a half. Cathal was born in 1972. He is in Limerick University. Aimee is in UCC. Paul is doing his Leaving in Glenstal and Mary is in Alexandra College in Dublin and is in second year.

When I am gone during the week we make up at the weekends. Two are off hunting this morning. They have had a very good life of it since we moved to Croom because all the family are interested in horses and they have been riding from ponies to hunters. Paul now rides the racehorses we have with Austin Leahy. So they have a great time when they are at home and never a dull moment.

Nobody in any other organisation has looked for me for many years. In the early years, yes. But either they took the view I was going to see it through at Kerry or they couldn't put up with me. I haven't had a job offer for at least fifteen years. And I am quite sure at this hour of my life I'm hardly going to get any. I was never coaxed by any political parties. I have very good friends in politics on different sides. I wouldn't go anywhere near it. I play a bit of golf in Ballybunion. We have a fourball going with Noel Cassidy, the professional at Castletroy in Limerick, Pat Lyons, the creamery manager in Feales Bridge, and Eamonn Stack from Ballybunion.

My advice to any young person is to strive for balance. Of course I would encourage them to get a good Leaving but don't get carried away to get that last extra point or points. Being balanced is more crucial than the result they get. Obviously they will be trying to get into college. Through that they have to think as Europeans and bring language with them. If they bring language with them they are assured of a job down the road. If they don't bring language they are very limited.

I would watch to see how young staff handle themselves and how they handle customers. We all like to have a good time in our twenties, but unfortunately we are in the era when those who want to have an exceptionally good time are less attractive to industry.

There are too many people in Ireland for the jobs to go around. No matter how hard we try to create jobs, modernisation continues to displace jobs and with computerisation we need fewer people to work. So the jobs becoming available are outside Ireland. If everybody stays at home they will not find work in Ireland. We must think of being European and be prepared to travel and that is the future of the graduates of the next decade.

My biggest regret is that we did not make the big decision to move house earlier to Croom. When you are away a lot, like I am, there must be enough activity around for the family in your absence.

JOHN B KEANE

(PLAYWRIGHT)

BEING born in Kerry is the greatest gift, in my opinion, that God can bestow on any man. The street where I was brought up, Church Street, was the single most important influence on me as a boy. The Street is Kerry, and Kerry is the Street. When you belong to Kerry you know you have a head start on the other fellow. You just know this by virtue of the fact that you are a Kerryman. You don't boast about it; you don't crow about it. You just know that because of your geographical location you are IT. You're the bees knees. You need no other assets. You need no talents, no finances, need to know nothing. The fact that you were born into Kerry is your special status in this topsyturvy world. It doesn't give you respectability or anything like that; God preserve us from too much of that anyway. It gives you status: it gives you a worthwhile place where you belong.

In belonging to Kerry you belong to the elements. You belong to the spheres spinning in their heavens. You belong to history. You belong to language. You belong to beauty. You belong to some of the finest scenery, classical, beautiful scenery not known anywhere else in the world. You belong to a great legacy of literature, romance and song. Chiefly romance, because the Kerryman is a great romantic at heart. And if you were to ask me the most resilient, profound aspect of my character it is my romantic attitude as a Kerryman. When I pass by places like Killarney my heart twinges. When I am in places of great beauty such as Dingle I always long to have the love of my life alongside me because these beautiful places generate great longings.

Kerry has always had a profound influence on poets going back the ages. Tennyson was the most profoundly influenced of all. He wrote

some great poems about Kerry. You might say that there is no day that when I awake I don't bless myself and thank God that I am in Kerry, that I can make a living in Kerry.

There are some great figures that we can look up to in Kerry. Walking out of a sportsfield after a North Kerry Championship game between Listowel and Ballylongford, I would say to any man, 'Look at Johnny Walsh of Ballylongford. If you could be like that man'. I remember Paddy Bawn Brosnan. Great men. Men I have great admiration for. Great men for their county. They gave their lives for the traditions of Kerry.

My heroes are football heroes. And my two heroes are still alive. There were also men like Mick O'Connell, Tom Long, Jacko, Bawn, Johnny Walsh, Spillane, Sheehy, Power, the Bomber, all of them; they were all my heroes. They embellished this great county, and did so with great skill and with great dignity. They were not just footballers, they were ambassadors as well. They were larger than life.

I remember one time after coming from Tralee where I had seen the great Joe Keohane play for Kerry, there was a crowd of old cronies in Paddy Griffin's small pub in Church Street. A lot of them would have been in their eighties. I think it was about 1941. They asked me if I had seen Keohane play. I said I did. One asked me if I had seen him eating. I said I had. 'What did he ate?' one asked. I said, 'He ate three steaks and about twenty spuds.' And if I told them he drank a barrel of porter after that they would have believed me. They would have believed anything about Keohane. He was a prodigious character. He was their hero as well as mine.

After football, I think literature comes a close second, wrapped together with song and dance. Then after that is language, the spoken language which I think is marvellous. There is a great raciness in the Kerry idiom. Kerry speech is wonderful. It is a mixture of two languages, especially in North Kerry; it is a mixture of Elizabethan English and Bardic Irish. It is mixed and refined down to this language we speak today, that racy, colourful, wonderful language which is the language of writers as well.

I had a very comfortable, cosy childhood, I would say. I remember going to the Library to school because the old school was undergoing repair at the time, and I spent some months in the Library and my earliest recollection was of my father teaching at the school at the time. My first teacher was Mrs Mai Crowley in the boys' school. She is still alive and was then one of the most beautiful girls in all of Kerry and that hasn't diminished in any way since. She still has all the old charm that she always had and a wonderful character and a great teacher.

I also grew up in a street which was a bit jaded. A grand but jaded old street called Church Street. It had seen better days, because at one time it had been more or less the centre of the butter market. Before I was born, from top to bottom it would have been full of horses and carts and asses and carts laden with butter, full all the way up the street with people and animals and produce. Then in my boyhood I remember the cattle fairs, particularly the quarterly cattle fairs when you couldn't draw a leg in Listowel and in Church Street in particular. The cattle were there in thousands, all over the town. Those were great times. Great for the fellows growing up, because you became acquainted with the two traditions: rural and urban. We knew nothing of the metropolitan tradition at that time. My novel *Durango* is based on that time too.

I grew up with Mossy Walsh, Tommy Murphy, Finbarr McAuliffe, Pat O'Brien, Fred Hassett, Paddy Glavin, Tommy Enright, John Murphy, Patrick Stack and many others I can't recall offhand. They were a fairly well behaved lot. Church Street was a tall intimate street; tall houses and, as I say, the remains of a one-time respectability, a bit jaded as thoroughfares go. It was full of wonderful folk, and many fine lunacies evident in those characters. It was a great place for a young creative writer. These characters and their idiosyncrasies and their mannerisms and methods of speaking all rubbed off on me and to them I will ever be indebted, because I did grow up facing wonderful characters, and I loved that street. I wrote a poem about that street one time which got me into trouble at school. I got a belt of a fist from the famous President of St Michael's, Fr O'Connor, when I told him that it was I who had written it. He was so horrified at the thought of any fellow wasting time writing poetry, when he should be studying Greek, that he erupted into a fierce rage. Apart from that I didn't regard him as a bad fellow at all. He had good points as well. I have very happy memories of school-days otherwise.

But it was the Street principally that left its impression on me. The old genteel Street. If I was asked to describe the Street then, I would describe it as an old lady wearing a moth-eaten, leopard skin fur coat and a refined accent, chronically short of cash, but very refined. Today I would describe it as a street just reawakening again after years of neglect. Today it's a livelier street than the Street where I was born. The Street where I was born had very few children. The families I remember were the Cains, they were bakers, the McAuliffes, the Flavins where the famous bookshop was. Maurice Walsh used to browse there as a boy. Seán Ó Faoláin wrote about it. Jimmy Wilmot was born in the Street, Bryan MacMahon lived and still does in the Street. I was very proud and fond of that Street. It was the most powerful influence. It was a testament to love, to a way of life that has gone and to wonderful people.

They were great characters there when I was a boy. The Street had the Carnegie Free Library at the top. More importantly it had the repository for all human remains, the graveyard. And I grew up in the vicinity of the graveyard. It was a great place to go wandering in my boyhood. You had the technical school, the guards barracks, the national and secondary schools. So you had all the education emporiums except the convent, in Church Street.

It was the ideal place for a writer. It was full of pubs where I was a well-known figure turning into a young man. Across the road was Journey's End, O'Grady's – the poet Bob Boland's sister actually had it. I had my first drink I would say at Ala Sheehy's, or Willie Keane's, or Curly Connor's. I'm not sure. I would say it was at Alphonsus Sheehy's and I'd say it was a pint of cider, because I can recall my mother saying to me one night when I was about eighteen, she asked me where I was and I didn't tell her the truth. She said, 'You were at Sheehy's because I could hear your voice above the others,' and she said, 'Do you know, you're not a bad singer at all'.

My father taught in Clounmacon, three miles from the town, where he was principal of a small school. He adored the Clounmacon people. You would be known out around that area as the Master's son. But in Listowel they wouldn't know him as a teacher. He had a wonderful library of books and I would say that before I was fifteen I read every-thing that could be read. I had all Dickens read before I was sixteen, Walter Scott, all those. Then I graduated along to the early works of Walter Macken and others like Steinbeck. The greatest book I read at that time when I was about nineteen was *Independent People*. It eventu-ally won the Nobel prize. It was truly a great book and the greatest book I ever read. But without a grounding in the Classics I probably would not have been able for that book at such a young age. There was no censorship in our house. There was elsewhere. I remember Macken's books were censored at the time, Ó Faoláin, O'Connor. We were reading all of those and we had no problem.

I had a very happy boyhood. My father was a relatively well-off man by local standards, but he was far from well-off in reality. It was always a struggle. We got a fairly decent education at St Michael's and after that we were left to fend for ourselves. But I grew up in a very happy, content home. My mother came from a Nationalist family, one of the Purtills. She was a member of Cumann na mBan and was the tar-get of the Tans many a time. She lived to be eighty-eight. She was a good actress. She acted with the Gaelic League and she could sing. My father was secretary of the Gaelic League in 1916. So I grew up in that atmosphere which was staunchly Nationalistic.

I have, however, a profound suspicion of all forms of exotic Nationalism, especially extreme Nationalism. When the Civil War came our household took the Treaty side, the Collins side. My uncle, Jack Keane down the street, took the opposing side. That was the story of the Civil War, brother against brother. When General O'Duffy came to town in 1932, I remember a baton charge at the bottom of Forge Lane where it enters Church Street, Colbert Street as it is now called after the great patriot, Con Colbert. All that day there were parades through the town to welcome O'Duffy, but there was a lot of fighting. I remember one appalling sight in the market-place where young boys had heaps of stones and they flung them out on the town square over the houses, indiscriminately. That was one of the most chilling aspects of that time.

There was fierce political excitement when de Valera would come to town. The street would be alive with bonfires and we would be commissioned by the Fine Gaelers in the street to put out the bonfires. They would give us a few pence and we would make mad dashes with buckets of water. Other children would be bribed to keep the bonfires going. De Valera used make wildly nationalistic speeches in the Square. The one thing that stays with me, there was no mention of the thing that mattered most: all our people were emigrating. My own family were starting to go. And there was never any mention of that. It was as though emigration never existed. And I firmly believe myself that maybe during the war, and especially after the Second World War, but for the money coming from England, the vast millions coming from England, that there would have been a revolution in this country, because we would have starved.

I remember, when I opened this public house in 1955, counting my money after the first Christmas and there was more English money than Irish money. That was to continue for several years. Then into the sixties the English money seemed to decline altogether. The Irish economy took an upturn under Lemass and we saw the best times Ireland ever saw for a number of years. Then recession set in again. I am convinced about that period from 1946 to 1960, that there would have been a revolution but for that money coming from England. In the envelopes there would be ten bob and maybe, glory of glories, a fiver to buy the Christmas. A fiver would buy what they called in them days 'the Christmas', which consisted of barmbracks, tea, sugar, butter, buns, jams, all the necessities. But all that money would come from the English letter. If it didn't come they were in great difficulty. They were then left with the turkey money. The food was always bought first, then the clothes and then the booze. There was plenty of drink at local Wren Dances after Christmas.

The Wren Dance was the great social occasion of rural Ireland. I was born in the town but I became a countryman. I took the creamery lorry to Lyrecrompane when I was eight years of age and I never stopped going back there. Consequently, when I started in business in Listowel,

I was more familiar and at ease with country people than with towns-people. They were two totally different types of people. As a result I used to get a lot of orders for the Wren Dance. I could sing and I could dance and I had a profound interest in traditional music. We started the great Wrenboy Competition here in Listowel, myself, Dr Johnny Walsh, Derry Tatten, Mick Relihan, Barney Hanley and Jimmy Hennessy whose idea it was. The only party and celebration in the year was the Wren Dance. The parish priest in Listowel, Canon Brennan, at the time was death down on Wren Dances. He could never explain why to us. He used to describe them as porter balls. He gave a reason one time – that they were always late for Mass after such dances. But they never held Wren Dances of a Saturday night. I went to a birthday party which lasted to dawn. But when the priest spoke about it afterwards, he didn't speak about the birthday party, he spoke about the Wren Dance and attacked it and the Wrenboys and their way of life. It really turned me against the clergy at the time because it was a terrible wrong, because these people were the last remaining bastion of culture that we had. They held on to the musical and dancing traditions until the emer-gence of Comhaltas.

Another tragic thing of those times was to go to Walsh's ballroom on a Sunday night. I remember something that never left my memory. Every Sunday night there was a break for the sets. Bunny Dalton or Mick Mangan would go on the stage and play. And the country lads and girls would dance these sets and reels. I was quite carried away by it. But you would also see a drunken townie making a parody of the beautiful country dances from a safe distance. Mimicry of the most vile kind, showing how little they understood of their own people.

I very nearly went for the Dáil for North Kerry one time. Gerard Lynch, my friend, was more anxious and I wasn't that keen. I was very interested in politics. Without politics you have nothing. You shape your country with politics, whether you like it or not. The way you make your furrow down the field with a spade, so you shape your country with political leaders. It is upon the calibre of those leaders that we depend. There was no Fine Gael TD in North Kerry and I met James Dillon in Lynch's corner house in the Square. He spent nearly an hour trying to talk me into going. That would be in the early 1960s. I wouldn't have made a good TD. Gerard Lynch was an excellent one.

I had acquired some fame at the time. It would not have been long after *Sive*. I was not interested in going, but I unreservedly gave my backing to Gerard Lynch when he recaptured the seat his father held and I worked with him. What I used love most of all in politics was the drama. I used love the count in Tralee. I saw powerful drama there. I saw Paddy Finucane, the Independent, emerging from the hall in Tralee with his hand covering his face, presuming he had lost his seat to Eamon Kissane. Whereas, in reality, a number of votes went astray through an accident and they were spotted by a man named Humphrey O'Connor and he advised Louis O'Connell and he brought it to the attention of the returning officer, Tommy Clarke. The votes were counted and Paddy Finucane was elected. That was an awfully dramatic moment.

I remember getting a lift home from John Joe Daly, secretary of the local Fianna Fáil party, and I was the secretary of the Fine Gael party. We were boyhood friends. We wouldn't let a small thing like politics come between us. We went into Paddy Keane's anyway, a pub across from my father's house. We met Johnny Moriarty, the bookmaker, who lived next door to me at the time. We were broke. Johnny said he had plenty so he bought drinks. Kissane was there. They were mourning the loss of his seat. We had no Fine Gael man at the time, so I had no axe to grind with anybody, although I would have been sympathetic to the farmers' candidate, Paddy Finucane, at the time. I remember Kissane made a statement saying de Valera had made a grievous error, not for the first time. He said the circumstances that obtained did not warrant a general election. They had a safe majority, but vanity, I suppose, took Dev to the country and he paid the price. Not the first time a political leader paid the price for such folly.

I am still very interested in politics and any man who isn't should be ashamed of himself. I don't care what politics you are as long as they are constitutional politics. Because the greater our interest in politics, the better chance we have of getting fair and just representation.

My Kerry identity came easily because I lived in a house which was

crazy on gaelic football, although I was to play rugby and to oppose the
Ban in later years. I was opposed also to compulsory Irish and, in the
eyes of my enemies, I was opposed to Irish which was untrue. I was
opposed to compulsory Irish. I was opposed to the GAA Ban which I
thought a dreadful thing. When I questioned the Ban and compulsory
Irish I got a lot of blind prejudice against me too. People were so bigot-
ed at the time they wouldn't see anything but what they wanted to see.
They wouldn't examine; they wouldn't criticise; they wouldn't question. These are the very qualities which are needed for the sane survival
of any country or community.

I was very nearly beaten to death, I mean death, at the back of the
Mansion House in Dublin on the infamous night of the Language
Freedom Movement meeting, but for a very stout friend, one Det Sgt
Tony Guerin, who came to my aid. A very courageous man. I got a
severe wallop into the side of the face. Another unknown person
showed us a way out and we got out through the back of an eating
place. We had to hide there for two hours. It was the enormous prejudice of the time. I was astonished to see so many Gaels turn a blind eye
on that night, men who pretended they had an interest in the Irish language. They did the country a very grave disservice and dealt free
speech a hammer blow.

Getting back to the Kerry identity: I was very aware of it as Kerry
was at the forefront of gaelic football. When I started to grow up they
won four All-Irelands in-a-row. That was my boyhood. You had the
dances, the character and the language. We all could speak Irish and
English. We loved both passionately. We were very proud and conscious of Kerry. And that still exists.

I think we are very proud of Kerry; I think we have a great lifestyle.
We have one great thing: we are able to laugh at our enemies. The
Kerry joke! It is often the practice of counties to make other counties the
butt of their jokes, especially when those other counties are more culti-
vated and more successful. We take no notice of those things. Let them
at it. We enjoy it. So the Kerry joke should be enjoyed and not criticised.

There is no such entity as a conventional Kerryman. If you try to
analyse him he generates confusion. He will not be pinned down and

you have as much chance of getting a straight answer from a cornered Kerryman as you have of getting a goose egg from an Arctic tern. He has a capacity for long perplexing silences. It is when he is speechless, however, that he is at his most dangerous. He is weighing up the opposition for an opening so that he can demoralise you.

I have always described the Kerryman as the greater, hardnecked, atlantical warbler, otherwise known as the Kerryman. He quests individually, and in flocks, for all forms of diversion, and is to be found high and low, winter and summer wherever there is the remotest prospect of drink, sex, confusion or commotion. I think that sums up my kind of Kerryman. We are Celts and I think we are the last bastion of Celticism. I know I am a true Celt. For instance I cannot account for certain things I do. I love every Sunday to go to football matches in far outposts of North Kerry like Ballylongford, Tarbert, Moyvane. I love to meet my friends afterwards to talk about relations and friends. To argue. The Celts were noted for arguing and tracing relations, going to funerals and for wrangling. Well, we haven't changed one bit since. Especially the North Kerry Celts.

My sporting culture is built around the North Kerry GAA Championship. I love other games as well. I like rugby and soccer. I never drink when I am driving, but I make up for it when I arrive. To me there is a wonderful Celtic way of life here. In a pub a few Sundays ago after a match, I was with my friends Liam Hanrahan and Cormac O'Leary, two Moyvane men. We were missing my great friend Johnny Walsh that day, he was missing as he had an operation. We quoted almost every poem under the sun. We met families through the generations. They had come to see the games. It was the language of North Kerry in that gathering. It's in this situation you will find me most Sundays. It's our culture; it's all we have left.

No matter what I do or say my fellow North Kerry people have to admit I am one of them: they'll all say, 'He's one of us. The hoor he's one of us, we'll put up with him'. But I think my neighbours in North Kerry have a sneaking regard for me all the same. While you mightn't hear them saying good things about me, they don't like it when somebody says something bad about me. They tolerate me. I have great friends in North Kerry, great singing and drinking companions. We meet regularly and have preserved our friendships. We meet and rejoice. I love these people and I love these outings to the football matches on Sundays. I love to watch the styles of the footballers – particularly the idiosyncrasies in footballers that have been derived from parents and grandparents who I would have seen play and with whom I played.

Two of my own sons wore the green and gold, John got to Croke Park for an All-Ireland Minor Final. In my day I played with Gus Cremin and Eddie Dowling, the best footballer who never won an All-Ireland medal; Mick Deenihan, Jimmy's father; Jimmy Galvin of Finuge; Phil Trant; Jimmy Sullivan; Paddy Scanlan of Tarbert; Billy McCarthy, Duagh; Mossie Walsh; Henry O'Donnell of Tarbert and Brendan Scannell of Tarbert.

Because I played rugby, I was suspended for a year and that broke my heart. I played rugby with Castleisland; not for love of rugby, but for the love of the girl I married. I had no car and the only way I could get to meet her was to play rugby with Castleisland. I like the comraderie of rugby which was different from the GAA at the time. After the rugby match you would be taken to a hotel for a meal. Nothing like that happened with the GAA. We got wrong political signs at the time. We were expected to hold on to the old festering bitternesses of the Civil War. And for too long it dominated North Kerry football and Kerry football. I know some whose Kerry footballing careers were blighted because they wore the wrong shirt. Frank Sheehy came back to Listowel in 1953 and declared a general amnesty for rugby players. Politics is now out of the GAA and it is probably the most important institution in this part of the world because it brings us together. We understand it and it understands us. Gaelic football is suited to our temperament. I can't do without it, I am so attached to that game.

My most important friendship is with my wife. We are friend and lover, which is a great relationship and she is the greatest woman ever to enter my ken. Without her I don't know what I'd be – I would probably be in jail in South America or some place. Or maybe hung in some back street in Cairo. All I know is that she has brought joy and colour into my life and we are extremely happy. We have had ups and downs, tragedies in our lives and all that, but we have survived. We will survive anything together. Mary is from Knocknagoshel. Some people say that Knocknagoshel is a state onto itself. That it belongs to no particular continent, world or planet. So she is a very independent minded woman like all the Knocknagoshel people. But in common with all the Knocknagoshel people, she has great charm and is a great worker and she gave me the opportunity to write.

She believed in my writing when nobody did. When I'd be getting back plays from the Abbey Theatre, sometimes with the pages stuck together, the same way as I sent them, she'd be there to console me. She'd hide them and then give them to me when I wouldn't take it so hard. But the Abbey made up for it since. But I did feel at times that my heart would surely break with all the rejections I was getting. I thought it must be a conspiracy because I knew that *Sive* was worth doing and *Sharon's Grave* was. They should have done those plays, but they didn't even bother with them. It was very disappointing. She kept me going and then I met other people, James N Healy, the wonderfully courageous Phyllis Ryan and I eventually arrived. I have four novels written, I have nine books of letters, twenty plays, fourteen books of humorous essays, three books of short stories and a book of poems. I have fifty-one works now published and Mary must take most of the credit.

Other friends who helped and encouraged me include Dr Johnny Walsh, Bryan MacMahon who taught me, and my father who was the great influence of my life from the point of view of writing and reading. He was a great man to discuss writing with. Dr Johnny was one of my truly great friends as is Johnny Walsh from Ballylongford and Mossie Walsh from Listowel and all my younger friends who are still around like Pádraig Kelly and Jerome Murphy.

I am deeply religious. Not conventional, but I am a great man to pray. I visit the church every day and yet I try not to be hypocritical. I go to Mass and Communion regularly. I am a chronic sinner, of course. There's no doubt about that and I only hope God isn't taken in by the last minute repentance of a scoundrel when I die. I believe in the hereafter. For just reason. Suppose you and I were to go on a secret mission and I knew you to be a sound man who would not let me down on that mission. And I would not have any doubt about you because of our friendship and past experience. That is what is known as surety or certainty. Christ was being crucified. He told the thief, 'You shall be with Me this day in paradise.' Knowing Christ, knowing His record, knowing His achievements, knowing His lifestyle, I believe what He said. I believe that if He said to that man: 'You will be with Me this day in paradise', that He would be there to meet him.

I could give you other reasons. But I give you that one reason which I think is absolutely valid. Imagine a man of the quality of Christ making a promise like that on His death cross. We know that He is going to keep it. I wouldn't bother my behind projecting what heaven might be like. That would be a futile exercise. There is no evidence whatsoever to tell us what it's like.

The only thing I would be terrified of is that it would be full of Holy Josies. I would like to see a few crusty old wretches like myself. I'm sure that Christ in His infinite forgiveness won't keep anybody out.

INDEX